CAMBRIDGE CLASSICAL JOURNAL
PROCEEDINGS OF THE CAMBRIDGE PHILOLOGICAL SOCIETY
SUPPLEMENTARY VOLUME 46

*Series editor:* HENRY SPELMAN

# SENSING GREEK DRAMA

*edited by*

ZACHARY CASE, MARCUS ELLIS
AND ANTONIA MARIE REINKE

Published by The Cambridge Philological Society,
www.classics.cam.ac.uk/seminars/philological

© The Cambridge Philological Society 2024

ISBN: 978-1-913701-46-8 Hardback
ISBN: 978-1-913701-47-5 Ebook

This book is available direct from Oxbow Books,
10 Hythe Bridge Street, Oxford, OX1 2EW,
www.oxbowbooks.com

Printed by H2 Associates (Cambridge) Ltd.

# SENSING GREEK DRAMA

*edited by*
ZACHARY CASE, MARCUS ELLIS
AND ANTONIA MARIE REINKE

# Contents

# Introduction

'Interpretation takes the sensory experience of the work of art for granted, and proceeds from there. This cannot be taken for granted, now'.[1]

Greek drama is an art form that intensely engages with the senses. The fact of theatrical performance, with actors and choruses performing in real time before an audience, makes drama one of the most rewarding forms for thinking in terms of sensory experience. The plays directly affect the five senses of the spectators, who primarily watch and listen to the stage action, and who experience touch, taste and smell at times as well – for instance, when actors make physical contact with the front row (e.g. *Peace* 881–909), when spectators eat treats tossed to them (e.g. *Peace* 962–5), and when the thunder-machine emits the foul smell of the hides from which it was made (e.g. Apollodoros *Bibliotheca* 1.9.7; Sophocles fragment 10c.6 Radt). At the same time, a significant part of comic and tragic stage action involves characters experiencing and giving voice to – and sometimes failing to articulate – their own sensory experiences. From Oedipus' self-inflicted blindness to Philoctetes' agonisingly stinky foot, Dicaeopolis' tasty 30-year peace treaty to the frog chorus' amphibian croaks, drama is often concerned with enacting the full multi-sensory range, as well as exploring the relationships between the auditory, visual, tactile, gustatory and olfactory. What is more, the sensory universe of drama often exceeds the traditional array of the five senses: when Creon denies burial to Polyneices' corpse there is, of course, the stench of his rotting corpse; but there is also a palpable feeling of unease, an atmosphere of dread and devastation that defies easy sensory categorisation. Both within the world of the plays and in the world of the audience, Greek drama is a true feast – and a profound challenge – for the senses.

One moment of particular sensorial intrigue comes at the very beginning of *Peace*. In it, two slaves are kneading dung to feed an overpoweringly 'foul-smelling and gluttonous' (κάκοσμον καὶ βορόν, 38) dung beetle that will carry their master, Trygaeus, to heaven. Less than 10 lines into the play, once the beetle's boundless appetite for dung has been established by the two slaves working to knead and feed as quickly as possible (ὡς τάχιστα, 1, 8), one of the slaves makes a triple address to the audience:[2]

ἄνδρες κοπρολόγοι, προσλάβεσθε πρὸς θεῶν,
εἰ μή με βούλεσθ' ἀποπνιγέντα περιιδεῖν. (9–10)

[1] Sontag 2009: 13.
[2] trans. Henderson 1998b.

You dung collectors, for god's sake lend a hand,
unless you want to watch me suffocate!

ἑνὸς μέν, ὤνδρες, ἀπολελύσθαι μοι δοκῶ·
οὐδεὶς γὰρ ἂν φαίη με μάττοντ᾽ ἐσθίειν. (13–14)

There's one charge, gentlemen, that I think I'm clear of:
no one will accuse me of tasting what I'm kneading.

ὑμῶν δέ γ᾽ εἴ τις οἶδέ μοι κατειπάτω
πόθεν ἂν πριαίμην ῥῖνα μὴ τετρημένην. (20–1)

If any of you knows where I can buy an unperforated nose,
please tell me!

Aristophanes is conjuring up the smell and taste of shit and its nauseating power to great comic effect. In the absence of real and *über*-potent faecal matter on stage, it is the language that leaves a repugnant stench and repelling aftertaste. After nearly 50 lines of complaining about the job and its offensiveness to the nostrils (as well as to the tastebuds), the slaves break the 'fourth wall' once again as they turn to one another to mimic a conversation between conceited spectators about the meaning of all this:

Οι.β. οὐκοῦν ἂν ἤδη τῶν θεατῶν τις λέγοι
νεανίας δοκησίσοφος· 'τόδε πρᾶγμα τί;
ὁ κάνθαρος δὲ πρὸς τί;'
Οι.α. κᾆτ᾽ αὐτῷ γ᾽ ἀνὴρ
Ἰωνικός τίς φησι παρακαθήμενος·
'δοκέω μέν, ἐς Κλέωνα τοῦτ᾽ αἰνίσσεται,
ὡς κεῖνος ἀναιδέως τὴν σπατίλην ἐσθίει'.
ἀλλ᾽ εἰσιὼν τῷ κανθάρῳ δώσω πιεῖν. (43–9)

SECOND SLAVE. Well, by now some young smart aleck in the audience may be saying, 'What's going on? What's the point of the beetle?'

FIRST SLAVE. Yes, and then the guy sitting next to him, some Ionian, says, 'In my view it's an allusion to Cleon, because he shamelessly eats loose shit'. But I'm going inside to give the beetle a drink.

The tone is dripping with sarcasm: the slaves mock this straightforwardly allegorical reading of the dung beetle as Cleon by simply ignoring it. Part of the failure of this interpretation, we might suggest, is that it avoids engaging with the sensory dynamics of the scene, above all the overpowering smell. The 'young smart aleck' (νεανίας δοκησίσοφος) and 'some Ionian' (Ἰωνικός τις) engage in sense-less conversation and fail to catch a whiff. Modern-day scholars, by contrast, have shown that smell is established as a central theme in *Peace* from the very start and remains so throughout, as the play's trajectory from war to peace maps onto an osphresiological movement from bad smells to good smells.[3] The senses expressed within Greek drama play an important role in shaping meaning.

They also play a key role in bridging the space between characters and spectators. In the case of the opening of *Peace*, the spectators are made to be complicit in Trygaeus' peace-making project by their ability to control their own stench. When Trygaeus enters astride the dung beetle, he addresses the mass of odorous bodies that is the audience:

ὑμεῖς δέ γ᾽, ὑπὲρ ὧν τοὺς πόνους ἐγὼ πονῶ,
μὴ βδεῖτε μηδὲ χέζεθ᾽ ἡμερῶν τριῶν·
ὡς εἰ μετέωρος οὗτος ὢν ὀσφρήσεται,
κατωκάρα ῥίψας με βουκολήσεται. (150–4)

As for all of you, for whose sake I'm performing these labours,
stop farting and shitting for a period of three days;
because if this thing picks up the scent while airborne,
he'll toss me off head first, and go off to pasture.

The smells that waft around the theatre here infuse the stage action as much as the smells that are described within the plot. The possibility that the beetle might get distracted immediately presents itself when Trygaeus claims to spot a shitter in the Piraeus who threatens to throw it off course (157–72), and when he warns the crane operator to be careful not to trigger a disruptive emission from his own arse (173–6). Trygaeus' fear of the real world influencing his journey is not without grounds, funny as the idea is presented, given that he is an actor suspended up high on a crane. If he falls, he will hurt himself – no joke indeed (οἴμ᾽ ὡς δέδοικα, κοὐκέτι σκώπτων λέγω, 173). What this scene exemplifies in a characteristically comic mode is that there is a sensory continuum between embodied characters and embodied spectators. Everyone is a live participant in the sensory experience that is theatre.

3   See e.g. Sommerstein 1985: xvi, Bowie 1993: 135–7, Tordoff 2011.

The opening of Aristophanes' *Peace* attests to the richness of the world of the senses in Greek drama and indicates the extent to which our understanding of tragedy and comedy may be revitalised if we read characters, audiences, plays and poetics through a sensory lens. *Sensing Greek Drama* seeks to do precisely that. This project works within and beyond a number of recent developments in the scholarship of classics and related fields.

The 'sensory'[4] and 'affective'[5] turns in the arts, humanities and social sciences – which we understand as a broad emphasis on the sensorial and affective dimension of human experience[6] – have opened up new directions in classical scholarship. Among the most significant so far has been Routledge's series *The senses in antiquity*, with individual volumes dedicated to synaesthesia, smell, sight, taste, touch and sound. Perspectives range widely within these works: individual articles consider literary, historical, philosophical, philological and even medical iterations of the themes in question.[7] A related phaenomenon – and similarly drawing on the emerging, although perhaps less widely recognised, 'aesthetic turn'[8] – has been the renaissance of aesthetic questions in the field of classics. Felix Budelmann and Tom Phillips draw attention to a resurgence of interest in aesthetics in Greek literature and culture;[9] there have also been significant developments in this regard in the study of Latin literature.[10] Whether broadly perceived as that which concerns pretty things or more narrowly as a philosophy of art, aesthetics is inextricably bound up with sensory processes. The term itself is drawn from αἰσθάνομαι, the Greek verb 'to perceive', and as a term it commonly refers to the characteristics of the artwork in question that are particularly bound up with its effect – that is, how its audience perceives it. Accordingly, aesthetics represents the other side of the coin to the issue of the sensory: it encompasses the material that, in artistic contexts, is fed to the senses.[11]

---

[4] E.g. Low 2012, Howes 2018.

[5] For a general overview see Clough and Halley 2007, Gregg and Seigworth 2010.

[6] This definition draws on Lawrens 2012: 3–4. 'Affective' involves both body and mind, reason and passion, and encompasses 'both our power to affect the world around us and our power to be affected by it' (Hardt 2007: ix).

[7] Butler and Purves 2013, Bradley 2015, Squire 2016, Purves 2017, Rudolph 2018a, Butler and Nooter 2019. A similar approach is offered by Toner 2014.

[8] Martindale 2004: 167–8 uses this term semi-ironically to a future of aesthetic criticism he envisages. It is currently in vogue in a variety of fields. Cf. e.g. Winchester 1994, Opondo and Shapiro 2012, Kompridis 2014.

[9] Budelmann and Phillips 2018b: 5. This scholarly trend encompasses Porter 2010, Peponi 2012, Sluiter and Rosen 2012, Destrée and Murray 2015a, Gurd 2016, Grethlein 2017, Liebert 2017, Budelmann and Phillips 2018a, Childs 2018, Kidd 2019.

[10] Cf. esp. Martindale 2001–2, Martindale 2005, Martindale 2010, Martindale, Evangelista and Prettejohn 2017.

[11] Kristeller 1980: 174 famously characterises the concept of aesthetics as unequivocally modern. In defence of its use in classics, see recently Peponi 2012: 2–4 who, along with a useful discussion of the origins of the term (it originates in the eighteenth century and, although not originally used in this manner, quickly came to be associated with the study of the fine arts), suggests it can be used for the grouping of and interest in *technai* in antiquity; also Halliwell 2012: 16–17, Destrée and Murray 2015b: 1–5.

*Sensing Greek Drama* is situated at the intersection of these three rising trends: the sensory turn, affect theory and neo-aesthetics. The chapters presented here further our understanding of the nature and function of the ancient senses within the 'test case' represented by the theatre. They do not intend to encompass the entirety of ancient drama, however. By focusing on a relatively narrow range of dramatic texts, this volume is best able to support meaningful links across individual chapters and to exemplify the value of engaging with the senses – an approach that we hope will inspire future research. In addition, some chapters interrogate the nature of the senses themselves by introducing sensory categories that do not map on to the traditional division into five adopted by the Routledge series (notwithstanding the Routledge volume on synaesthesia, which is itself a particular sensory effect). These chapters emphasise the blurred boundaries between the senses and highlight the manner in which (the portrayal of) attempts to apply them to the world at large can raise profound questions about identity and ways of being.

Most importantly, rather than focusing on (one of) the senses per se, as does the majority of the Routledge series and the lion's share of other classical scholarship on the senses so far,[12] the principal purpose of *Sensing Greek Drama* is to adopt the senses as a heuristic tool, exploring their highly valuable ability to cast light on Greek drama – which, as a performed genre, is an arena *par excellence* for sensory engagement of all kinds. Approaching these works from the perspective of the senses and using them to get a grip on the material contained in the plays that stimulates these senses provides the key to a new appreciation of the complex artistries of Greek drama – and beyond this a means to tie such aesthetic considerations into other features of their stylistic, formal and conceptual make-up.

As such, *Sensing Greek Drama* also complements Mario Telò and Melissa Mueller's book *The materialities of Greek tragedy: objects and affect in Aeschylus, Sophocles, and Euripides*,[13] which particularly draws affect theory into the realm of Greek tragedy. However, while one stated aim is to 'defamiliarize the texts of Aeschylus, Sophocles and Euripides by analyzing them within the theoretical framework of the new materialisms',[14] and the book thus, to some extent, shares our broad intention to refresh understanding of Greek

---

[12] Cf. Hamilakis 2013 (proposing that archaeology should explore sensorial experience), Cazzato and Lardinois 2016 (addressing the many roles of the visual in lyric; note that the themes considered include visuality as a feature of poetics – this study also forms part of the trend of studies focussed on aesthetics noted above), Betts 2017 (the senses in Roman culture), Papadis 2018 (covers sense-perception in Aristotle and Alexander), Bochicchio, Mazzeo and Squillace 2019 (a study of smell ranging across a variety of Classical disciplines), Platts 2020 (a socio-historical study based on Rome), Weiss 2023a (a phenomenological study of Greek drama focussing on the visual).

[13] Telò and Mueller 2018a.

[14] Telò and Mueller 2018b: 3.

drama, it is mostly concerned with objects and theories of materialism in Greek tragedy – and indeed the contribution that tragedy can make to contemporary theoretical debate on this head. Furthermore, the volume is almost exclusively concerned with tragedy. By contrast, our project encompasses both comedy and tragedy equally, and its emphasis is on the senses themselves and their potential to help us – as it were – make sense of Greek drama. Ultimately, it aims to harness the potential of the senses to act as a theoretical device that brings new momentum to the field of Greek drama as a whole.

In addressing the senses in Greek drama, our project adopts a wide range of methodological and theoretical matter to enhance our grip on the senses. In addition to the underlying current of affect theory, chapters in this volume engage with the questions of reception both ancient and modern,[15] ancient proto-theoretical conceptualisations of the process of sensing drama, modern theorisations of the ancient poetic sphere (e.g. the concept of the New Music), theoretical frameworks imported from kindred fields in the arts and humanities (e.g. film studies), postmodernism, humanism, feminism, phenomenological approaches, aspects of cognitive theory rooted in linguistics, psychology and science – the latter even leading to a not insignificant role for neuroscientific research. This wide-ranging critical arsenal is vital to the project of bringing new insight to the field of Greek drama, allowing us to negotiate various tensions in scholarship and to move beyond certain themes around which it has concentrated.

Indeed, our approach is deliberately eclectic, as overdominance of any one approach or theory can only be to the detriment of the field of Greek drama. Accordingly, the chapters in this volume offer a broad sweep. Many range between and combine traditional philological methodologies and a variety of modern theoretical approaches. Some engage senses and sensory theory to produce novel readings in a socio-political vein, often in dialogue with voices on the political wing of contemporary critical theory. Others privilege alternative approaches based less overtly on politicised theoretical matter. Instead of adopting an overarching position in the volume, we have decided to utilise the productive lens of the senses, with the rich and varied perspectives it opens up, to provide a variety of novel and refreshing insights into Greek drama. This is not to disregard the traditional approaches to interpreting Greek drama that have come before us. One of the most influential approaches over the last 30–40 years has been scholarship that places the civic and socio-political at the centre of Greek drama. The most significant original inspirations for such work, in the anglophone sphere, are

---

[15] A rarity in the existing scholarship on the senses despite their persistent implication – emphasised in particular by Martindale 1993, Martindale and Thomas 2006 – in the reading of any ancient text. One exception to this trend is Grand-Clément and Ribeyrol 2022 on the artistic reception of ancient smells from the late eighteenth to the twenty-first century.

Simon Goldhill's landmark article 'The Great Dionysia and civic ideology'[16] and John Winkler and Froma Zeitlin's edited volume *Nothing to do with Dionysos? Athenian drama in its social context*, which appeared a few years later.[17] This trend, which is often highly logocentric, has come to be of enormous significance.[18]

Another important strand of scholarship on drama is performance studies, originally championed in classics by figures such as Oliver Taplin[19] and Niall Slater,[20] and exemplified by the more recent works of Edith Hall et al.,[21] especially in conjunction with the Oxford Archive of Performances of Greek and Roman Drama.[22] The shift away from predominant logocentrism and emphasis on the status of the works in question as enacted, embodied drama that this has brought to the fields of Greek tragedy and comedy is, quite obviously, foundational to our project: the richest moments of sensory engagement with these works are tied to their real time performance, whether the original production or subsequent revivals down to the present day. One especially significant aspect of this is consideration of the role and impact of sound in tragic performance.[23] Here, exploration of the influence of the so-called 'New Music' – a modern scholarly term encompassing a number of poetic and musical revolutions in lyric that appear to have taken place at the end of the fifth century – has served, to an extent, to centre consideration of the role of the sonic in performance on the question of lyric style: the language of the New Music is often thought to have been distinguished by a particularly 'noisy' quality.[24]

Study of performance, however, cannot entirely escape the text. Indeed, other than the surviving texts, our evidence for the nature of theatrical performance in Classical Athens is scarce, and often – for instance, that of an archaeological stamp – difficult to interpret with any certainty. Many of our chapters seek to negotiate this tension by

---

[16] Goldhill 1987; see also Goldhill 1986.

[17] Winkler and Zeitlin 1990.

[18] On this feature of scholarship in comedy cf. Dobrov 2010: 31–2. For recent examples of such broadly socio-political treatments of tragedy and comedy see Carter 2011, Ruffell 2011, some articles in Marshall and Kovacs 2012, Reig and Riu 2014, Rosenbloom 2014, Sommerstein 2014, Lamari 2017, Lauriola and Magnelli 2017, Shipton 2018, Cairns 2019a, Most 2019, Sells 2019, Thatcher 2019, Rosen and Foley 2020, Barzini 2021.

[19] Taplin 1977 is seminal.

[20] E.g. Slater 1985, Slater 2002.

[21] Hall, Macintosh, Michelakis and Taplin 2000, Hall, Macintosh and Taplin 2005, Hall and Wrigley 2007, Hall and Harrop 2010, Hall, Braund and Wyles 2019.

[22] http://www.apgrd.ox.ac.uk/.

[23] See e.g. Nooter 2012, Gurd 2013, Gurd 2016, Nooter 2017, Weiss 2017, Weiss 2018a, Weiss 2018b.

[24] On the New Music, and its influence on tragedy see e.g. Csapo 1999–2000, Csapo 2003, Csapo 2004, D'Angour 2006, Csapo 2008, Csapo 2009, Csapo and Wilson 2009, Power 2010: 82–9, 500–54, Csapo 2011, D'Angour 2011: 184–206, Steiner 2011, LeVen 2014, Ellis 2022.

addressing verbal sensory triggers of all kinds. By this means, the ghosts of senses past rise before us from the shadows of the text, enriching our understanding both of the experience of performance in the fifth century and of the dramas themselves. This aids in bridging the gap between logocentric and performance-based approaches, contributing to a more holistic understanding of Greek drama.

Finally, and most generally, scholarship on Greek drama has a particularly vexed history of being torn between historicising and universalising impulses.[25] *Sensing Greek Drama* presents an opportunity to reflect on both. Focusing on the senses in Greek drama is one way to be firmly historicist: it compels us to pay close attention to the texts as written and performed in their original contexts, and to try to understand their sensory impact on the embodied audience watching on. At the same time, it is one way to acknowledge the universality of Greek drama: we still possess the same five senses that those Greeks did, and our capacity to comprehend the sensations enacted in the plays is predicated on a shared sense of being human that transcends historical specificity, and this lends itself to theoretically informed studies. The point, to reiterate, is not to fall on one side or the other of the scholarly divide.

The chapters in this volume testify to the continuing endurance of both approaches, and to the ways in which a focus on the senses encourages us to think across divides – between historicist and universalist readings but also, in particular, between actors and audience, subject and object, form and performance. The four parts of the volume indicate some of the most important areas that such thinking may affect: our understanding of dramatic form, language and poetics, of the politics and social implications of the theatre, of its treatment of life and death, reality and artifice and the impact Greek drama has on its audiences. While the chapters in the individual parts share a particularly close correspondence, they also look to other parts of the volume. Indeed, as will become clear, the constraints of having parts do not prevent the chapters from speaking to each other across editorial boundaries. Part of this stems from the fact that the study of tragedy and comedy is not, as in many other publications, segregated into two separate parts, but the chapters move freely from tragedy to comedy and back again. This is to stress both the benefit of contemplating the two genres alongside each other – not incidentally, they were once staged in immediate succession at the same festivals – and the thematic focus of this volume. All the parts are intended, not as closed entities in themselves, but as different entry points to a shared project: the exploration of Greek drama through the lens of the senses.

The first part (*Senses and Form*) begins this exploration by casting a fresh, and deliberately diverse, perspective on dramatic form. In the course of three chapters, it takes us from the politics to the poetics of the formal aspects of Greek drama, and from

---

[25] Case 2021a esp. 46–7, with further references.

tragedy to comedy. Ben Radcliffe's 'Monads on the Sonic Fold: Disquiet in Sophocles' *Antigone*' opens the section with a study of 'disquiet' – that is, the 'surplus of acoustic form' in Sophocles' *Antigone*. Drawing on a rich array of theory, including Deleuze, Honig and Rancière, the chapter traces the political force of the play's many utterances, from bird cries to inarticulate wailing, that break the conventional expectations of sens-ible speech. Radcliffe's radical dissection of dramatic language demonstrates that tragic (non-) sense resides in an inextricable fusion of form and meaning. Marcus Ellis' contribution, 'Euripidean Lyric through the Eyes of Aristophanes', takes up Radcliffe's concern with the non-sensible – an accusation repeatedly levelled at Euripides' lyrics in the works of Aristophanes. In the light of modern-day cognitive theory and the 'New Musical' avant-garde of Euripides' own time, Ellis argues that Aristophanes' parodies pick up on a particular quality of Euripidean lyrics: their inherent visuality. They blend ideas in a dense and complex juxtapositional structure that triggers mental operations associated with vision as well as hearing. Afroditi Angelopoulou's 'The Dynamics of Physical, Aesthetic and Cultural Taste in Aristophanes', in turn, takes us from the visuality of Euripides' poetry, as it becomes apparent in Aristophanes' mockeries, to Aristophanes' own poetics. By discussing scenes of gustatory experience across the Aristophanic corpus, and especially in *Wasps*, she reveals the importance of the creative interplay between physical, aesthetic and cultural taste for Aristophanes' comedies. Each of the three chapters in this part, then, calls our attention to the manner in which dramatic moments that particularly confound and/or engage the senses shape Greek drama at the formal level, from the bare bones of its linguistic ingredients to the larger concerns of its poetic make-up and political relevance.

The next part of the volume (*Senses and Power*) continues Ellis' and Angelopoulou's study of Aristophanes, while also returning us to Radcliffe's interest in the politics of the sensory. Zachary Case's, '"But not a word about me" (περὶ ἐμοῦ δ' οὐδεὶς λόγος): Sensing Xanthias in Aristophanes' *Frogs*', casts the spotlight on one of the slaves in Aristophanic comedy. Inspired by Rancière and feminist humanism, Case argues that Aristophanes deliberately presents Xanthias as a sensing being, sharing the human experience of pain. Thus, the comedian challenges, in Case's view, the rigidity of the slave-free boundary that many scholars ascribe to Classical Athens, and in a way that is not simply a matter of comic inversion. Another social boundary, and its comic blurriness, are at stake in Antonia Marie Reinke's 'Smell, Sex and Gender in Aristophanes' *Lysistrata*'. Reinke discusses how smell in the play oscillates between a fleeting accessory and a fundamental indicator of gendered self and explores Aristophanes' presentation of male and female gender as equally unstable: ultimately, Aristophanic gender identities, and the smells they give off, are as hard to pin down as reality itself amidst the comedy's manifold layers of dramatic artifice. Jointly, Reinke and Case show that the study of the senses prompts us to re-visit, and scrutinise afresh, the social hierarchies of the dramatic world and Athens as well.

The next part (*Senses and Vitality*) has two chapters that lead us from the political to the ontological, as they place the fuzzy area between life and death centre stage. Katharine A. Craik's 'Seeing in Euripides' *Alcestis* and Shakespeare's *The Winter's Tale*' argues that, in both Euripides and Shakespeare, vision ultimately fails to reliably draw the line between the living and the dead. This is especially true, as Craik shows, since viewing within the plays can never truly escape the illusionary mode of theatrical viewing. Thus, Craik takes up some of the threads that appeared earlier in the volume – Ellis' contemplations of visuality, Reinke's interest in theatrical illusion – while also adding an important reception perspective. Chiara Blanco opens up the volume in different ways: her 'Touching Death in Euripides' *Alcestis*' considers the Euripidean tragedy in light of the artistic production at the time. Like Craik, Blanco is interested in liminality in *Alcestis*, but she detects it in the resemblance between the haptic encounters of Alcestis and Admetus and the *dexiosis* (handshake) motif of contemporary funerary reliefs. Both Craik and Blanco illustrate how the senses could be used in Greek (and Shakespearean) drama to destabilise the edges of the world of the living.

The two chapters in the final part of the volume (*Senses and Audiences*) hark back to its beginning, as they open the focus, once again, to a wider understanding of the senses, and especially to moments of sensory confounding. Both chapters address dramatic notions of shock and surprisal in Greek tragedy and their capacity to touch characters and audiences alike. Drawing on affect studies and phenomenological approaches to theatre, Naomi Weiss' 'Bodies That Shock: The Erinyes and Lyssa' explores the visceral impact that Aeschylus' furies and Euripides' personified Madness invite in their onlookers. These terrifying figures are most present on stage, Weiss argues, in the somatic traces they leave in others. The chapter's focus on the body also recalls Case's contemplation of physicality as a common denominator between human beings. Weiss' interest in dramatic shock is complemented by Peter Meineck's 'Making Sense of Surprisal: *Thaumastos* on the Ancient Stage – A Cognitive Approach'. Meineck works within a rich theoretical framework, reaching from ancient theatre criticism to modern-day cognitive theory, and identifies surprise as a key tenet of Greek drama as a genre: it is by confronting spectators with temporary challenges to their sensory apparatus that ancient theatre prompts their active cognitive engagement, which ultimately enables their empathy and self-reflection. Weiss and Meineck allow us to see the senses, especially as they are probed and tested, as a conduit between dramatic illusion and real-life audience.

As this brief survey of the volume may indicate, a focus on the senses promises a new and important perspective for the study of Greek drama. It allows us, in particular, to appreciate the many ways in which the ancient plays challenge easy categories, boundaries and definitions. But there is more at stake in this volume. We live in sensorially interesting times.

We all experience sensory overload, bombarded as we are by mass media and engulfed by information. The effect of this might be understood to be a form of the sensory deprivation that emerges in some of the chapters in this volume: given how overly stimulated we are, each sensory experience becomes dulled in its own right. This is particularly true of those of us who live most of our lives through screens, in particular throughout and in the wake of the COVID-19 pandemic: indeed, a curious symptom of catching the virus was literally to deprive some of us of the senses of smell and taste. The looming normalisation of Virtual Reality only threatens to compound the sensory numbness that has been well on its course in an age of capitalist overproduction and overconsumption, according to Susan Sontag writing in the 1960s. For Sontag, in her famous essay 'Against interpretation' advocating critique of form ('erotics') over content ('hermeneutics'), literary criticism can provide a curative to this anaesthetic condition:

All the conditions of modern life – its material plenitude, its sheer crowdedness – conjoin to dull our sensory faculties. And it is in the light of the condition of our senses, our capacities (rather than those of another age), that the task of the critic must be assessed. What is important now is to recover our senses … The aim of all commentary on art now should be to make works of art – and, by analogy, our own experience – more, rather than less, real to us.[26]

We do not need to agree with Sontag's polemic against the instrumentality and violence of interpretation as such to appreciate her reflection on the task of the critic in modernity. By exploring Greek drama in all its sensorial complexity, perhaps we can recover our own senses too.

*Zachary Case, Marcus Ellis and Antonia Marie Reinke*

[26] Sontag 2009, 13-14

# PART I

## Senses and Form

# Monads on the Sonic Fold: Disquiet in Sophocles' *Antigone*

*Ben Radcliffe*

'There is I, on the one hand, and this noise on the other ... if it is the other'.[1]

Carl Orff's *Antigonae* (1949) opens with a breathless cry, as Antigone sings the first verse of Hölderlin's translation on a single, unwavering note.[2] Orff's operatic adaptation of Sophocles' original is known for its austere style, which emphasises rhythm and prosody over melodic complexity, blending a style of declamatory singing with an orchestra featuring unusual percussive instruments. But Antigone's part stands out for its tonal simplicity: in her opening dialogue with Ismene, Antigone sometimes allows her voice to rise and dip at the beginnings and ends of verses, but her otherwise uniform vocal line imbues her character with a sense of control and determination that contrasts sharply with Ismene's quavering replies. Antigone is matched in this respect only by Creon, who delivers many of his proclamations and interrogations in a flat baritone. Despite their antagonism, Antigone and Creon share a common voice, a musical *ēthos* that registers the literally univocal quality of their feuding convictions.

Orff's musical interpretation directs our attention to the acoustic force of the voice and its role in the political conflicts that drive Sophocles' drama. The civic spaces of Thebes resound with Creon's declarations and Antigone's equally unambiguous expressions of defiance: Antigone tells her sister in the opening scene that Creon 'is coming here to make clear proclamations (σαφῆ προκηρύξοντα) to those who do not already know' (33–4).[3] After she is caught performing burial rites for Polyneices, she is asked by Creon whether she was aware of his ban and replies, 'Yes, I knew it. How could I not? It was manifest (ἐμφανῆ) to everyone' (448). As Judith Butler and Bonnie Honig

---

[1] Beckett 1994.

[2] On Orff's *Antigonae* and his other adaptations of Greek drama see Steiner 1984: 169–70, Levi 2002, Pernerstorfer 2005, De'Ath 2016.

[3] In what follows, line numbers refer to *Antigone* unless otherwise noted. On the meaning of *kērugma* in *Antigone* and in contemporary Athenian politics see Fletcher 2008.

have argued, Antigone's claim is subversive precisely because she voices it in a public, political space that she shares with Creon, and her confident declarations echo his own clarion commands. Indeed, Helene Foley suggests that the tragic impasse of *Antigone* amounts to 'the failure of *Antigone*'s multiple voices to communicate with each other' – that is, to the failure of the public sonosphere to facilitate a political settlement.[4]

But *Antigone* admits other kinds of acoustic presence that do not fit this model of failed civic communication. Thebes is filled with inchoate shouts, garbled speech and animal cries that grow more intense and impinge more insistently on Antigone's and Creon's *logoi* as the drama progresses.[5] *Antigone* foregrounds the materiality of such sounds as they 'sting the mind', 'touch thoughts' and 'strike the ears' (317, 858, 1188), bypassing the channels of linguistic sense-making to impact the psyche on an affective level. Sean Gurd and Sarah Nooter have highlighted the para-political and pre-conscious force of the voice in Athenian tragedy, a force that can redouble, displace, or negate the voice's propositional content.[6] Following their lead and drawing on the work of Gilles Deleuze, this chapter examines the political and dramatic valences of noise, understood as a surplus of acoustic form that stimulates an affective state of uneasy anticipation ('disquiet'). I focus especially on *phthongos* and related terms,[7] tracing how such sounds pass through and reconfigure the various partitions that constitute Thebes' political topography – the boundaries between city and country, between private and public spaces and between the *psukhai* of its intransigent protagonists.[8]

As Antigone herself observes, the conflict between her determination to bury her brother and Creon's ban on such a burial cannot be processed through *logos*: ὡς ἐμοὶ τῶν σῶν λόγων | ἀρεστὸν οὐδὲν μηδ᾽ ἀρεσθείη ποτέ | οὕτω δὲ καὶ σοὶ τἄμ᾽ ἀφανδάνοντ᾽ ἔφυ ('just as nothing in your *logoi* is acceptable to me – and may it never please me – | so too my views are by nature displeasing to you', 499–502).[9] The consequences of this impasse are far-reaching. The political process requires movement – some fusion, mediation or abstraction among private interests and perspectives – but for much of the plot of *Antigone*, the *logos*, the conventional medium of collective discourse and

---

[4]   Foley 2018: 145.
[5]   Human shouts: 423, 1001, 1079, 1210, 1226–7, 1252; garbled or incomprehensible statements: 320, 692, 1187, 1206; animal cries: 424, 998–1022.
[6]   Gurd 2013, 2016, Nooter 2017; on the mourning voice and its relation to tragic (anti-)politics see Loraux 2002. On approaches to reading ancient soundscapes see the chapters in *Sound and the Ancient Senses* (eds Butler and Nooter 2019), esp. Gurd 2019, LeVen 2019, Nooter 2019.
[7]   On the valences of *phthongos* and cognate terms see n. 49 below.
[8]   Creon and Antigone do change their outlooks over the course of the drama, but their mutual intransigence lasts through the third episode (for Creon, into the fifth) and fixes the drama's disastrous course; see Foley 2001: 196–200 on the protagonists' ethical intractability.
[9]   The translation of *Antigone* is my own. The edition of the text is Lloyd-Jones and Wilson 1990.

political rationality, has been captured and immobilised by two singularities. It is left to the voice's disquieting, residual presence to draw Thebans out of their monadic isolation and toward some processing of their communal crisis.

Noise is conventionally understood as a kind of privation – as sound without sense, as the unformed, uninformative other of articulate speech. Jacques Rancière has shown how, in political contexts, 'noise' can designate the voices of those regarded as unqualified to participate in the public sphere, including workers, slaves, women, migrants and other disenfranchised classes.[10] Rancière refers especially to Aristotle's distinction between *phōnē* and *logos* in *Politics*: the voices of the disenfranchised are supposed to express individual states of pain and pleasure but not the political discursivity that concerns the common good.[11] Vocal noise, in this sense, fits into the terms of Hegel's interpretation of *Antigone*. It would express the singular needs of the human animal, of the *oikos* and the (female) sphere of social reproduction, in which Hegel locates the ethical basis of Antigone's claim. Speech, by contrast, would achieve the universality and rationality of politics and the (male) public sphere, personified by Creon.[12] Bonnie Honig has suggested that a permutation of this Hegelian framing underlies readings of *Antigone* that interpret the heroine's voice, especially her acts of lamentation, as an expression of a wordless, universal capacity for suffering that transcends the terms of Thebes' civil conflict and resists the tyrant's appeal to *raison d'état*.[13]

Honig's own reading of *Antigone* draws on Rancière's work to complicate this binary opposition, suggesting that Antigone 'works the interval' between *phōnē* and *logos*, composing impure utterances out of words, cries, intonation and a sophisticated partisan rhetoric. Honig's reading of Antigone's voice focuses narrowly on her final dirge (806–82 and 891–928), but this approach is productive for our purposes because it decouples the opposition between Antigone and Creon from the opposition between speech and noise.[14] Both protagonists promulgate (mutually antithetical) *logoi*, and both produce and respond to non-verbal and para-verbal expressions. Honig also underscores how

---

[10] Rancière 1999: 39–42, 2010: 37–40. See Zachary Case's discussion of Rancière in this volume. For other Classicists who discuss Rancière see recently O'Gorman 2018 and Telò 2020b. O'Gorman draws on Rancière specifically to explore the figure of popular noise (*clamor*) in Roman historiography. *Antigone* includes passing references to rumour and gossip among the Thebans (see Fletcher 2008 on the political implications), but I focus on the more palpable and dramatic expressions of noise in the play.

[11] Arist. *Pol.* 1253a; see Nooter 2019: 200.

[12] Hegel discusses *Antigone* in the *Phenomenology* and the *Philosophy of Right*; for details see Mills 1996, Butler 2000: 2–5, Burke 2008, Robert 2010: 417–23. Of the many efforts to historicise and complicate the opposition between *oikos* and *polis* in *Antigone*, Sourvinou-Inwood 1989 is the most influential.

[13] Honig 2013: 40. Butler 2000: 2 makes a similar claim.

[14] Honig 2013 focuses primarily on the opposition between *logos* and the 'voice', although she uses 'noise' interchangeably for the latter e.g. in her discussions of Rancière (p. 144) and Adriana Cavarero (p. 143).

noise, precisely through its messy entanglements with politically authorised speech, can serve as a site for contesting the boundaries of public life. Thus, according to Honig, Antigone remixes elements of women's lament, funeral oration and historiography in order to broadcast her own dirge to the Theban public, despite Creon's prohibition.[15] On the other hand, even though this interpretation usefully deconstructs the speech/ noise binary, it refrains from defining noise as anything in particular: noise might consist of intonation, inflection or exclamations (but are these ever absent from spoken language?) – whatever is supposed to mark the voices of those excluded from public life. 'Noise' remains fundamentally privative, an empty square or void that allows the boundaries of *logos* to be reorganised in the course of political disputes.

This way of conceptualising noise is too abstract to do justice to the rich depictions of sound and acoustic texture in Sophocles' drama. For this, we need to specify an ontology of noise. Consider, for instance, a notorious scene that at first appears to exemplify the gendered, Hegelian division between speech and noise. In the second episode, the Guard reports to Creon how he observed Antigone performing funeral rites for Polyneices. When she discovered that her brother's corpse had been unburied again outside the city walls, 'she wailed the sharp cry of a bitter bird, as when she sees the nest in her empty lair orphaned of hatchlings' (κἀνακωκύει πικρᾶς | ὄρνιθος ὀξὺν φθόγγον, ἐς ὅταν κενῆς | εὐνῆς νεοσσῶν ὀρφανὸν βλέψῃ λέχος, 423–5). Antigone's utterance (*phthongos*) is framed by the Guard as an expression of animal suffering, singular and unreproducible. But when the Guard recounts Antigone's cry, his own discourse becomes distended with verbal redundancies that seem to strain against language's form-carrying capacity: notice how 'sharp' repeats 'bitter', 'cry' repeats 'wailed', 'orphaned' repeats 'empty' and 'lair' repeats 'nest'.[16] This pleonasm gives the impression that the intensity of Antigone's cry has passed into the Guard's discourse on a formal level. Indeed – as we will see shortly – noise may be regarded precisely as *a surplus of sensory form* that can infiltrate any sort of vocal emission, from a wordless cry to a complex narrative.

It will be useful to consider some contemporary theorisations of noise that offer ways of thinking about its capacity to transmit form. A pioneering researcher in information theory, Claude Shannon, defined noise as a perturbation that interferes with the transmission of signals, like the buzzing distortions in the background of bad radio receptions.[17] Such sounds are acoustically richer than the signals that they interrupt: to maintain its linguistic intelligibility, the speaking voice is constrained to a limited range of sonic patterns, whereas noise (especially 'white noise') oscillates freely through a wide

---

[15] Honig 2013: 128–40

[16] On the use of λέχος here see Worman 2020: 152. Oudemans and Lardinois (1987: 177) interpret the naturalising imagery here as an expression of cosmic disorder.

[17] See Gunders 2002.

range of frequencies and intensities. In the case of radio static, each blip registers the vagaries of the signal's complex passage through the atmosphere and various receivers, an inhuman order of electromagnetic fields and thermal fluctuations. In this sense, noise is rich in information, but the information that it carries is not useful to most listeners. The crucial insight of Shannon's formulation is that noise is not simply opposed to form, information or even to a kind of meaning. It is not, for instance, like the pure sonority of the voice prior to its articulation into signifiers, like matter without form.[18] Noise tends to be overly formed and excessively meaningful, although it may not have interpreters who would or could appreciate its meaning; it presents information so densely that it can hinder the transmission of any consolidated, interpretable information in the signal.[19]

Alongside Shannon's notion of noise as a surplus of acoustic form, my main conceptual reference in what follows is the work of the philosopher Gilles Deleuze. His understanding of sensory experience, which has been deeply influential in contemporary affect theory, is especially valuable for examining how noise can overflow the channels of linguistic intelligibility and activate other modes of apprehension that operate just at or beneath the threshold of conscious awareness. In a passage of his 1968 work *Difference and repetition*, Deleuze reflects on two ways of regarding the phenomenology of noise. Taking the sound of crashing waves as an example,[20] Deleuze suggests that such a sound is perceived as 'clear' – one can readily recognise it as the sound of a wave – but also as 'confused', since one cannot consciously perceive the sound's component elements, the countless reverberations caused by each colliding drop of water.[21] These sonic components produce conscious aural experience by interacting with our sensory and cognitive apparatus, but they have a generative dynamism of their own that cannot be exhausted by their conscious effects. Deleuze suggests that noise is more interesting for this second, para-conscious aspect than for the vague conscious impression ('clear–confused') that it produces.

---

[18] See Agamben 1998: 7–8 and 1993: 6–8 on ancient theorisations of the distinction between *phōnē* and *logos*. For Butler 2015: 57, noise appears as the 'residue' of the voice that the symbolic cannot manage to reduce to itself; see Cavarero 2005 esp. 34–61, 165–72.

[19] The fraught relay between sensation, information and cognition in drama is a recurring topic in this volume: on productive perturbations in the information content of speech and images see Marcus Ellis' chapter. Likewise, Peter Meineck's chapter frames perceptual entropy in terms that resonate with Shannon's distinction between signal and noise. Although I am concerned primarily with acoustic noise in what follows, noise is not, according to Shannon's definition, restricted to the domain of sound: an image can be noisy if it presents an unfiltered surplus of visual information, for instance. Similar to 'noise' thus defined is the notion of 'dissonance' in Gurd 2016: both terms designate a kind of sonic multiplicity that overwhelms the placid flow of narrative discourse. Kristeva's notions of the semiotic and the chora overlap with the concept of 'noise' that I develop here; see Randhawa 2014 for a Kristevan reading of *Antigone*.

[20] Deleuze develops the example and the distinction between clear/confused from Leibniz; see n. 25 below.

[21] Deleuze 1994: 213–14.

Noise, for Deleuze, thus constitutes a kind of tattered boundary where the aural subject registers the swarming intensities of the acoustic environment. Deleuze develops this concept in his monograph on Leibniz and Baroque art.[22] In the following passage, he describes how the 'tiny perceptions' that constitute certain kinds of noise can produce an animated affect that he calls 'disquiet':

> Tiny perceptions are as much the passage from one perception to another as they are components of each perception. They constitute the animal or animated state par excellence: disquiet. These are 'pricklings', or little foldings that are no less present in pleasure than in pain. The pricklings are the representative of the world in the closed monad.[23]

Disquiet includes various states of agitation – anxiety, dread, apprehension – that feature pervasively in Athenian tragedy.[24] But what is particularly valuable for reading *Antigone* is Deleuze's notion that the soul, subjective interiority, forms a 'closed monad', a kind of windowless chamber severed from its outward-facing façade.[25] A monad appears atomic and unitary from the outside, but it contains an intricately folded ideational structure that mirrors the fractal structure of the physical world outside. Soul and matter approach each other asymptotically, without ever touching, but at their non-interface, both become infinitely pleated with unconscious and non-conscious vibrations, with a noisiness that somehow straddles the impassable divide between mind and matter. The paradox and the value of this concept is that it locates channels of sensory receptivity even in a hermetically sealed subject – tiny psychic modulations (noise) that can add up to a charged potential for action (disquiet).[26]

We are not likely, of course, to find an exact equivalent to this complex topology of mind and matter in *Antigone*, but Deleuze's concept does shed light on some of the recurring issues that surround the drama's representations of noise. As I discussed earlier, one of the central political problems in *Antigone* is the failure of its civic voices to communicate with each other: the two protagonists are, until the final scenes, driven

---

[22]  Deleuze 1993.

[23]  Deleuze 1993: 99.

[24]  As de Romilly 1958: 61–3 observes, Aeschylean choruses are frequently struck by an inarticulate fear that they nevertheless strive to articulate.

[25]  Deleuze's characterisation of monads is based on his interpretation of Leibniz, esp. *La Monadologie* (1714), but it is also a synthesis of Leibnizian concepts and Deleuze's philosophy, informed by Deleuze's interpretation of Baroque architecture; see Smith 2012: 43–58.

[26]  See Naomi Weiss's contribution to this volume on the capacity of tragic affects to break down intercorporeal boundaries.

by their internal convictions and appear insensible to the objections of their friends and fellow citizens. We will see how the drama repeatedly spatialises this intransigence, representing it as the enclosure of the protagonists' souls and bodies in states of monadic isolation. The question that *Antigone* pursues is whether and how some form-imparting capacities of the voice can bypass this intersubjective barrier and reconstitute a shared sensorium.[27] Through what topological sleight-of-hand can voice or affect or sense pass between sealed chambers?

In the third episode of the drama, Haemon attempts to convince his father to temper the cruel sentence that he has issued against Antigone:

μή νυν ἓν ἦθος μοῦνον ἐν σαυτῷ φόρει,
ὡς φῂς σύ, κοὐδὲν ἄλλο, τοῦτ᾽ ὀρθῶς ἔχειν.
ὅστις γὰρ αὐτὸς ἢ φρονεῖν μόνος δοκεῖ,
ἢ γλῶσσαν, ἣν οὐκ ἄλλος, ἢ ψυχὴν ἔχειν,
οὗτοι διαπτυχθέντες ὤφθησαν κενοί. (705–9)

So don't carry within yourself only one mentality,
as if the only thing that is correct is what you say and nothing else.
For whoever thinks that he alone has intelligence,
or a tongue or a soul that no one else has,
such people, when unfolded, are seen to be empty.

In this appeal, Haemon implies that Creon has constituted himself as a monad (μοῦνον ... μόνος), a folded-up being that is, in truth, nothing but its own self-regarding aversiveness.[28] If Creon were unfolded (διαπτυχθείς), he would be only void (κενός). This cognitive and ethical self-closure is caught up in Creon's attitude toward his own and others' voices. After their exchange takes a turn toward open confrontation, Haemon criticises his father for speaking but not listening (βούλει λέγειν τι καὶ λέγων μηδὲν κλύειν, 757), although it is perhaps fairer to say that Creon is receptive to a narrow channel of aural information and thus hears only what he wants to hear. He consistently misunderstands the sense of his interlocutors' words and fits their intentions into a fixed, paranoid schema.[29] As Haemon intimates, the consequences of Creon's monadicism are

[27] The characters of *Antigone* are exposed to a shared, deracinating sensory experience at the end of the drama, but I do not claim that this experience necessarily amounts to communal reconciliation. On the (all too tidy) restoration of normalcy in the play's conclusion see Griffith 2010: 131–4; on *Antigone*'s critique of communal immanence see Stocking 2008.
[28] On Creon's isolation and its relation to his political power see Oudemans and Lardinois 1987: 182.
[29] Foley 2001: 185–7, Kierstead 2017.

politically calamitous: a community is a collectivity, never 'of one man', whereas Creon would 'rule the vacant earth, alone' (καλῶς γ᾽ ἐρήμης ἂν σὺ γῆς ἄρχοις μόνος, 737–9).[30]

This is not to say that Creon is entirely closed to voices that fall outside of his narrow band of discursive receptivity. During the first episode, Creon expresses annoyance at the Guard for bringing the unwelcomed news that someone has buried Polyneices' corpse:

Φυ. εἰπεῖν τι δώσεις, ἢ στραφεὶς οὕτως ἴω;
Κρ. οὐκ οἶσθα καὶ νῦν ὡς ἀνιαρῶς λέγεις;
Φυ. ἐν τοῖσιν ὠσὶν ἢ 'πὶ τῇ ψυχῇ δάκνῃ;
Κρ. τί δὲ ῥυθμίζεις τὴν ἐμὴν λύπην ὅπου;
Φυ. ὁ δρῶν σ᾽ ἀνιᾷ τὰς φρένας, τὰ δ᾽ ὦτ᾽ ἐγώ.
Κρ. οἴμ᾽ ὡς λάλημα, δῆλον, ἐκπεφυκὸς εἶ. (315–20)

GUARD. Will you let me say something, or should I just turn and go?
CREON. Are you even now unaware of how your voice pains me?
GUARD. Are you stung in your ears or in your soul?
CREON. Why are you trying to define where my pain is?
GUARD. The culprit distresses your mind; I your ear.
CREON. Oh, how clear it is you were born to be a babbler!

Part of what Creon finds offensive is that his servant presumes to analyse him into parts (ears and soul) rather than regarding him as a monad whose pain (λύπην) is unanalysable.[31] But the Guard correctly discerns that Creon's agitation is complex: he is initially so upset by the Guard's news that he silences the Chorus with a threat (παῦσαι, πρὶν ὀργῆς καὶ 'μὲ μεστῶσαι λέγων, 280), but he is also annoyed by the sound of the Guard's voice, which has a dense, meandering quality (as Creon remarks at 241–2). Indeed, the Guard's voice is distinctly noisy: Creon dismisses him as 'born to be a babbler' (λάλημα … ἐκπεφυκὸς εἶ, 320).[32] These two sources of distress – the voice's content and the voice's noise – correspond somehow to two sensory organs – ears and soul.

Which harms which? The Guard answers his own question ('the culprit distresses your mind; I your ear', 319), but it is not clear if the problem can be resolved so easily. That is, it is not clear if the intense disquiet, the 'animal or animated state', that Creon exhibits in this scene and in the following scenes is simply a response to the information

---

[30] In practice, Creon's power is not absolute but has to be negotiated with his subjects, especially the Chorus of elders; see Fletcher 2008 and Hawthorne 2009.

[31] Characters in *Antigone* refer to *phrenes*, *phronēma* or their cognates in almost every speech; see Cropp 1997. On the opposition between wisdom and foolishness in *Antigone* see Lauriola 2007.

[32] On the comic characterisation of the Guard see Tatum 2015.

that he has comprehended (i.e. Antigone's disobedience), or if it also responds to a kind of information that he refuses to acknowledge, the *lalēma* of his interlocutors' objections and counterarguments, which evidently does more than 'sting his ears'. Throughout the drama, Creon's peremptory bluster and his silencing of dissenting voices seem to suppress an increasing disquiet, an inner reservation about his own course of action.[33] We will see below how the noisiness of voices does finally alter Creon's course, but too late.

Antigone's intransigence is initially figured as a kind of immobility: Ismene calls her 'hard' (ὦ σχετλία, 47); Creon calls her thoughts 'stiff' (τὰ σκλήρ᾽ ἄγαν φρονήματα, 473) and compares her to 'the stoutest iron' (τὸν ἐγκρατέστατον | σίδηρον, 475–6).[34] This characterisation is developed in the second half of the drama, however, along lines that converge with the figure of Creon's self-closure. Antigone's punishment is to be sealed in a 'rocky vault' (774; cf. 849) – an image that blends Antigone's own hardness with the monadic closure previously ascribed to Creon's mind.[35] During her exchange with the Chorus in the fourth episode, Antigone attempts to rebut their claim that her appalling fate is unprecedented (821). She likens herself to Niobe (823–31), who was petrified after the destruction of her children but continues to weep, held in a state between life and death that resembles Antigone's living entombment. But besides serving as a reflection of Antigone's pending fate, Niobe, I think, also serves as a comment on Antigone's character and her place in the Theban sonosphere.

Consider a second resonance between Antigone's condition and Niobe's: Niobe is the figure of a monad, an insensate stone façade within which a living soul is preoccupied with its singular miseries (λυγρότατον ... ξέναν, 823). This might not seem like an accurate portrait of Antigone, who is emotionally expressive and politically proactive, but there are elements of this picture that resonate with Antigone's situation.[36] Antigone alludes to Niobe's tears – she is 'melting' and has 'all-tearful brows' (828, 831), and these emissions seem to express her grief outwardly, marking some linkage between the stony surface and the mind confined within. But the expressivity of Niobe's tears is a notorious conundrum:

---

[33]  Thus when Creon does change his mind (e.g. 770–1; 1091–114), the reversal seems abrupt, as if it had been building for some time under the surface of his discourse.

[34]  Similar language is applied to Creon e.g. by Haemon at 711.

[35]  On the somatic characteristics of Antigone's tomb see Worman 2020: 153–6. Stalpaert 2008 develops the resonances between subjecthood and entombment in recent receptions of *Antigone*.

[36]  Antigone's isolation in Thebes becomes more complete as the drama progresses. Her initial effort to form an alliance with Ismene is fraught and ambiguous (Stocking 2008: 159–61, Tyrrell and Bennett 2008, Goldhill 2012: 231–41, Honig 2013: 184–9), but by the fourth episode she is repeatedly referred to (by herself and by others) as 'alone' and 'deserted' (773, 887, 919, 923, 941). See Tyrrell and Bennett 1990: 446 and Winnington-Ingram 1980: 144.

καί νιν ὄμβροι τακομέναν,
ὡς φάτις ἀνδρῶν,
χιών τ᾽ οὐδαμὰ λείπει,
τέγγει δ᾽ ὑπ᾽ ὀφρύσι παγ-
κλαύτοις δειράδας· (828–32)

And rains and snow,
so goes the saying of men,
never leave her as she melts,
but under her all-tearful brows
she wets the mountain ridges;

The petrified Niobe is forever weeping, but she is also forever drenched in rain and snow (οὐδαμὰ λείπει, 830), and the two sources of water are effectively inseparable. In fact, the rain and snow may be the only source of water, the tears being illusory expressions of an interior projected by the surface.[37] But the issue of the tears' semiotic content is submerged by the flood of water that dampens the mountain ridges surrounding Niobe's autotaph (τέγγει … δειράδας, 831–2). The tears *affect* as much as they signify. Niobe is silent, but her lacrimal emissions carry an excess of para-somatic form that amounts to a kind of visual noise, coursing along the boundary between monad and matter and overloading the onlooker's interpretive resources with disquieting resonances.[38]

This scene marks a decisive shift in the development of Antigone's voice, the point at which it becomes formally akin to Niobe's (pseudo-)tears. In her initial exchanges with Ismene and Creon in the prologue and second episode, her voice is direct and brusque, preferring concise commands (41, 82), stark polarities (e.g. 37–8, 442) and brief explanations (499–502), as I discussed earlier. It is only after Creon issues his death sentence that Antigone returns to the stage (801–943) with a more reflective and

---

[37]  On the ambivalent formal and affective character of tears see Brinkema 2014: 1–25. Segal (1964: 54) sees Niobe as an almost utopian figure for Antigone, 'organically fused with the natural world'.

[38]  The Chorus develops this problem in the song that follows Antigone's final departure, when they compare her to a trio of mythological figures (Danae, Lycurgus and the Phineids) who suffer similar fates, although the terms of the comparisons are notoriously varied and obscure (see Bernadete 1999: 116, Griffith 1999: 283–5, Kitzinger 2008: 57–60, among many others). But the problem of the monad and its paradoxical boundaries appears in each of these figures: Danae is sealed in a bronze chamber, but Zeus's 'gold-streaming seed' (950) miraculously passes through the walls and into her womb. Lycurgus is imprisoned in a cave for opposing the cult of Dionysus, and in this condition, 'the blooming force of his madness drips away' (959–60), that is, his state of mind is somehow materialised and cathartically passes out of his body. Finally, the Phineids are blinded when their stepmother gouges their eyes out, a gruesome breach of the boundary between mind and body (970–6).

effusive disposition.[39] Creon even mocks her mournful self-absorption: 'don't you know that if one were required to pour out songs and dirges before dying, no one would ever stop?' (ἆρ᾽ ἴστ᾽, ἀοιδὰς καὶ γόους πρὸ τοῦ θανεῖν | ὡς οὐδ᾽ ἂν εἷς παύσαιτ᾽ ἄν, εἰ χρείη χέων, 883–4).[40] Creon repeatedly attempts to cut off Antigone's outpouring of lament (885–6, 929–30), which starts to resemble Niobe's endless stream of tears, imagined in the previous scene.

Indeed, critics have suggested that Antigone is too effusive during her final speech and that, by speaking too much, she compromises herself and her characterisation. The passage at 904–15, where she argues for Polyneices' value as an irreplaceable sibling, has elicited particular editorial controversy because of its dramatic incongruities and its apparent inconsistency with Antigone's earlier statements explaining her actions.[41] As Bonnie Honig has argued, Antigone also mimes other voices both within and beyond the text of *Antigone*, including Creon, Herodotus and possibly Thucydides.[42] For Honig, the political force of Antigone's voice in this scene lies precisely in its noisy surplus of form, in the way in which she 'parodies, mimics, lampoons, and cites the stories, figures, and speech of the powerful, insinuating her views into their discourse' (146). But perhaps this reading too hastily resolves Antigone's polymorphism back into a single political intention, when in fact the strains of her dirge resist our efforts to trace their emission back to a unitary source, just as Niobe's doubtful tears confound the viewer's efforts to fix their source in her entombed person. Indeed, the Chorus takes the plurality of Antigone's soul as a given, declaring after the end of her final speech that 'the same soul-gusts of the same winds still possess her' (929–30).[43]

As a punishment, Antigone's entombment is designed to reflect and amplify her social and ethical isolation: thus, even as she mourns her state of desertion by friends and family (ἔρημος πρὸς φίλων, 919), Creon decrees that she will be 'deserted, alone … folded up in a covered tomb' (κατηρεφεῖ | τύμβῳ περιπτύξαντες … μόνην ἔρημον, 885–7).[44] But the prospect of living entombment also transfigures Antigone's effectivity as a speaking being in her final appearance. A flood of voices pours from her (ἀοιδὰς καὶ

---

[39]   Scodel 2018 and Sommerstein 2018: 25–6 also note that, after Creon's sentence, Antigone's attitude toward her own death changes from eager anticipation to bitter regret; see Winnington-Ingram 1980: 138–40, Oudemans and Lardinois 1987: 186–8, Neuburg 1990.

[40]   The MS εἰ χρεί᾽ ἢ λέγειν is corrupt; I use Blaydes' emendation (χέων for λέγειν) because of the resonance with Niobe's shedding of tears. See Griffith 1999: 275.

[41]   See Murnaghan 1986, Cropp 1997, Griffith 1999: 277–9.

[42]   Honig 2013: 128–40; on the citation of Herodotus see Murnaghan 1986: 198, Neuberg 1990, Griffith 1999: 227.

[43]   Cf. a similar expression for Capaneus at 137; see Beradete 1999: 114.

[44]   Antigone describes herself as a *metoikos* among the living (852, 868), a designation that Creon echoes (890); see Mueller 2011.

γόους … χέων, 883–4) but, as the controversy surrounding this passage suggests, there is a certain indirection between the speaker and the speech, as if, in an echo of Niobe, the relation between Antigone's self and her expressivity has already been perplexed by the stony barrier awaiting her in the following scene. Under these conditions, Antigone's words may be less consequential for the argument that they make than for the disquiet that their noisiness instils in listeners. Despite his bluster, Creon may have been waiting and listening silently onstage during Antigone's long exchange with the Chorus (781–883),[45] and even though he issues another impatient command to have Antigone led to her tomb (885), there is yet another 'freeze' in the action as she delivers her final, formally excessive, noisy speech. The freeze is justified by dramatic expediency – Antigone needs more stage time – but it may also register the diegetic impact of Antigone's voice on the Chorus, Creon and his attendants, who seem temporarily immobilised or entranced when she launches into her mournful reflections, despite their apparent unresponsiveness to the content of her speeches.

Before we examine the role of noise in the final two scenes, it will be useful to turn back to the first stasimon, the Chorus' famous anthropology, and consider how it meditates on the role of the voice in the partial closure of individual and collective human subjects.[46] The ode begins by celebrating humanity's control over the natural environment and other kinds of animal life (including the 'tribe of birds', 344). In the second strophe, it turns to consider the construction of refuges from nature, human environments like the city and the home that repel destructive forces like weather and disease:

καὶ φθέγμα καὶ ἀνεμόεν φρόνημα καὶ ἀστυνόμους
ὀργὰς ἐδιδάξατο καὶ δυσαύλων
πάγων ὑπαίθρεια καὶ δύσομβρα φεύγειν βέλη
παντοπόρος· (355–9)

And voice and wind-quick thought and city-managing
impulses they taught themselves, and how to escape
the open air of inhospitable frosts and the stormy missiles,
resourceful in everything;

[45] Winnington-Ingram 1980: 100 and Griffith 1999: 274.
[46] Oudemans and Lardinois 1987: 120–31. See Staley 1985 and Crane 1989 on the ode's literary and intellectual context.

The first word in the stanza, *phthegma*, is often translated as 'language' or 'speech',[47] but it is a cognate of *phthongos* and really designates 'the sound of the voice', including the cries of animals.[48] Although 'noise' does not have an exact equivalent in the Greek lexicon, *phthegma* and *phthongos* are often close approximations, referring not to some particular variety of sound (they are applied to human speech, to music and to sounds emitted by animals and machines) but to any acoustic intensity that forcefully impacts a listener.[49] We will see how these terms occur with increasing frequency in the drama's final scenes and serve, I think, to thematise and even hypostatise noise.[50]

The use of *phthegma* at 355 is strung together with a sequence of associated capacities, including thought and affect, in a polyptoton (καὶ … καὶ … καὶ) that marks out an indeterminate space of possibilities, without subordinating one capacity to the others.[51] It is peculiar that this passage, which is framed by humanity's triumph over animal life and its modes of sheltering against the natural elements, should foreground the animal quality of the human voice and the windiness of human thoughts.[52] The monadic impassivity of humans toward the natural world that they master is subtly compromised by the resonance between what is included and what is excluded from

---

[47] E.g. Jebb 1900, Lloyd-Jones 1994 and Mulroy 2013 translate *phthegma* as 'speech', Rayor 2011 as 'language'. The preference is presumably because φθέγμα is the object of ἐδιδάξατο – humans 'teach themselves' language. But the expressivity of the voice, both in and beyond language, is also a capacity that can be formed and developed.

[48] Nooter 2017: 62, referring to the description of Io's voice in *Prometheus Bound*: 'φθέγμα … express[es] the most material aspect of voice, not a linguistic or musical voice, but a grunt, a snort, an animal cry'. Variants of this triad of faculties appears elsewhere in the drama; see Bernadete 1999: 46–7, 129. Segal 1964: 53 notes the ambivalence of the vocabulary in the ode, including *orgas*, *phronēma* and (of course) *deinos*.

[49] LSJ s.v. φθόγγος and φθέγμα. To be sure, not every instance of these terms in the corpus matches my characterisation, but the instances in early Greek poetry do tend to underscore the affective and involuntary impact of sounds rather than their cognitive appraisal. For example, *phthongos* occurs six times in Homer: horses yearn to hear their masters' voice issuing commands to them in the thick of battle (*Il.* 5.234); Odysseus' 'heart is snapped' when he first hears the deep, booming voice of Polyphemus (*Od.* 9.257); Circe warns the Ithacans to avoid the Sirens' polyphonic, enchanting utterances (*Od.* 12.41, 159; 23.326); Penelope's maids awake her from a deep sleep with their voices (*Od.* 18.199). Both *phthongos* and *phthegma* are common in Attic tragedy, and a full examination would exceed the needs of the present discussion. But it is worth noting that in Sophocles' other works, *phthongos* occurs only in *Oedipus at Colonus*, where it designates the mournful wailing of Antigone and Ismene (1610, 1669). *Phthegma* occurs eight times in Sophocles besides *Antigone* (excluding fragments), referring to animal vocalisations (*El.* 18), voices that one longs to hear (*El.* 1225, *Ph.* 1445), voices that inspire loathing (*OC* 863, 1177; *Aj.* 1144) and mournful weeping (*OC* 1623). Other cognates include *phthongē* and *phthengomai*, which do not occur in *Antigone* but occupy a similar semantic field.

[50] There are five instances of *phthongos* (424, 1001, 1187, 1214, 1218) and two of *phthegma* (353, 1148) in *Antigone*; notice that all but two of these seven instances are in the final quarter of the drama.

[51] See Deleuze and Guattari 1987 on the 'conjunctive synthesis'.

[52] On the ode's framing of the 'limitations of human agency' see Kitzinger 2008: 20–30.

human spaces – between 'wind-quick thought' and the frosty sky, between human speech and the animal voice. This kind of ethological imagery recurs in the following scenes, most notably when the Guard compares Antigone's wailing to 'the sharp cry of a bitter bird' (κἀνακωκύει πικρᾶς | ὄρνιθος ὀξὺν φθόγγον, 423–4), as we saw earlier.

The figure of the birdcall returns again in the drama's pivotal scene, its *peripeteia*, which is also by a large margin its noisiest scene. In the fifth episode, Teiresias seeks out Creon to report disturbing news: he has observed unfavourable bird-signs and sacrifices, certain proof that Creon's policy is leading the city to ruin. Teiresias' account of the sound of the birds is a descriptive *tour de force*, registering the blind seer's special attentiveness to aural information. He begins his account with the sounds that he encountered in the augur's seat:

ἀγνῶτ᾽ ἀκούω φθόγγον ὀρνίθων, κακῷ
κλάζοντας οἴστρῳ καὶ βεβαρβαρωμένῳ·
καὶ σπῶντας ἐν χηλαῖσιν ἀλλήλους φοναῖς
ἔγνων· πτερῶν γὰρ ῥοῖβδος οὐκ ἄσημος ἦν. (1001–4)

I heard an unknown noise from the birds,
shrieking with an ugly and incomprehensible frenzy;
and I recognised them rending each other in their murderous
talons; for the whirring of wings was not lacking signification.

Some of the language is simply descriptive – the birds make a *phthongos*, which consists of 'shrieking' and 'whirring' sounds – but the noise is also distinctly unpleasant (κακῷ 1001) and incomprehensible (βεβαρβαρωμένῳ, 1002 ἄσημος 1004). The issue of the sound's (in)comprehensibility is raised repeatedly: the birds' *phthongos* is first called 'unknown' (ἀγνῶτ᾽, 1001); then their whirring is 'not lacking signification' (οὐκ ἄσημος, 1004); and at the end of his speech, Teiresias concludes that the birds' 'cries' were 'not clearly signifying' (οὐδ᾽ ὄρνις εὐσήμους ἀπορροιβδεῖ βοάς, 1021; cf. 1013). This oscillation between sense and nonsense (οὐκ ἄσημος | οὐδ᾽ ... εὐσήμους) is characteristic of noise's disruptive surplus of form which can, like Leibniz's wave, sound 'confused' in gross but contain vast reserves of information in its micrological substructure, in the countless collisions of 'murderous talons' and 'rushing wings'.

An expert seer like Teiresias can discern the relevant *sēmata* in the noise: the birds have feasted on human blood, the corpse of Polyneices, and because of this sacrilege the channel between human and divine spheres has been severed, presaging disaster. This religious pollution takes on ecological dimensions, as the birds stage a revolt of nature against the *polis*, refusing to 'signify clearly' and suspending the order of human dominion extolled in the Ode to Man. The birds' *phthongos*, the point of indistinction between human language and animal cry, now compromises the other monads that have organised the drama to this point. Heeding their sound, Teiresias directs the Thebans to (attempt to) release Antigone from her sealed tomb and to break Creon out of his isolating sense of self-regard.

Commenting on the rhetorical effect of Teiresias' speech, Mark Griffith calls it 'a voice from another dimension'.[53] The directness and forcefulness of the seer's arguments contribute to this effect – no one else, not even Antigone, has stated the case against Creon so convincingly. But the power of the speech also has to do with Teiresias' express effort to convey the aural texture of the otherworldly bird cries that he has heard; and in this, he seems to succeed, overloading his account with vivid acoustic description and a 'sonorous and elevated' diction.[54] Sonic presence serves as a kind of visceral argument that will, Teiresias hopes, compel Creon to accept his religious prescriptions: 'you will understand when you hear the signs of my craft' (γνώσει ... κλύων, 998). Creon initially maintains his haughty façade and refuses to heed Teiresias' advice, but he instantly reverses course after Teiresias departs, admitting to the Chorus that he is 'disturbed' (ταράσσομαι, 1095) by the seer's words and agreeing to the Chorus' plan to free Antigone and bury Polyneices at once.

The noise swells to a shattering intensity in the following scene. Indeed, the amount of sonic detail becomes overwhelming; we, as audiences, are as overloaded as the characters by the (a)signifying density of the text's noisy crescendo. After the Chorus completes its final stasimon, the Messenger arrives to recount the tragic denouement. He has time to relate the bare facts of what has transpired in the cave, when Eurydice joins him and the Chorus, for she 'perceived their words' (τῶν λόγων ἐπῃσθόμην, 1183) while she was leaving the palace to make prayers to Athena:

καὶ τυγχάνω τε κλῇθρ' ἀνασπαστοῦ πύλης
χαλῶσα, καί με φθόγγος οἰκείου κακοῦ
βάλλει δι' ὤτων· ὑπτία δὲ κλίνομαι
δείσασα πρὸς δμωαῖσι κἀποπλήσσομαι.
ἀλλ' ὅστις ἦν ὁ μῦθος αὖθις εἴπατε·
κακῶν γὰρ οὐκ ἄπειρος οὖσ' ἀκούσομαι. (1186–92)

I happened to be releasing the bolts of the gate,
[so that it could be] pushed back, and the sound of family disaster

53 Griffith 1999: 298.
54 Griffith 1999: 298.

struck me through my ears; and I fell back in terror
into my slaves, and I fainted.
But whatever your story was, tell it again;
for I will listen, since I am not inexperienced with disasters.

Eurydice focuses on the perceptual experience of what she has heard but leaves the
content underdetermined: she 'perceived' some *logoi* (which ones – the Messenger's?
The Chorus'? Both?) and has been acutely disturbed by 'the sound of family disaster',
a phrase that oddly underscores the acoustics of the *kakon* rather than its meaning.
Eurydice reinforces the physicality of the news by construing the *phthongos* as an active
force, a home invader: it slips through her barely opened door and 'strikes' her in her ears,
recalling the Guard's notion that a voice can 'sting' either the ears or the mind (317); but
Eurydice's ears and mind are struck at once, and she suffers a lapse of consciousness as
the cataclysmic news lingers indistinctly on the boundary between her sense organs and
her *psukhē*. In the same movement, the noise compromises another kind of boundary:
the hitherto inviolable domestic space of the palace, which serves as the backdrop to the
action of the drama. Eurydice was not even mentioned before her appearance,[55] since
her security within the monadic privacy of the *oikos* was simply taken for granted, but
now this space too has succumbed to the surge of noise that encompasses every corner
of Thebes with its disquieting intensity.[56]

The Messenger resumes his account with an extended narrative of the events that
have transpired offstage. After burying Polyneices' corpse in a tumulus, Creon, the
Messenger and his attendants near Antigone's tomb:

φωνῆς δ᾽ ἄπωθεν <u>ὀρθίων κωκυμάτων</u>
κλύει τις ἀκτέριστον ἀμφὶ παστάδα,
καὶ δεσπότῃ Κρέοντι <u>σημαίνει</u> μολών·
τῷ δ᾽ ἀθλίας <u>ἄσημα</u> περιβαίνει βοῆς
ἕρποντι μᾶλλον ἄσσον, οἰμώξας δ᾽ ἔπος
ἵησι δυσθρήνητον, ᾽ ὦ τάλας ἐγώ,
ἆρ᾽ εἰμὶ μάντις; ἆρα δυστυχεστάτην
κέλευθον ἕρπω τῶν παρελθουσῶν ὁδῶν;
<u>παιδός με σαίνει φθόγγος</u>. ἀλλά, πρόσπολοι,

[55] Reeve 2009: 228 suggests, however, that Creon may allude to his (dysfunctional) relationship with Eurydice
in an earlier scene.
[56] Rehm 2006: 194–5. Eurydice was opening the outer gate (πύλης) when the sound struck her, and she
probably enters the scene through the gates rather than through the side entrance that the other characters
have been using, except for Antigone and Ismene; see Griffith 1999: 327.

ἴτ᾽ ἆσσον ὠκεῖς, καὶ παραστάντες τάφῳ
ἀθρήσατ᾽, ἁρμὸν χώματος λιθοσπαδῆ
δύντες πρὸς αὐτὸ στόμιον, εἰ <u>τὸν Αἵμονος</u>
<u>φθόγγον</u> συνίημ᾽, ἢ θεοῖσι κλέπτομαι᾽. (1206–18)

Someone heard the voice of shrill wailing far off,
around the unhallowed portico,
and went to signal (this) to the master, Creon;
As he draws nearer, indecipherable (sounds) of wretched
shouting surround him, and he groans
and emits a most mournful speech: 'O unhappy me,
am I a prophet? Am I walking on the most unfortunate
path of the ways that are passing by?
The voice of my child greets me. But, attendants,
come closer quickly, and standing by the tomb,
see, once you have entered the stone-torn joint
of the mound into the actual mouth, if I do hear the voice
of Haemon, or if I am deluded by the gods'.

The Messenger stresses the avian quality of the voice that the party perceives outside of
the cave. The adjective ὀρθίων ('shrill', literally 'steep') is almost an anagram of ὀρνίθων
( 'of the birds' ), and this shrill/bird voice is added to Teiresias' birdcalls as yet another
omen of the unfolding disaster: Creon groans as he thinks he recognises the voice's
source and realises that by interpreting this new *phthongos* (1218), he has become, after
Teiresias, the second prophet of his own doom.

   This voice exhibits the same kind of entropic excess as the birdcalls: the servant who
initially hears the voice 'signals' (σημαίνει) its presence to Creon, who soon perceives its
source, but the sound itself is called 'unsignifying' (ἄσημα), and Creon is not certain that
it comes from Haemon.[57] The voice's noisiness presumably reflects both its intensity
and its complicated passage from the depths of the cave, through a cleft in the rocky
exterior and over the intervening country. The listeners do not know this course with
any precision, but they perhaps glean some traces of this acoustic information in their
impression that the sound issues from 'around' or 'near' what the Messenger calls
the *pastas* (ἀμφὶ παστάδα, 1207), an ambiguous term referring either to the portico
surrounding a temple or to the innermost chamber of a home, thus by implication both
the inside and the outside of Antigone's tomb. Both are in fact points in the noise's actual

[57]   Cf. Teiresias' description of the birdcalls as οὐκ ἄσημος but also οὐδ᾽ ... εὐσήμους (1004, 1021).

trajectory. Like the water pouring down the stone face of Niobe, Haemon's cry carries a surplus of resonances that exceeds the listeners' conscious understanding but fills them with an intense disquiet, an almost unbearable anticipation directed toward the scene's disastrous finale.

The noise now takes on a material consistency, 'surrounding' (περιβαίνει, 1209) Creon and 'greeting' him in a personified form (παιδός με σαίνει φθόγγος, 1214) as it accelerates him toward the tomb.[58] At the climax of the drama, the rising noise actively draws the characters into the sonic fold of the tomb, an echo chamber in which their voices and bodies are to be refolded in a new – and, as it turns out – ghastly configuration. When Creon enters the cave and discovers the scene within, he joins his own voice to the uproar, completing the series of *phthongoi* that have passed and reverberated between Antigone, the Guard, Teiresias' birds, Eurydice and Haemon:

ὁ δ' ὡς ὁρᾷ σφε, στυγνὸν οἰμώξας ἔσω
χωρεῖ πρὸς αὐτῷ <u>κἀνακωκύσας</u> καλεῖ· (1227)

But when he saw them, he groaned dreadfully
and advanced inside toward them, and he called out, wailing.

This is one of the two instances of ἀνακωκύω in *Antigone*, both of which are in crasis with καί: the other appears in the avian metaphor that the Guard applies to Antigone when she finds Polyneices' corpse unburied (ἡ παῖς ὁρᾶται <u>κἀνακωκύει</u> πικρῶς, 423). And indeed, Creon here discovers his own 'nestling', Haemon, in a state of extreme peril.[59] The repetition of kappa (<u>κἀνακωκύσας καλεῖ</u>) in the Messenger's account may register the amplified, echoing acoustics in the cave during the complex choreography that follows, as sounds, words and bodies are folded and unfolded by the cave's catalytic loudness. With his wailing cry, Creon echoes the birds and Antigone, forming a kind of alliance with their departed voices; in this desperate spirit of reconciliation, he approaches and calls to Haemon, attempting to reestablish some kind of familial assemblage with him. But Haemon, enraged, emits spit at his father instead of words (<u>πτύσας</u> προσώπῳ κοὐδὲν ἀντειπών, 1232) and,[60] after lunging at him in a failed sword attack, 'folds' his arms around Antigone's corpse (προσ<u>πτύσσεται</u>,

---

[58] On the canine resonance of the expression see Oudemans and Larindois 1987: 181.

[59] Hiscock 2018 unpacks the ambiguous details in this scene surrounding the suicides and the word *autokheir*; see Loraux 1987: 31–2 and Johnson 2006.

[60] Haemon's silence (κοὐδὲν ἀντειπών, 1232) foreshadows Eurydice's response to the Messenger's account: after hearing about her son's suicide, she departs without a word (1244–5), troubling the Messenger and the Chorus with a sense of dread that is soon validated by the news of her own suicide in the palace.

1237) and takes his own life.[61] As Mario Telò observes,[62] the phrases πτύσας προσώπῳ and προσπτύσσεται form an inverted echo that figures the act of spitting as a kind of (un)folding,[63] momentarily joining father and son in a violent assemblage of spit, step and sword, then unfolding them as Haemon turns back to Antigone, joined with her in a final embrace. The noisiness of the scene is more than acoustic: lines of affinity, kinship, voice and violence are condensed into the narrow spatial and textual confines of the cave (1219–43). This surplus of form is then volatilised and ignited, leaving a new situation in Thebes that few of the characters could have imagined from the outset of the drama.

With the deaths of Antigone, Haemon and Eurydice, Creon is left to lament his misfortune and mourn his son and wife (but pointedly, not Antigone) in dialogue with the Chorus. The resolution of *Antigone's* tragic conflict, its Aristotelian *lusis*,[64] also contains a *dialusis*, a 'liquidation' of hostilities in a civil conflict. Nicole Loraux has vividly demonstrated how the notion of civil conflict (*stasis*) involves the division of a community into two mutually exclusive factions; such political monads regard every citizen as either an ally or an enemy and pressure uncommitted parties to pick sides.[65] Athenian political thinkers supposed that this condition of political immobility could be forestalled or resolved by 'mixing' the opposing parties in a balanced regime.[66] Mixture (*mignunai, kerannunai*) is an evocative metaphor, since it suggests a kind of movement that, much like noise, works on a micrological level to undermine the separateness and integrity of opposing bodies.[67] The antagonism between Antigone and Creon amounts to a kind of limited *stasis* that follows immediately upon the full-blown civil war between Eteocles and Polyneices. Under the stimulus of noise, this static division is gradually (and then precipitously) broken down as characters are discharged from their private monads – Creon from his closed *psukhē*, Antigone from her tomb, Eurydice from the palace – and mixed together in a shared sensorium, crisscrossed by a thickening sequence of cries that drive the plot toward its resolution.

After resolving a state of civil conflict, a *polis* might hope to restore its unity either by reconciling the formerly opposing parties or by cementing the political supremacy of

[61] Many commentators have discussed the erotic quality of the death scene; see recently Miller 2014, who relates the imagery to Haemon's destabilisation of gender binaries.
[62] Telò 2020a: 246–9.
[63] Cf. the earlier instances of πτύσσω and compounds at 709 (διαπτυχθέντες – someone like Creon would be empty if 'unfolded') and 886 (περιπτύξαντες – Antigone is to be 'enfolded' by her tomb).
[64] Arist. *Poet.* 1455b; see Halliwell 1986: 211. Discussing resolution in Greek tragedy, Goldhill (2012: 21–2) notes the language of loosening and binding used by characters in *Antigone*.
[65] Loraux 2006: 93–122.
[66] Loraux 2006: 109; on the medical resonances of 'mixture' as a metaphor for political harmony see Brock 2000: 31–2 and Mitchell-Boyask 2008: 39–44.
[67] Cf. Creon's expression at 1311, 'I am mixed with miserable grief!' (δειλαίᾳ δὲ συγκέκραμαι δύᾳ).

the victors.[68] The conclusion of *Antigone* (1257–1353) seems to gesture toward these recuperative possibilities by amplifying the voices of the drama's male elites, Creon and the collection of elder Thebans in the Chorus, who are left alone on stage to have the last word about the emotional and ethical import of the events that have transpired.[69] This moment of clarification, which coincides with the cathartic disclosure of Creon's ruin, would seem to repudiate the noisy excess of the tragic climax, reinstalling a chastened patriarchy to authorise an interpretation of the plot. But, as is often the case in Attic tragedies, and especially in *Antigone*, the interpretive dilemmas that give the drama much of its fascination actually remain unresolved as the plot and the political conflict find their resolution.[70] Even Creon and the Chorus' monopoly of the stage is interrupted by the chilling report of Eurydice's final words – she did not, according to the Messenger, die in silence but was 'singing evil-doings at [Creon], child-killer, until the very end' (λοίσθιον δὲ σοὶ κακὰς | πράξεις ἐφυμνήσασα τῷ παιδοκτόνῳ, 1304–5). The 'evil-doings' are semantically overloaded here, suggesting both an accusation (for what Creon has done to destroy their children) and a curse (against his future *praxeis*). The formal surplus of the reported words, as well as their musical quality (ἐφυμνήσασα), recall the Guard's densely repetitive description of how Antigone wailed like a mother-bird bereft of her children when she encountered Polyneices' unburied corpse (432–5). Whether there can be any political or poetic recuperation in the presence of these persistent, disquieting voices is a question that the drama leaves unanswered. At the very least, it is difficult to feel confidence in the Chorus' stolid admonitions to Creon that life must go on (1334–5).

The drama's refusal to consolidate its own lines of interpretation amounts to a kind of metadramatic noisiness that should undermine any certainties we might entertain about what kinds of responses – relief, pleasure, exhaustion, agitation, disgust? – the drama is supposed to produce in its audiences. Perhaps it is not surprising, then, that the god of tragedy is depicted so equivocally in his handful of appearances in *Antigone*.[71] In the fifth stasimon, the Chorus envisions Dionysus as 'supervisor of the night-time voices'

---

[68] See Gray 2015 on the variety of post-*stasis* settlements, from the conciliatory to the exclusionary, in the late Classical and Hellenistic periods; on the Athenian settlement after the democratic restoration in 403 BC, see Loraux 2006.

[69] Creon recognises the ruin of his life and his own culpability (1261–9, 1317–18, 1340–3), although he also attributes his recklessness to the agency of a malign god (1272–4). The Chorus spells out the lesson (ἐδίδαξαν, 1353) that moderation and reverence toward the gods are the foundations of human happiness.

[70] See Griffith 1999: 43–54 on *Antigone's* 'baffling open-endedness' and the various contradictions that the drama raises but does not resolve.

[71] There are references to Dionysus at 153–4, 955–65 and 1115–54; Winnington-Ingram 1980: 110–16 discusses the irony of the Chorus' invocation of Dionysus (1115–54), a god whose unsettling duality is signalled throughout the drama.

in songs and dances around and far beyond the city (νυχίων … φθεγμάτων, 1146–7). This euphoric picture sees the god pass instantly from the 'ivy-clad heights of Nysa' to the 'streets of Thebes' as the divine chants sound around him (1132–5), annulling the boundary between city and environment in a noisy contraction of space and time.[72] The Chorus celebrates this scene of reconciled nature just before the final episode, when they still hope (in vain) that Dionysus will heal the city's 'disease' with his 'purifying foot' (καθαρσίῳ ποδὶ, 1144).[73] Dionysus' foot and *phthegmata* – a likely allusion to the dancing and singing of the tragic stage – are invoked as a cure to the (political) ailments staged within the tragedy itself.[74] In the event, the city's divisions are resolved, but the Chorus' hopes are dashed when the deaths of Antigone and Haemon are announced moments after the end of their hymn.[75] As if to refuse the figure of efficient catharsis, Creon laments soon after that 'the harbour of Hades', now packed with dead family members, is 'difficult to purify' (δυσκάθαρτος Ἀιδου λιμήν, 1284).[76] Indeed, as the drama concludes, the voices of the dead Thebans – and soon of Creon and the Chorus – fall silent, but their noisiness persists in audiences' *psukhai*, in what Deleuze calls 'folds of the soul' that interrupt any effort to distil a single, authoritative voice from the disquieting uproar of *Antigone*.

---

[72]  Macedo 2011 maps the spatial organisation of the hymn into horizontal (near/distant to Thebes) and vertical (mountains/coast) dimensions – Dionysus traverses these divisions even as he unites the cosmic with the local.

[73]  On the Chorus' optimism see Kitzinger 2008: 66. The 'disease' may refer to the religious pollution of the city, brought on by the neglect of Polyneices' corpse, but it also alludes to the disease of political *stasis* that began with the exile of Oedipus; see Scullion 1998. On *stasis* as *nosos* see Mitchell-Boyask 2008: 40–1.

[74]  Macedo 2011 argues that the ode alludes reflexively to the tragedy's performance context of the City Dionysia; Scullion 1998 argues that Dionysus' 'purifying foot' (1144) is a reference to ecstatic ritual dances intended to cure mental illness and, figuratively, the 'illness' of the Theban *stasis*; see Henrichs 1994–5 (esp. 77–9) on the Chorus' self-referentiality as a bridge between the fictional world of tragedy and the ritual reality of tragic performance.

[75]  Cf. Griffith 1999: 321 ('but κάθαρσις can be painful') and Cullyer 2005: 20 ('Delphic Dionysus does bring katharsis to the city, but at the price of yet more deaths').

[76]  See Telò 2020a on tragedy's anticathartic aesthetics, esp. p. 249 on *duskathartos*.

# Euripidean Lyric through the Eyes of Aristophanes
*Marcus Ellis*

Among all that is at stake in negotiating the rift between Greek drama as originally received and the texts and testimonia that remain to us today, and attempting to recover from the latter the spectacular sensory impact of the art form, aesthetics stands as a matter of particular significance. Ultimately, in fact, the sensory and the aesthetic are inseparable. As discussed in the introduction, aesthetics can be understood as encompassing all features of a given work of art which impact the senses of its audience, affecting their perception of it.

Consequently, the potential for mutual illumination through combined study of the aesthetic and the sensory represents a vital opportunity for advancement in contemporary scholarship on Greek tragedy. This a field in which the rising interest in aesthetics in the study of Greek literature and culture more broadly, following the wider 'aesthetic turn' in the arts and humanities, has so far made relatively little impact;[1] yet the effect of tragic artistry on an audience is a key and eternally contested issue of the genre, resonating from ancient authors such as Aristophanes and Aristotle down to modern tragedy and tragic theory, and is intimately bound up with its enduring popularity outside of academia, for instance in modern performance.

A driving force not only in this aesthetic renaissance but in the affect theory that forms a keystone of this volume, further revealing the profound and intricate association of aesthetics and sensation, is the thought of Maurice Merleau-Ponty. His insistence, intended to challenge both idealist and empiricist philosophy, on the 'primacy of perceptual experience' – and especially his characterisation of perception as embodied knowledge of the world, and his situation of consciousness in the body[2] – lies at the heart of a general shift

---

[1] Ellis 2022 represents a broad attempt to remedy this. On aesthetics in Greek literature see Porter 2010, Peponi 2012, Sluiter and Rosen 2012, Destrée and Murray 2015a, Cazzato and Lardinois 2016, Gurd 2016, Grethlein 2017, Liebert 2017, Budelmann and Phillips 2018a, Childs 2018, Kidd 2019.

[2] For these characterisations of Merleau-Ponty's thought cf. Armstrong 2005 – largely drawing on Merleau-Ponty 1945.

in emphasis in the arts and humanities from the intellectual and semantic to the sensory and embodied, foundational to many trends in critical theory. Taking their cue from the latter, several chapters in this volume similarly focus on embodied experience.

Modern formalist aesthetic philosophy, too, sharpens conception of the relation of aesthetics and sensation in art. It complements the phenomenologically-inspired emphasis on embodied perception by foregrounding the object perceived. Form – defined as that which is directly accessible to the senses and can be immediately experienced – is central to such philosophy's understanding of artworks of all kinds; such formal features may be, but are not always, entirely distinct from meaning.[3] This current of ideas, in which the conception of a work's artistry is moved away from questions of content, is an important setting for the hypothesis presented in this chapter: namely, that Euripidean lyric appeals to the senses in a unique manner through its formal, structural and stylistic characteristics.

Consideration of the immediate impact on the senses of tragic artwork, however, necessarily raises the question of the effect it has beyond this immediate impact – that is, how the latter is processed by the mind receiving the sensory input. Indeed, the idea that it might be possible entirely to separate the questions of the senses and of the mind in its intellectual aspect seems dubious: as soon as a sensory input is registered – as soon as we are conscious of it – it has already entered the sphere of mental analysis.

Accordingly, my chapter aims to push the limits of our conception of the sensory, forging beyond Merleau-Ponty and affect theory to encompass mental process, to underscore the porousness of the boundary between embodied sense and intellectual interpretation – and thus to weave the latter back into the sensory framework that is the focus of this volume. Here, neuroscience and contemporary developments in cognitive theory – concerning the way both sensory data and the concepts they sometimes convey are received, processed, manipulated and deployed by the mind – afford valuable tools to break new ground in conceptions of Euripidean tragic aesthetics through an emphasis on mental operations triggered by textual features of all kinds, deepening and nuancing our account of the relation between, and function of, form and content in his work.[4] Content, it emerges, often plays the role of a constituent part in Euripides' formal lyric artistry – furnishing components from which it is created – as well as comprising an emotive or striking 'message' this lyric form is designed to convey.

Drawing on these considerations, I present a novel theory of how Euripidean lyric engages the senses – and the mind that is inextricably bound up with them. To

---

[3]  For a nuanced account see Zangwill 2001.

[4]  For further perspectives on the relation of the senses to cognitive processes see the chapters by Chiara Blanco and Peter Meineck in this volume.

anticipate, I propose two related theses. Firstly, that late Euripidean lyric in some respects displays a structural similarity, quite independent of content, to physical, visual art objects. Secondly, and more significantly, that late Euripidean lyric can be understood to trigger a mental response that resembles typical responses to visual art – again, regardless of the content presented. Overall, this chapter illuminates the remarkably sophisticated way in which Euripidean verse *itself* captures the senses *qua* text: its inherent visuality, a quality that it is somewhat counterintuitive to associate with poetry, is rooted in its very structural and formal qualities – in other words, in some of its most abstract literary characteristics.

In the process, the approach taken paves the way for a cautious probing of the extent of the subjectivity of aesthetic experience. Underlying the question of the cognitive effect of the creative arts is the consideration of whether it might be possible to identify any commonality in responses to given aesthetic features.

I would like to stress from the outset – to avoid confusion – that my concern is not with explicitly visual imagery. Some of the examples presented do involve such imagery, but that is not the reason for their inclusion; rather it is certain structural features, to be described below, that lead me to draw attention to them. While this chapter complements work that emphasises the richness of Euripides' explicit visual imagery,[5] its themes are ultimately of a markedly different stamp.

My starting point is an account of the sensory experience of tragic lyric offered by a contemporary: the comic poet Aristophanes. Caution is, of course, in order when reading any text through comic reception.[6] However, while such sources inevitably involve some parodic distortion, when – as in this chapter – read against Euripidean lyric itself in order to corroborate their suggestions and avoid any misleading avenues, they prove useful indicators of particular idiosyncrasies of Euripidean composition. Indeed, distortion of an exaggerative stamp – which will often be encountered in any attempt to shed light on one text by reading it through reception in another,[7] and is certainly to be expected in parody – may *itself* bring to light features of the work parodied that would otherwise have remained obscure.

---

[5]  Zeitlin 1994 is a landmark study. See also e.g. Barlow 1971, Stieber 2011, Torrance 2013: 63–134. On a rather different aspect of visuality in tragedy – namely the spectatorial 'act of seeing theatre' (4) – see Weiss 2023a. Dedicated to plays that 'interrogate the spectator's own viewing experience', and the question of 'the extent to which such plays share elements of visuality with the … medium of vase painting' (4), this book adopts a 'phenomenological approach' which 'foregrounds the experience of the spectator and their engagement with performance, in terms of their own bodied presence within a material event' (12).

[6]  LeVen 2014: 71–112, for instance, argues at length that comedy is unreliable as a source for late fifth-century lyric avant-gardism and the qualities it was supposed to possess.

[7]  On such reading practices cf. Martindale 1993, Martindale and Thomas 2006.

The Aristophanic characterisation of Euripidean lyric with which I am here concerned suggests that, although the approach I take to Euripidean lyric is rooted in modern theory and philosophy, similar concepts were already associated with it in the ancient world. His literary reception of Euripides, effectively an ancient 'reading' of his poetry, aids us in *seeing* Euripidean lyric in a new light.[8]

## Euripidean Lyric and Visuality in *Frogs*

In the poetic contest between the traditionalist Aeschylus and the radically progressive Euripides that forms the climax of Aristophanes' *Frogs* (405 BC), Aeschylus interrupts a bizarrely florid and confusing parody of Euripidean choral lyric he is performing with the following exchange:[9]

> Αι. ὁρᾶις τὸν πόδα τοῦτον;
> Ευ.                                              ὁρῶ.
> Αι. τί δαί; τοῦτον ὁρᾶις;
> Δι.                                              ὁρῶ. (1323–4)

> AESCHYLUS. Do you see that foot?
> EURIPIDES. I see it.
> AESCHYLUS. And this one, see that?
> DIONYSUS. I see it.[10]

Kenneth Dover suggests that Aeschylus is referring by his first remark to the dance movements he is himself performing while singing, and by the second to the metrical abnormality Euripides has produced by his answer ὁρῶ – which adds an extra short syllable at the end of the line, disrupting a run of glyconics.[11]

---

[8]  Hunter 2009: 10–52 reveals that Aristophanes' *Frogs* – the comedy at issue – presents paradigms that were to become central to later criticism.

[9]  Text as in Wilson 2007. Some uncertainty surrounds the two replies ὁρῶ; in the MSS these are both assigned to Dionysus (cf. Borthwick 1994: 34), but editors variously divide them between the two or even (e.g. Henderson 2002) attribute them both to Euripides. However, my case, which focuses on the visuality attributed to Euripides' lyric though these comments, stands regardless of who speaks the lines in question.

[10]  Trans. adapted from Henderson 2002 throughout.

[11]  Cf. Dover 1993 ad loc.

There is certainly a pun here exploiting the ambiguity of πούς as a metrical/physical foot.[12] However, it is arguably more natural to assume that it plays on the physical appearance, and probably the dancing,[13] of another character – the Muse of Euripides, whom Aeschylus summons to aid his performance of pseudo-Euripidean lyrics:[14]

που 'στιν ή τοῖς ὀστράκοις
αὕτη κροτοῦσα; δεῦρο, Μοῦσ' Εὐριπίδου,
πρὸς ἥνπερ ἐπιτήδεια ταῦτ' ἄιδειν μέλη. (1305–7)

Where's that female percussionist who plays potsherds? Oh Muse of Euripides, come out here; you're the proper accompanist for a recital of these songs.

Aeschylus' pun, then, draws on the polyvalence of πούς to equate the metrical components of Euripides' lyric with visually observable body parts. In doing so, it suggests the status of the Muse as a visual incarnation of Euripides' lyric. The aura of visuality thus cumulatively attributed to the latter is particularly marked in the casting of both iterations of πούς – physical and metrical in reference – as objects of ὁρῶ. This staging of Euripides' lyric, that is to say, characterises it as somehow inherently visual, down to the level of its fundamental technical structure.[15]

This portrayal of Euripidean lyric in particularly visual terms is heightened by contrast with the aurally focused parody of Aeschylus that preceded it.[16] Both 'Aeschylean' songs presented by Euripides involve refrains repeated between lines, in the first instance ἰὴ κόπον οὐ πελάθεις ἐπ' ἀρωγάν, 'Aiee the strike! – draw you not near to the rescue?' (1265f., a citation from Aeschylus' Myrmidons), and in the

---

[12]  A near contemporary instance of the usage of πούς in a metrical sense is Pl. Resp. 400. Cf. Dover 1993 ad loc. The scholia offer a similar interpretation.

[13]  Cf. Barker 2004: 199.

[14]  Σ Ar. Ran. 1305 claim that this is a spoof of a scene in Euripides' Hypsipyle in which the title character sang, accompanying herself with the krotala, to amuse the infant Opheltes. Cf. Dover 1993 ad loc.; also Hall 2006: 173, de Simone 2008: 480 n. 7.

[15]  While Euripides' Muse is the only 'literary concept' represented in the numerous female personifications extant in Aristophanes, 'feminine metapoetic figures' are frequent in Old Comedy at large, for instance Comedy in Cratinus' Pytine and Mousike in Pherecrates' Cheiron; Hall 2006: 175–6, 181–3. In fact, Sommerstein 2005 suggests that Aristophanes was the originator of this trend. The staging of a personification of Euripides' lyric in Frogs is nonetheless distinguished by a particularly prominent visuality, above all due to the notable contrast with the parodies of Aeschylus' lyrics. Note that, while less marked, the attribution of fundamental visuality to Euripidean lyric stands even if 1323–4 is taken to refer to Aeschylus' foot.

[16]  On the importance of sound in Aristophanes' characterisation of Aeschylus cf. Scharffenberger 2006–7; on sonic features of Aeschylean tragedies themselves cf. Gurd 2016: 63–83.

second the nonsense word φλαττοθραττοφλαττοθρατ (1286f.), obviously intended to represent the monotonous sound of the lyre,[17] evoking the kitharodic nomes from which, Euripides claims, these songs were adapted.[18] The aural tedium of these lyrics is underlined by Dionysus' irritated comparison of them to 'rope-winders' songs', i.e. typically repetitive work songs.[19]

Aristophanes' framing of his parodies of Euripides' avant-gardist lyric with this emphasis on their visuality raises the question of whether genuine Euripidean lyric can be understood to be somehow inherently visual. A first step in uncovering the reasons behind this characterisation is to analyse the parodies themselves.[20] These provide the key to appreciating a distinguishing formal feature of Euripidean lyric that will prove fundamental to its sensory uniqueness.

## Juxtapositional Structures, 'Conceptual Blends' and Visuality

One of the most prominent stylistic idiosyncrasies of the parodies of Euripidean lyric is their juxtapositional structuring. This is evident at both a macrocosmic and microcosmic level in the text.[21] Take, for instance, the parody of Euripides' choral lyrics:

ἀλκυόνες, αἳ παρ' ἀενάοις θαλάσσης
κύμασι στωμύλλετε,
τέγγουσαι νοτίοις πτερῶν
ῥανίσι χρόα δροσιζόμεναι·
αἵ θ' ὑπωρόφιοι κατὰ γωνίας
εἰειειειειλίσσετε δακτύλοις φάλαγγες
ἱστότονα πηνίσματα,
κερκίδος ἀοιδοῦ μελέτας,
ἵν' ὁ φίλαυλος ἔπαλλε δελ-
φὶς πρώιραις κυανεμβόλοις
μαντεῖα καὶ σταδίους,
οἰνάνθας γάνος ἀμπέλου,

17 Cf. Dover 1993 ad loc.
18 Ar. *Ran.* 1282. On the lyre cf. Bélis 1991, Borthwick 1994: 22, Griffith 2013: 136.
19 Ar. *Ran.* 1296–7. Cf. Dover 1993 ad loc. On the metrical monotony of these songs see Scharffenberger 2006–7: 243–4, Griffith 2013: 134–6.
20 Silk 1993: 481–90 and Griffith 2013: 115–49 note that the depictions of Aeschylus and Euripides in *Frogs*, despite simplifications and exaggerations, ring true in many respects.
21 These terms are intended to capture the teeming 'worlds' of ideas that, as will become clear, such structures may evoke.

βότρυος ἕλικα παυσίπονον.
περίβαλ᾿, ὦ τέκνον, ὠλένας. (1309–22)

You Halcyons, who babble beside the ever-flowing waves of the sea, wetting and bedewing the flesh of your wings with rainy drops; and you spiders in crannies beneath the roof who with your fingers wi-i-i-i-ind loom-taut spoolings, a recital by the minstrel loom, where the pipe-loving dolphin leaped at the prows with their dark rams for oracles and race tracks, for the sparkle of the vine's winey blossom, for the anodyne tendril of the grape cluster. Throw your arms about me, child!

Here, we are faced with a series of images – halcyons, spiders, a dolphin, grapes – with no apparent connection to each other. The juxtapositional ordering of these images, which lacks any overt logical sequence, is remarkable.

This juxtaposition is made particularly jarring by the fact that, despite the lack of logical sequence, in two cases a grammatical link between the images forces us to try to combine them into some sort of meaningful whole. As Dover notes, the phrase 'where the dolphin …' is – bizarrely – attached to the 'corners of the ceiling where spiders spin their webs'.[22] A similar effect is achieved in the transition from the 'dolphin' image to the 'grape' image: οἰνάνθας γάνος ἀμπέλου, | βότρυος ἕλικα παυσίπονον is in apposition to μαντεῖα καὶ σταδίους (that is, it is also something for which the dolphin leapt),[23] and so a particularly baffling connection between them is set up.[24] This leaves the audience struggling to make some sense out of the passage: there is no refuge in simply treating it as a series of unconnected tableaux.

An example of juxtapositional structure at the microcosmic scale of individual words and phrases is the compound word κελαινοφαής in the phrase ὦ νυκτὸς κελαινοφαὴς ὄρφνα, 'Oh black-shining murk of night …' (1331), with which the parody of Euripidean monody opens. It is difficult to combine the concepts of 'dark' and 'shining' in any way that makes sense in the context of a reference to the darkness of night. The term could conceivably describe a gleaming black object, but this is obviously irrelevant here; perhaps it refers to the stars or to other nocturnal sources of very low light, but 'black-

[22] Dover 1993: 352.
[23] On this reading 1322 is a sudden and unrelated interjection; cf. Dover 1993 ad loc.
[24] Dover 1993 ad loc. comments that the effect is that of 'deliberate nonsense'.

shining' is at the least a rather awkward way of describing such things.[25] Aristophanes' parodies of Euripidean lyric are, in fact, full of features of this sort.[26]

The attributes of Aristophanes' parodies described above recall a recent assessment, by Felix Budelmann and Pauline LeVen, of the 'New Music'. This modern term is used by scholars to refer to a 'style of song performed by star performers in large theatres in the last quarter of the fifth and the first quarter of the fourth century ... characterised by the complexity of its instrumental, melodic and stylistic features'.[27] The musical and poetic movement in question is commonly understood to encompass non-dramatic poetry (above all dithyramb and nome),[28] and frequently also dramatic poetry.

The relevance of the New Music and its contemporary study to the interpretation of the parodies of Euripidean lyric in *Frogs* is hardly surprising. The lyric of Euripides' late, avant-gardist works has long been associated with the New Music[29] – Eric Csapo, indeed, characterises him as a forerunner in it[30] – and his affiliations with it are in fact implied by *Frogs*' parodies. The heavy use of anadiplosis and exaggerated melismata[31] – presumably reflective of the setting of the words to the melody – and their florid diction, often descending into verbiage,[32] recall the New Music's privileging of music over word[33] and its linguistic tendency to 'put more emphasis on sound than sense'.[34]

---

[25] Dover 1993 ad loc. attempts to deal with this difficulty by suggesting that we should take the -φαής element to 'serve simply as a suffix to a colour-term', although he concedes that 'white-shining' is an 'appropriate translation' for λευκοφαής in λευκοφαῆ ψάμαθον ('white-shining sand'; Eur. *IA* 1054). Tzetzes ad Ar. *Ran.* 1331 suggests that it simply means ἡ μέλαινα φαινομένη ('appearing black'); the Σ ad loc. posit the meanings σκοτεινή ('shadowy') and ἡ φῶς ἔχουσα μέλαν (the beautifully oxymoronic 'characterised by black light'). On κελαινοφαής as a parody of Euripidean oxymora see Silk 1993: 483. There is a possibility that this is a genuine Euripidean epithet: Page 1941: 84 prints [κελαιν]οφαῆ in Eur. *Hyps.* fr. 752f.4. If this reading is correct, *Frogs*' parody is particularly sharp: Aristophanes is highlighting the latent absurdity of an authentic Euripidean expression by placing it in the context of other highly eccentric juxtapositional structures.

[26] Cf. especially Ar. *Ran.* 1316, 1317–18 and the conglomeration of such tropes at 1332–7.

[27] Budelmann and LeVen 2014: 191. On the New Music see also Csapo 1999–2000, Csapo 2003, Csapo 2004, D'Angour 2006, Csapo 2008, Csapo 2009, Csapo and Wilson 2009, Power 2010: 82–9, 500–54, Csapo 2011, D'Angour 2011: 184–206, Steiner 2011, LeVen 2014.

[28] On which genres cf. e.g. Ford 2013, Franklin 2013, Power 2013.

[29] Kranz 1933 was particularly influential in this regard.

[30] Csapo 1999–2000: 405–15. See also Battezzato 2005, Steiner 2011, Griffith 2013: 136–49, Weiss 2018a: 116–30, Weiss 2018c.

[31] Ar. *Ran.* 1314, 1349, 1352–5.

[32] E.g. Ar. *Ran.* 1311–12.

[33] Cf. Borthwick 1994: 30–1.

[34] LeVen 2014: 164. Silk 1993: 483 notes that these parodies accurately capture Euripidean pleonasm and anadiplosis.

Furthermore, these parodies feature extensive imagery of rotation and whirling;[35] this is a common characteristic of New Musical compositions, frequently occurring in self-reflexive passages.[36]

Budelmann and LeVen suggest that a system of 'blending' or 'conceptual integration' (drawn from a cognitive theory developed by Gilles Fauçonnier and Mark Turner,[37] and thus rooted in the mind's fundamental processes) is especially characteristic of the language of Timotheus – arguably foremost among the New Musicians[38] – and indeed of the language of the New Music in general.[39] Blending is the combination of 'two different, often apparently incompatible, inputs in such a way that a new, third, thing emerges';[40] the 'inputs' consist of concepts, or sets of concepts, as does the 'blend' itself that they are combined to create. Budelmann and LeVen describe the operation of blending as follows:

> The speaker, or listener or reader, needs to identify a 'generic space', that is, the structure shared by two 'inputs', and map this structure, in turn, back onto the two inputs. So structured, the two inputs are projected onto one another and the result of the projection is the 'blend'.[41]

As far as literary texts go, they claim, blending is at the heart of features such as metaphor, metonymy, periphrasis, compound words and counterfactuals, to name but a few.[42] However – as will become clear – analysing such features as blends brings to light fascinating aspects not only of their conceptual structure, but also of their effect on the mind of the hearer or reader.

I suggest that it is the centrality of such a process to Euripidean lyric that Aristophanes is lampooning in his portrayal of it as full of bizarre and confusing juxtapositions. It is easy to see how a poetics that makes heavy use of the combination of conceptual inputs that are often seemingly unrelated into new structures is open to parody that characterises such combinations as downright nonsensical.

For my purposes, the possibility that – in light of Aristophanes' parodies and given the links of Euripidean compositions to the tradition of poetry now termed the New

[35]  See Ar. *Ran.* 1313–21, 1346–51, 1356–7.
[36]  Cf. Griffith 2013: 147–8, and on whirling imagery and the New Music in general Csapo 2008: 280–86.
[37]  See above all Fauçonnier and Turner 1998, Fauçonnier and Turner 2002.
[38]  Campbell 1993: 6.
[39]  Budelmann and LeVen 2014.
[40]  Budelmann and LeVen 2014: 193.
[41]  Budelmann and LeVen 2014: 194.
[42]  Budelmann and LeVen 2014: 193.

Music – blending might be particularly prominent in Euripides' late lyric is significant, as it is arguably the case that blends are characterised by formal, structural features that endow them with an inherent visuality.

Blends reveal an often unexpected parallel between the conceptual structure of two things – i.e. a set of corresponding attributes – that enables their combination, presenting a novel image or piece of information. They lack sequentiality, both in the structure identified in the inputs (its component attributes are a number of propositions that are simultaneously true and have no inherent sequence) and in the parallel relation between them.[43] Since they consist of a non-linear manipulation of a set of concepts that is itself non-linear – with the two inputs colliding to create a new 'output' – blends can be understood to have an effectively two-dimensional, intrinsically spatial quality. Furthermore – although the visual, as a sensory sphere, is in any case closely associated with apprehension of the spatial – in the context of a more general, widespread association of the visual and the verbal in ancient Greek culture,[44] the spatiality of verbally expressed blends would, I suggest, have particularly evoked an aura of visuality.

---

[43]  Cf. diagram at Budelmann and LeVen 2014: 194.

[44]  This note offers a window onto this topic through some examples especially germane to tragedy. Gorgias, whose thought has been understood as an influence on some of Euripides' works (cf. e.g. Wright 2005: 226–337), suggests speech arouses φρίκη and ἔλεος, 'shuddering' and 'pity', (Gorg. *Hel.* 9), in a manner often thought to prefigure Aristotelian understandings of tragedy; cf. Munteanu 2012: 37. Interestingly, Gorgias accords similar powers to ὄψις, 'sight'; indeed, 'even more than Speech … sight appears to be defined through its emotional effect on the soul, and especially through its production of "fear" (φόβος)': Gorg. *Hel.* 16–17, discussed by Munteanu 2012: 45, drawing on Ford 2002, 181. The close association, in Gorgias' theory, of vision and word is manifest in his belief that 'vision acts on the mind as if it has written a text' – ὄψις ἐνέγραψεν: Gorg. *Hel.* 17; Munteanu 2012: 47. Aristotle famously characterises tragedy as eliciting ἔλεος and φόβος, 'pity' and 'fear', at Arist. *Poet.* 1449b24–8. This work is notable for 'its influence in perpetuating logocentric accounts of tragedy'; Wiles 2007: 238. ὄψις, by contrast, is listed last in the six elements of which he claims tragedy consists, and described as ἀτεχνότατον … καὶ ἥκιστα οἰκεῖον τῆς ποιητικῆς, 'falling quite outside the art and not integral to poetry' (trans. adapted from Halliwell, Fyfe, Russel and Innes 1999 here and below); Arist. *Poet.* 1450b16–20. Despite this, Munteanu takes a relatively positive view of the role accorded to vision in the *Poetics*, arguing, on the basis of Arist. *Poet.* 1453b1–5, 7–10, that Aristotle merely 'subordinated' spectacle to the 'poetic art' in drama; Munteanu 2012: 81–2, drawing on Janko 1984: 229 and Halliwell 1998: 337–43. The statement at Arist. *Poet.* 1453b1 that ἔστιν μὲν οὖν τὸ φοβερὸν καὶ ἐλεεινὸν ἐκ τῆς ὄψεως γίγνεσθαι, 'it is possible for the pitiful and fearful to arise from spectacle', certainly leaves no doubt that, in Aristotle's view, spectacle, as well as poetry, could contribute to the effects that were the hallmark of tragedy. Not only (near) contemporary literary theory, but literature itself offers examples of a conceptual linkage of the visual and the verbal. One of the earliest instances of this is Hom. *Od.* 8.63–4 on the Phaeacian bard Demodocus. The fact that song is given in exchange for sight here establishes an equivalence between the two. (For alternative readings of these lines cf. Garvie 1994 ad loc., Buxton 1980: 27–30, Bassi 2016: 66.) Visual–verbal synaesthetic features are exhibited in Aeschylean and Sophoclean tragedy – for instance Aesch. *Th.* 103, κτύπον δέδορκα, 'I see the din'; Gurd 2016: 83–9.

Blends, that is to say, can be understood to have an inherently visual quality, regardless of the nature of the concepts that constitute their inputs. This quality, as will become apparent, is more or less salient depending on how they are deployed. For now, I note one contributing factor to the distinguishing visuality of Euripidean blends as received in the fifth century BC – namely that, in the context of a dramatic performance in which space would have been experienced by an audience primarily in visual terms,[45] the visuality inevitably implicated in the spatiality of blends would have been felt with heightened force.

Indeed, the spatiality and visuality of blending is further intimated by the fact that it seems impossible to escape the spatial and visual in describing it. Witness not only its conceptualisation in terms of 'mapping' and 'projection' by Budelmann and LeVen, but the fact that they, and others, find it expedient to present blending with the help of diagrams illustrating the non-linear manner in which the different conceptual inputs come together to be combined as one.[46] This accentuates the conceptual two-dimensionality of the process.

The non-linearity of blends encourages us to interpret them in a manner akin to what neuroscientific studies of eye-movement have shown to be our standard mode of engagement with visual representations. We explore both in a non-linear manner, returning to or reflecting on points that interest or confuse us, jumping from one area of the image or set of concepts to another rather than experiencing them in a linear sequential fashion.[47]

It might be objected that, ultimately, language conveys its information in sequence, and thus cannot achieve the full non-linearity of communication of a visual representation. Nonetheless, my argument stands, as it remains that the communicative function of the language of blends is significantly non-sequential. It creates, and invites contemplation of, intricate and frequently extraordinary linkages of (aspects of) images or ideas, rather than simply relating a series of events or facts. Furthermore, although it is theoretically always possible to process linguistic communication in a non-linear manner, blending specifically *encourages* a non-linear processing of the information proffered.[48]

---

[45] With some minor exceptions such as throwing nuts into the audience during comedy: cf. Ar. *Vesp.* 58–9. Note also on this point the strong association of choral performance and visual art; cf. Power 2011: 80–9, Kurke 2013: 146–60.

[46] Budelmann and LeVen 2014: 194, inspired by Fauçonnier and Turner 2002.

[47] On such features of engagement with visual art cf. e.g. Jarbus 1967, Land and Tatler 2009, Grethlein 2017: 32, 164–5.

[48] In a somewhat similar vein Csapo comments that various Euripidean New Musical odes 'are in words what a triglyph and metope frieze is in images' (Csapo 2009: 96) and that 'Instead of building events up into a story, or propositions up into an argument, Euripides' verse offers us an almost purely paratactic sequence, a gallery of images' (Csapo 2003: 72, basing these features on an analysis of Eur. *El.* 432–41; he draws on Cropp 1988: 128).

The parodic insight into the qualities of Euripidean verse offered by *Frogs*, then, suggests the following hypothesis. Aristophanes' characterisation of his poetry as full of complex juxtapositional structures illuminates Euripides' use of blending, a process typical of the New Music. Such blending endows it with an inherent visuality – to recap, both a structural similarity to, and a capacity to engage the interpretative faculties in a manner parallel to, visual art objects. This is not dependent on content – the nature of the individual inputs in any one case – but rather arises from literary form: the way the inputs are combined, a constant across all blends. It is this inherently visual quality that was recognised by Aristophanes.

## Visuality and Blending in Euripides' *Iphigenia in Aulis*

Blending in fact pervades Euripidean odes. The lyric of *Iphigenia in Aulis* (hereafter *IA*) offers illuminating examples of its function in his compositions. First performed posthumously, probably in 405 BC, along with *Bacchae* and the fragmentary *Alcmaeon in Corinth*,[49] it is one of the very latest extant Euripidean tragedies. Unlike *Bacchae*, which has frequently been understood as a reactionary work,[50] *IA* represents the final development of late Euripidean avant-gardist lyric, closest in time to its parodic refraction in *Frogs*. In consequence, it constitutes an informative test case for the hypothesis proposed at the end of the last section.[51]

### *Microcosmic Blending*

A usefully representative instantiation of the structural nature and effects of individual Euripidean blends occurs in the third stasimon of *IA*, which contrasts the wedding of Peleus and Thetis with the imminent sacrifice of Iphigenia. The centaurs who attend the

---

[49] Stockert 1992: 3.
[50] Cf. Billings 2018: 57–9. Dodds 1960: xxxvi–xxxviii and esp. Seaford 1996 are notable instances of this trend.
[51] The textual history of *IA* is, of course, notoriously complex. There is no space here to address this issue in full; suffice it merely to say that the third stasimon, from which all following examples are drawn, is considered by recent editors to be either genuinely Euripidean or written in close imitation of his style to complete a play commonly thought to have been left unfinished at his death (cf. Stockert 1992: 129–31, 496–511, Diggle 1994: 399–401, Kovacs 2003: 102). Even assuming that it was not written by Euripides, it would remain valuable evidence for the characteristics that were thought by contemporaries to be the distinguishing features of his style, and would thus be a revealing case in point for the visuality of Euripidean lyric. For a similar approach to the textual problems of the play cf. Torrance 2013: 83. Another modern contribution of note on these issues is Gurd 2005, who champions an alternative approach to including as much of what is (or might be) *IA* as possible in our appreciation of it. Advocating reading practices which embrace the 'rich plurality of textual versions possible and extant' (163), he characterises the text of *IA* presented in Diggle 1994 – with its system of indicating the relative probability that a passage is or is not of Euripidean origin – as 'the screen through which … [the] chaos of attempts [to make sense of the text] takes place as a symphony of multiple voices' (194).

wedding are described as the θίασος ... ἱπποβάτας Κενταύρων (1059–60).[52] This phrase contains two separate examples of blending, the combination of the inputs θίασος and ἱπποβάτας, and also the compound word ἱπποβάτας itself with the inputs ἱππο- and -βάτας. ἱπποβάτας is an unusual and ambivalent word. There are various possible interpretations of its combination of the inputs of 'horse' and 'movement/treading up/ upon'. It is distinctly reminiscent of the word αἰγιβάτης, an epithet of Pan,[53] which has traditionally been understood to mean either 'mounting on she-goats' or 'treading like a goat'. By analogy, ἱπποβάτας could be taken either as 'mounting on mares'[54] or as 'treading like a horse'. However, another possible interpretation of this word is suggested by the precedent of Aeschylus' *Persae*, where ἱπποβάται is used to mean 'horsemen' (26);[55] this raises the possibility that here, too it could mean 'riding a horse'.

When ἱπποβάτας is understood as an instance of blending, these various meanings can be seen as different nuances simultaneously suggested by the integration of ἱππο- and -βάτας, which are mapped onto each other through the shared structure of 'movement'. The first two nuances evoke the wildness of the centaurs by foregrounding their bestial nature. The third nuance calls up an ostensibly counterintuitive and nonsensical image – that of centaurs riding themselves. However, underlying this apparent absurdity is an emphasis, through the characterisation of the centaurs as a rider, on the human aspect of the centaurs' nature and a subjugation to it of the horse aspect. Thus, this nuance humanises (and civilises) the centaurs in contrast to the first two.[56]

The complex nexus of correspondence and tension between various nuances arising from the first blend is augmented and reinforced by the second, the combination of θίασος and ἱπποβάτας used to describe the group of centaurs. The term θίασος pulls in two directions: while it is true that it could well be taken to evoke riotous Dionysiac behaviour,[57] it is also the case that θίασοι formed a part of civilised religious practice as well as the darker, 'wilder' aspects of Dionysiac worship.[58] Thus, if it is blended

---

[52]  *IA* text as in Diggle 1994. Where appropriate, I have not directly translated some of the blends on which my discussion is based in order to avoid constricting their significance, but rather indicate their various potential meanings through discussion of their inputs etc.

[53]  See e.g. Theoc. *Ep.* 5.6.

[54]  For use of the word to mean 'stallion' see Str. 8.8.1, *Hippiatrica Berolinensia* 14.2; cf. LSJ s.v.

[55]  Cf. Stockert 1992 ad Eur. *IA* 1059.

[56]  Euripides may be tapping into an existing dichotomy in the conception of centaurs. The François Vase (mid sixth century) juxtaposes depictions of a centaur – Cheiron – at the wedding of Peleus and Thetis, and of the war between the centaurs and the Lapiths. For a parallel, but slightly later, 'humanising' of centaurs (probably fourth century; see Stern 1996: 5, Hawes 2014: 227–38), cf. Palaeph. 1, who suggests that the myth of centaurs arose when people mistook horsemen for a new kind of creature.

[57]  Cf. Stockert 1992 ad loc.

[58]  See Henrichs 1969 for inscriptional evidence of the role of *thiasoi* in established religion.

with ἱπποβάτας through the shared structure of 'civilisation versus wildness', various opposing nuances offer themselves, as it simultaneously reinforces and contradicts both the wild, bestial nature and the civilised humanity of the centaurs evoked by ἱπποβάτας.

Through the above, the unique potentialities of a blend-based analysis vis-à-vis traditional concepts such as metaphor and metonymy emerge. Recognising θίασος … ἱπποβάτας Κενταύρων as an instance of blending facilitates an appreciation that the expression is characterised by a polysemy that, although complex, confusing and even contradictory, is nonetheless unified rather than disparate: all the various complexities of nuance arise from the same confluence of concepts and are thus aspects of a single whole rather than a series of disparate alternatives. Reading it as a complex metaphor, by contrast, encourages us to 'decode' the construction as a rather arcane way of expressing the concept of 'a group of centaurs', and to select one meaning that we believe it is intended to convey: to implant from one concept – that of the metaphor – into another – that of its referent.[59]

More importantly, in revealing this polysemy, the lens of cognitive blending brings to light further structural characteristics that, I contend, are at the heart of the inherent spatiality and visuality of Euripidean lyric. The non-linear relation of the various nuances in the unified polysemy of a blend, its 'outputs' (so to speak) – which are all conjoined at its central collision and fusion of inputs much as spokes at the hub of a wheel – reinforces the sense, which I first identified as arising from the non-linear relation and combination of the inputs of a blend (rather than its resulting nuances), that a blend has a quasi-spatial structure of an inherently visual quality.

Finally, and most significantly, the theory of blending foregrounds, and affords an account for, the effect of such features on the perceiving mind of the hearer or reader – as discussed, a vital theme in a project dedicated to the senses. As we come to grips with the conceptual structures identified, the mind meanders back and forth from one nuance to another and contemplates the way in which they bleed into each other. The varied nuances arising from a blend, as well as the nature and relation of its constituent parts, provoke the non-linear process of thought that is typical of our engagement with visual artworks and symbols, and that points to the visuality of the blends that elicit it.

### The Macrocosmic Function of Blends

The preceding analysis left untouched the question of the collective effect of blends in late Euripidean lyric, which must be addressed if we are fully to evaluate the hypothesis that his poetry is distinguished by a quality of inherent visuality, entirely independent of content, that it owes to such features. A mere emphasis on the ubiquity of such structures in his

---

[59]   See Budelmann and LeVen 2014: 203 on the advantages of a blend-based analysis.

works will not suffice: blending is a universal phenomenon, as the original proponents of the theory make clear.[60] Rather, the manner of their deployment, as well as other features of Euripidean verse that affect how they are perceived, must be considered.

Contrasting real Aeschylean and Euripidean lyric facilitates appreciation of the distinctive features of the latter at which the parodies in *Frogs* are directed. Accordingly, I offer a comparison of the entirety of the third stasimon of *IA* with an Aeschylean lyric treatment of the sacrifice of Iphigenia, namely the end of the *Agamemnon* parodos (458 BC), which represents an acme of Aeschylus' lyric composition – two passages of comparable scope and length.[61] As ever, my principal occupation is with blends as conceptual *structures*, rather than with the concepts communicated themselves – although the latter also form an important part of the discussion.

The section of the *Agamemnon* at issue is – unsurprisingly – full of blends of a variety of description. Some of these stand alone, for instance the portrayal of the inability to sail affecting the Greeks as κεναγγής (188), a compound originating in the adjective κενός and the noun ἄγγος. The integration of the concepts of 'empty' and 'vessel' simultaneously suggests various possible outputs; the emptiness of their food vessels, but also of their stomachs.[62] This blend is distinctly polysemic, although it lacks the more complex and contradictory overtones of θίασος … ἱπποβάτας Κενταύρων – which are also a characteristic of the parodic 'Euripidean' blends in *Frogs*.[63]

However, a great many of the blends in this section of the *Agamemnon* parodos build up into an overarching structure of meaning. In the speech the chorus put in Agamemnon's mouth as he vacillates over how to respond to Artemis' demand for the sacrifice of Iphigenia, he refers to her as δόμων ἄγαλμα (208). This expression integrates the inputs 'Iphigenia' and ἄγαλμα, the latter being a complex term that can refer to any delightful or beautiful object, especially a statue, an idol, or indeed a dedication.[64] Iphigenia's preciousness and beauty are emphasised; but she is also characterised as a beautiful *thing* of the sort commonly devoted to gods. The latter nuance of the blend not only dehumanises her but suggests that she is in some respect like an offering. A disturbing ambiguity results.

The nexus of meaning originating in the convergence of the concepts of 'Iphigenia' and 'beautiful thing/sacrificial object' is sustained through many of the following blends of the *Agamemnon* parodos. Her sacrifice is characterised as προτέλεια ναῶν, 'preliminary

---

[60]  Fauçonnier and Turner 2002. Cf. Budelmann and LeVen 2014: 193, who similarly point out that the pervasive presence of such structures in Timotheus' poetry is not enough to account for its distinguishing qualities.

[61]  Eur. *IA* 1036–97; Aesch. *Ag.* 184–247. Text of the latter as in West 1990.

[62]  Fraenkel 1950 ad loc. favours the former meaning, Denniston and Page 1957 ad loc. the latter.

[63]  I owe my understanding of this particular Aeschylean blend to Dr Thomas Nelson, who offered useful feedback on this chapter at the conference in which this volume originated.

[64]  Cf. discussion of the term in Bloesch 1943.

marriage rites on behalf of the ships' (227).[65] The significance of the previous blend
steers us away from the more bizarre ideas intimated by this strange expression – ruling
out the ghosts of the sense 'marriage rites *undergone by* the ships' evoked by the latter
input – and allows us to understand it as conceptualising one ritual involving Iphigenia,
sacrifice, as another, marriage. The former – *prima facie* a horrible and unnatural act, as
is emphasised by the chorus elsewhere[66] – thus acquires an aura of appropriateness;
Iphigenia's characterisation drifts a little further towards that of a sacrificial animal.

Similar blends occur with a rising frequency in the following two stanzas. Agamemnon
commands Iphigenia to be lifted above the altar – an act the chorus compares to the
typical treatment of a yearling goat, δίκαν χιμαίρας (232)[67] – and forcibly silenced:

> στόματός τε καλλιπρώιρου
> φυλακᾶι κατασχεῖν
> φθόγγον ἀραῖον οἴκοις,
> βίαι χαλινῶν τ᾽ ἀναύδωι μένει· (235–8)

[Agamemnon told his attendants to] restrain speech that might lay a curse on the
house by putting a guard on her fair-prowed mouth – by force, by the silencing
power of a bridle.[68]

This further advances the integration of the concepts of Iphigenia and ritual offering, as
does the closing reference to her virgin purity as ἀταύρωτος (literally, 'unbulled' 245),
'possibly a technical cultic term for a sacrificial heifer.'[69] The depiction of her mouth as
καλλίπρωιρος (not just 'beautiful' but 'fair-prowed')[70] and the striking πρέπουσα τὼς |
ἐν γραφαῖς ('standing out as if in a picture'; 241–2, describing Iphigenia's appearance
as she casts pitiful glances on her sacrificers)[71] both further the conceptual blending of
Iphigenia with beautiful, artistic, but ultimately lifeless objects.

---

[65] Cf. Fraenkel 1950 ad loc.
[66] Cf. e.g. Aesch. *Ag.* 218–21 for an especially marked example of this.
[67] Cf. Fraenkel 1950 ad loc.
[68] Trans. adapted from Sommerstein 2008 throughout.
[69] Sommerstein 2008: 29 n. 54. Cf. Denniston and Page 1957 ad loc. on the meaning of this term.
[70] Fraenkel 1950 ad loc. notes that the use of πρῶιρα merely as a metaphor for the front of something is not
uncommon. However, in this context, it clearly contributes to the characterisation of Iphigenia as *object*. Hence,
*pace* Denniston and Page 1957 ad loc., the latter element of this compound adjective is far from meaningless.
[71] The effect of this phrase is augmented by κρόκου βαφὰς δ᾽ εἰς πέδον χέουσα a couple of lines above (Aesch. *Ag.*
239). Whether one takes this to indicate that Iphigenia has cast off her garments (Fraenkel 1950 ad loc.) or
that they hang down beneath her as she is held over the altar (Denniston and Page 1957 ad loc.), the scene is
suddenly awash with artificial colour, laying the ground for its explicit characterisation as an artwork.

Indeed, such imagery resonates beyond Iphigenia in the *Agamemnon* parodos. Two separate passages blend the concepts of 'Agamemnon' and 'wind',[72] endowing him with the characteristics of a natural force; on the one hand terrible and destructive, on the other hand possessed of no active will or ability to choose how it influences events. The latter instantiation of the image is complemented by the preceding statement that Agamemnon ἀνάγκας ἔδυ λέπαδνον, 'put on the yoke of necessity' (218); here Agamemnon is integrated with the concept of 'ox'. This expresses his subjection to fate and lack of agency – he is driven like one. It also suggests the bestial brutality of the sacrifice of Iphigenia he is about to carry out.

It is thus the case that many of the blends in this passage chart the slippage of Agamemnon and Iphigenia from humanity into non-humanity; the use of bovine imagery in either case emphasises the parallel. Of course, there is a degree of modulation in the meaning evoked in this process, and some variation in how it is realised between the two of them. Iphigenia is drawn into the realm of beautiful sacrificial offerings, whereas Agamemnon is endowed with the mindless and unwilled savagery of a beast or natural force. Nonetheless, the significance of each of these blends – in some individual cases complex or unclear – is reinforced and shaped by the others, which together form a framework on the human/non-human axis; together, they construct a broad sweep of meaning, communicating in bold terms the horror of the events portrayed. Interestingly this is remarkably similar to the function of blends in the work of the New Musician Timotheus.[73] As Budelmann and LeVen emphasise, his blends are often combined into 'integration networks'[74] that support and clarify the meaning of each.

It is most illuminating to compare the relation between the blends in the third stasimon of Euripides' *IA*. There are many examples of such structures in addition to θίασος … ἱπποβάτας Κενταύρων. The strophe opens with a reference to the ἰαχή raised by Hymenaios at the wedding of Peleus and Thetis; this is accompanied, *inter alia*, by the φιλόχορος κιθάρα (1037). If the opening element of the compound φιλόχορος is understood to have the possessive force often typical of it in Homer and the earlier poets,[75] this blend could be taken as no more than an expression of the appropriateness of the kithara to choral performance. If it is taken more actively, attributing to an instrument the love of chorality typical of a performer, it suggests that everything involved in the performance shares a common will to artistic creation, augmenting both its vitality and its supernatural aura.

Other blends in the strophe include the χρσεοσάνδαλον ἴχνος of the Muses (1042); since ἴχνος, although it can be used poetically to mean 'foot', has the fundamental

---

[72] Aesch. *Ag.* 187, 219–20.
[73] Notwithstanding the fact that the individual blends in the works of the latter are frequently more confusing than the Aeschylean examples I have discussed.
[74] For this term, taken from Fauçonnier and Turner 1998 see esp. Budelmann and LeVen 2014: 196.
[75] Cf. LSJ s.v.

significance of 'track' or 'footstep'[76] there is, in addition to the obvious indication that the Muses are wearing golden sandals, a sense that the ornamental quality of their footwear bleeds into and remains in any place they have trodden – the tracks made by golden sandals become golden themselves. The reference to χρυσέα γύαλα (1051–2) blends the concepts of 'gold' and 'hollow' to depict the cups into which Ganymede pours the wine, foregrounding their artistry as instantiated in their shape and material. The compound word λευκοφαής (1054) is another blend, combining the elements of 'white' and 'gleaming' to present an especially radiant impression of the sand.

The antistrophe is marked by blends of a more striking character. The description of the centaurs who attend the wedding, θίασος ... ἱπποβάτας Κενταύρων, is preceded by a statement that they came ἅμα δ᾽ ἐλάταισι στεφανώδει τε χλόαι (1058); the last three words blend the concepts of 'wreath-like' and 'foliage'.[77] This polysemic blend could be understood in two distinct ways.

The most straightforward – commonly adopted by commentators – is to take στεφανώδης χλόα in isolation from ἐλάται to refer to wreaths worn by the centaurs.[78] In this case, the nuance accentuated – 'wreath-like *foliage*' – lessens the latent contradiction of the wreaths (redolent of order and graceful beauty, suggesting cultural spheres ranging from symposia to athletic victory celebrations) with the uncivilised, wild aspects of the nature of the centaurs.

However, στεφανώδης χλόα could also be taken with ἐλάται in a hendiadys. Notably England, working from an alternative version of the text, **ἀνὰ** δ᾽ ἐλάταισι στεφανώδει τε χλόαι – preserved in L and adopted by some modern editors, although not by Diggle, whose text forms the basis for this chapter – does precisely that, translating 'among the pines with their green crowns'.[79] Read thus, Diggle's text (with ἅμα in place of ἀνὰ) would then signify 'holding green-crowned pines'. Such an interpretation foregrounds the blend nuance 'green-crowned', serving, in the context of the phrase as a whole, subtly to introduce aestheticisation (wreath-like qualities) into the natural world.[80]

---

[76] LSJ s.v.

[77] Blends often take the form of such periphrastic noun–adjective combinations; cf. Budelmann and LeVen 2014: 199.

[78] The interpretation favoured by Stockert 1992 ad loc., Collard and Morwood 2017 ad loc., Andò 2021 ad loc. The textual variant printed by Kovacs 2002, ἅμα δ᾽ ἐλάταις **σύν** στεφανώδει τε χλόαι – and his translation – also support this reading.

[79] England 1891; note that this reading is rejected by Stockert 1992 ad loc., who is one of the modern editors to print ἀνὰ. He suggests, drawing on Paley 1860, Breitenbach 1934: 111, Panagl 1971: 214, that ἀνὰ should be taken with ἔμολεν – communicating the sense 'the centaurs came up with ...'.

[80] Note that my argument regarding the blend's polysemy stands regardless of which textual variant is adopted.

Later in the antistrophe, Achilles is characterised as Θεσσαλίαι μέγα φῶς (1063). Combining the concepts of 'Achilles' and 'light', it evokes Achilles' heroic glory and power, especially to deliver;[81] it also invites us to see Achilles as pure, and of a dazzling visual appearance; finally, it characterises him as ethereal and essentially non-physical. Although perhaps less eye-catching than some other blends featured in this ode, since the association of Homeric heroes – and especially Achilles – with brilliance is commonplace,[82] the polysemy of this expression is nonetheless evident.

The predictions regarding Achilles of which the last blend forms a part are said to have been delivered by the μάντις ὁ φοιβάδα μοῦσαν εἰδώς – Chiron (1064–5). This is a particularly challenging combination of two blends. The first, already difficult due to the complex of concepts represented by each word involved, consists of two nouns in apposition: φοιβάς – 'priestess of Apollo', and thus also more generally 'prophetess'; and μοῦσα – 'muse', also by extension 'music' or even simply 'art'.[83] Given that this blend is presented as the particular object of knowledge of a μάντις, a seer, it is marked as in some sense a metonymy for prophecy – thus introducing the second blend in the compound, namely of the concepts introduced by φοιβὰς μοῦσα and 'prophecy'. A variety of nuances arise from this convoluted web of inputs. If the force of φοιβάς is reduced to that of an adjective connoting the Apolline, and μοῦσα is taken at its most abstract, then the relatively prosaic meaning 'Apollonian skill' emerges – similar enough to 'prophecy' that the second blend is rather unremarkable. More intriguing are the possibilities 'Apollonian muse' and – better – 'muse who [or possibly even 'music which …'] is a priestess of Apollo'. When merged into the second blend, these latter nuances – attractive for their particular closeness to the respective conceptual cores of the interrelated networks of ideas signified by φοιβάς and μοῦσα – lead us to see prophecy as a thing of aesthetic beauty: part of Apollo's artistic, not only his mantic, sphere of influence.

The epode opens as follows:

σὲ δ᾽ ἐπὶ κάραι στέψουσι καλλικόμαν
πλόκαμον Ἀργεῖοι, βαλιὰν
ὥστε πετραίων
ἀπ᾽ ἄντρων ἐλθοῦσαν ὀρέων
μόσχον ἀκήρατον, βρότειον
αἱμάσσοντες λαιμόν·

[81]   For this nuance in particular, see parallel Euripidean uses of light imagery at *Hec.* 841, *El.* 449, *IT* 849, *Or.* 243, *Bacch.* 608, *IA* 1502. Cf. Stockert 1992 ad loc., Collard and Morwood 2017 ad loc.
[82]   A notable example of this – although with much more negative connotations than the instance in *IA* – is Achilles' comparison to the destructive dog-star at Hom. *Il.* 22.25–32.
[83]   Cf. LSJ s.vv. Collard and Morwood 2017 ad loc. foreground the meaning 'poetic art'.

οὐ σύριγγι τραφεῖσαν οὐδ'
ἐν ῥοιβδήσεσι βουκόλων,
παρὰ δὲ ματέρι νυμφοκόμον
Ἰναχίδαις γάμον. (1080–9)

But as for you [Iphigenia], the Greeks shall garland the fair tresses upon your head like a dappled, unblemished calf from a rocky mountain cave, bloodying your mortal neck, you who were not raised to the syrinx or the piping of shepherds, but at the side of your mother to be a bridal catch for the sons of Inachus.[84]

Most notable here is the blending of the concepts of 'Iphigenia' and 'unblemished calf'. Unlike most of the Euripidean blends I have discussed, the various nuances arising from it are strengthened by other features of the passage. As a result, the complexity of its conceptual structure, its non-linear polysemy, is especially apparent. Her crowning, an act equally applicable to a human and a sacrificial animal, underscores Iphigenia's similarity to the latter; the image of her neck covered in blood emphasises the horror of the sacrifice; and the remark that she was not raised like a sacrificial animal underlines its unnaturalness.[85] All this serves to clarify the disturbing paradox that emerges from the blend in question: on the one hand, it emphasises Iphigenia's possession of the ideal maidenly characteristics of purity and virginity;[86] on the other, it casts her as removed from the human sphere – and thus as an appropriate sacrificial victim.[87] A second, less prominent blend is the description of Iphigenia as a νυμφοκόμον … γάμον. Here Iphigenia acquires dignity, beauty – and the abstract and inanimate quality of the concept with which she is identified.

The ode ends with a quick-fire succession of personifications which blend personhood and abstract concepts. For instance, Modesty and Virtue are endowed with physical features in the words ποῦ τὸ τᾶς Αἰδοῦς ἢ τὸ τᾶς Ἀρετᾶς | σθένει τι πρόσωπον, 'where does Modesty's or Virtue's face hold any sway' (1090–1);[88] this personification of Ἀρετα continues in the description of it as 'left behind'.[89] By this means, not merely personhood but physical characteristics are integrated with these concepts, heightening the horror of

---

[84] Trans. adapted from Kovacs 2002.

[85] Cf. Budelmann and LeVen 2014: 195 on the subject of features external to blends that support them.

[86] Cf. Stockert 1992 ad loc.

[87] This blend obviously recalls, and may well have been inspired by, the Iphigenia–beast blends in the *Agamemnon*. It is worth noting that a secondary effect of the perspective afforded by cognitive blending theory is, in bringing to light this striking collision of concepts, to revive the devastating impact of the conception of human death as sacrifice – which might otherwise have been disregarded as a standard tragic trope.

[88] Trans. Kovacs 2002.

[89] Eur. *IA* 1093–4.

the outrages committed against them by casting them almost as an infliction of pain. The personification of τὸ ἄσεπτον and Ἀνομία imparts a striking immediacy to their malign power (1092–3, 1095).

The quality of goldenness obviously features in both χρσεοσάνδαλον ἴχνος and χρυσέα γύαλα; in fact, the aura of brightness evoked by λευκοφαής and the attribution of qualities of light to Achilles could be thought to resonate with this golden imagery to a certain extent. It might thus be suggested that these blends form a support network in a similar manner to those of the *Agamemnon* parodos. This, however, is not the case. Rather than a sustained integration of the same or similar concepts over a series of different expressions and images, χρσεοσάνδαλον ἴχνος and χρυσέα γύαλα correspond only in respect of one input, which is very distantly echoed in the description of Achilles as μέγα φῶς; λευκοφαής is a blend which resonates to a degree with the 'golden' element in the first two blends at issue and the 'light' element in the latter. Such nebulous and uneven links are entirely different from the intense build-up of meaning in the *Agamemnon* blends.

The nuance of στεφανώδης χλόα suggesting the centaurs are crowned with wreaths might be thought to parallel the human and civilised versus wild and bestial blending structure associated with the centaurs by θίασος ... ἱπποβάτας Κενταύρων. Yet the supporting structure is, again, not especially strong: the individual concepts blended are only distantly related and, more importantly, the primary focus of the latter blend is humanity versus bestiality, whereas that of the former is nature versus civilisation.

Similarly, the characterisation of Iphigenia as a calf might be understood to form a minor blend network with θίασος ... ἱπποβάτας Κενταύρων. However, while both blends integrate elements of the human and the bestial, they occur in such different contexts that they can scarcely be said to combine into a broader theme. The former is a virtuosic exploration of the complex identity of one of the categories of guests at Peleus and Thetis' wedding, adding to the dazzling brilliance of the scene; the other emphasises the disturbing paradoxes of Iphigenia's sacrifice.

Thus, even where there are hints of overarching networks of blends in this passage, they remain mere traces; they are also interleaved, meaning that even such limited integration networks as exist are constantly interrupted.[90] There is nothing approaching the uncompromising drive towards dehumanisation of the blends in the final section of the *Agamemnon* parodos.

This comparison reveals that, in this instance, Euripidean blends represent a series of fascinating and suggestive conceptual nexuses, but that these nexuses do not support each other and contribute to a crescendo of meaning in the manner of

---

[90] On the confusing effect of changes of integration networks when they occur in Timotheus cf. Budelmann and LeVen 2014: 197.

Aeschylean blends. When they are taken together, it becomes apparent that meaning, while remaining important,[91] is sometimes a secondary concern; in the absence of such supporting networks, Euripides' blends do not function to foreground and communicate meaning in the same manner. Of course, blending invariably creates meaning. Yet the brilliant, flashy *combination* of concepts, the highly formalist structural artistry of blending that is a root cause of its inherent visuality, lies at the heart of Euripidean poetics – and it is these processes, as much as the meaning created, which his lyric is designed to put on display. This differentiates Euripides' verse not merely from Aeschylus' but from Timotheus' whose blends, as noted above, also combine into sustained structures of meaning. In consequence, the inherent visuality of Euripidean blends is especially prominent.[92]

As well as these differing uses of conceptual integration, this comparison also brings to light a significant distinction between Aeschylus and Euripides in the language itself used to convey these concepts. The Aeschylean passage, especially the towards the end of the description of Iphigenia's sacrifice,[93] is full of challenging vocabulary and syntax. One individual instance of such features is the expression πέπλοισι περιπετῆ, used of Iphigenia at her sacrifice (233). There are widely differing interpretations of περιπετής, ranging from 'with her clothes falling about her'[94] to 'falling around his [Agamemnon's] robes, as a suppliant'.[95] There is also an unusual preponderance of hapaxes in this section.[96]

The third stasimon of *IA*, by contrast, is far less complicated from the perspective of vocabulary and syntax. There are various epicisms: the centaurs μέγα ... ἀνέκλαγον, 'proclaimed loudly', Chiron's prophecy about Achilles (1062); the act of prophecy is indicated by the verb ἐξονομάζεν (1066); Achilles, it is predicted, will carry out his heroism in the Trojan war κεκορυθμένος, 'furnished', in the armour forged by Hephaestus

---

[91]   E.g. the Iphigenia–calf blend still serves to communicate the horror of her sacrifice.

[92]   Interestingly Konstan 2023, reflecting on how best to navigate the textual difficulties of *IA*, specifically its sense of incompleteness, suggests that *IA* deliberately evokes a host of alternative histories to the storyline it actually presents through the inclusion of narrative 'stubs' that are never pursued. This is perhaps, on a much larger scale, not entirely unlike the non-linear polysemy arising from the blends of its lyric language – although the fact that, in the latter, various alternative, often contradictory, meanings are suggested more strongly and with more equal force constitutes an important difference. The play is characterised by a complex structural multiplicity of import at all levels.

[93]   Aesch. *Ag.* 238–47. See Fraenkel 1950 ad loc.

[94]   Cf. Fraenkel 1950 ad loc.

[95]   Denniston and Page 1957 ad loc. drawing on Lloyd-Jones 1952.

[96]   Cf. e.g. Fraenkel 1950 ad Aesch. *Ag.* 196. For further linguistic difficulties in this passage see (on grammar) Fraenkel 1950 ad Aesch. *Ag.* 190–1, 193, 194, 215–17, 231, 237, Denniston and Page 1957 ad Aesch. *Ag.* 215–17, 221; (on vocabulary) Fraenkel 1950 ad Aesch. *Ag.* 187, 188, 210, 213, 214, 230, 231, 245, Denniston and Page 1957 ad Aesch. *Ag.* 188–9, 194, 213, 220, 234.

(1073).[97] The performers at Thetis and Peleus' wedding are – probably for metrical reasons[98] – described as hymning them with ἀχήμασιν rather than ἰαχήμασιν (1045; both mean 'cries' or 'shouts'). These, however, are very minor linguistic idiosyncrasies, and certainly do not present the same linguistic ambiguities and barriers to understanding as Aeschylus' *Agamemnon* parodos.

The fact that the challenges of Euripidean lyric do not lie in its linguistic complexity, and its distinction in this regard from that of Aeschylus, is corroborated by the specific difficulty of the blends in this ode. For instance, the inputs in θίασος … ἱπποβάτας Κενταύρων are lucid from the perspective of vocabulary and syntax; however, their combined significance – the nexus of concepts they express – is anything but.

Not only the macroscopic arcs of meaning which Aeschylean blends construct, but also the general difficulties of his language and syntax draw our attention away from the blending process itself and from its associated visuality. Furthermore, integration networks of blends of the sort featured in Aeschylus' verse often serve to reduce the polysemy of their constituent blends – a characteristic that, as discussed, is one of the principal causes of their inherently visual quality in Euripides. As illustrated in my analysis of προτέλεια ναῶν (227), such integration networks prime us to interpret the blends which constitute them only in terms that conform to an overarching train of imagery, and to disregard possible alternative meanings.[99]

In Euripidean lyric, by contrast, the simplicity of the vocabulary and syntax means that we are confronted directly with, and induced to focus principally on, the blending of the concepts signified by his language. Furthermore, since these blends are not moulded into comprehensive structures of meaning, the structural non-linearity associated with polysemy is unrestricted. Accordingly, the quality of inherent visuality that arises from it is also particularly conspicuous.[100]

It is significant that the distinctions of Aeschylean and Euripidean poetry just outlined seem to have been remarked in the ancient world. I have already discussed

[97] Cf. Stockert 1992 ad loc. on these epicisms. Epicism also features elsewhere in the lyric portions of the play; see e.g. the commentary on the parodos in Stockert 1992.

[98] Cf. Stockert 1992 ad loc., Collard and Morwood 2017 ad loc.; there may also be a shadow of a pun on ἄχος, subversively presaging the unhappy future of the marriage and its issue. Note that there is a lengthy history of interpreting Achilles' name itself in similar terms; cf. Σ Hom. *Il.* 1.1.

[99] Lebeck 1971, although lacking my focus on blends, the variations in their deployment and consequently in the prominence of their structural non-linearity, works on the basis that the 'significance of each part [of the imagery in the *Agamemnon* parodos] can be appreciated only with reference to the whole' (19).

[100] It is true that the integration networks in Timothean blends are sometimes interrupted or confusingly intertwined in a way that those in Aeschylus are not, and that some of his blends could be characterised as polysemic to the point of confusion; cf. discussion at Budelmann and LeVen 2014: 195–8. However, the lack of integration networks is still much more marked in Euripides, hence the uniquely visual quality of his blends.

the representation of blends and their associated visuality as a distinguishing feature of Euripidean poetry in *Frogs*. Notably, one of the principal qualities attributed to Aeschylus' poetry in *Frogs* is its complex vocabulary. Take for instance Euripides' complaint:

σαφὲς δ᾽ ἂν εἶπεν οὐδὲ ἕν—

…

ἀλλ᾽ ἢ Σκαμάνδρους καὶ τάφρους κἀπ᾽ ἀσπίδων ἐπόντας
γρυπαιέτους χαλκηλάτους καὶ ῥήμαθ᾽ ἱππόκρημνα,
ἃ ξυμβαλεῖν οὐ ῥᾴδι᾽ ἦν. (927–30)

And he wouldn't say a single intelligible word … but only Scamanders, or moats, or shields bronze-bossed and blazoned with griffin-eagles, and huge craggy utterances that weren't easy to decipher.

Dionysus readily agrees, remembering his failure to comprehend what Aeschylus meant by ξουθὸς ἱππαλεκτρυών , 'a zooming/yellow [?] horsecock' (932).[101] Euripides further states that when he took over the art of Tragedy from Aeschylus he put it on a diet, since it was οἰδοῦσαν ὑπὸ κομπασμάτων καὶ ῥημάτων ἐπαχθῶν, 'bloated with bombast and obese vocabulary' (940);[102] naturally, this also implies the relative absence of such features in his own verse.

An evaluation of Euripidean poetry which, although much more positive, recalls that of *Frogs* is presented by Longinus, who lists Euripides among the poets who achieve grandeur by the skilful arrangement of common, even vulgar, words, and claims τῆς συνθέσεως ποιητὴς ὁ Εὐριπίδης μᾶλλόν ἐστιν ἢ τοῦ νοῦ, 'Euripides is a poet of word arrangement more than of ideas' (40:2–3).[103] Longinus is referring to iambics rather than lyric, and he is occupied with questions of diction rather than the fusion of concepts involved in blending; however, this passage nonetheless supports the theory that juxtapositional logic, combined with simple language, is a prominent element in Euripidean poetry.

---

[101] On the ambiguity of ξουθὸς cf. Dover 1993 ad loc.

[102] On such features of Aeschylus' language in *Frogs* cf. Scharffenberger 2006–7: 243, Griffith 2013: 120–2.

[103] Trans. Halliwell, Fyfe, Russel and Innes 1999. Halliwell 2022: 414 understands this remark to refer to 'expressive placement of words'. He also draws attention (411) to similar discussion, in conjunction with a reference to Euripides, of the 'intense effects' that can be achieved by word arrangement regardless of vocabulary at Arist. *Rhet.* 1404b24–5.

## Conclusion

Through the unique artistry of its blends, structural and formal features endowing it with qualities of two-dimensionality and spatiality – and in consequence of physical, visual objects – late Euripidean lyric effects a remarkably complex sensory experience. It triggers mental operations typical of engagement with the visual – and does so independently of the content communicated. A sense which, *prima facie*, has little inherent association with lyric poetry *qua* art form[104] thus takes centre stage. Far from being confined to the spectacular aspects of performance, or to moments of explicitly visual imagery, visuality emerges as a primary and fundamental feature of the text of Euripidean tragedy itself, permeating its very form. When, along with Aristophanes' Aeschylus, we 'see' the blending structures of Euripides' poetry, our visual and verbal receptive faculties are drawn together in a striking synaesthetic experience.

This invites further reassessment of the role and function of Greek texts as sensory objects, especially of how they might be understood to engage senses of all descriptions in a manner substantially independent of performance and indeed of content. We thus stand to gain a new avenue of insight from the extant textual evidence into the sensory experience of audiences and readers ranging from ancient Greece to the present day.

Furthermore, this chapter paves the way for a broader re-evaluation of Euripidean lyric. For many years critics, taking their cue from Aristotle's strictures in his *Poetics*,[105] characterised various late Euripidean odes as problematically irrelevant, or mere empty aestheticism.[106] In reaction to this was spawned what Csapo terms a 'productive minor industry' of vindications of their relevance.[107] The emphasis, typical of the latter, on 'criteria of mood and imagery rather than thought' for dramatic relevance is important;[108] yet the repeated insistence on this point itself suggests a general awareness that the question of their relevance is in fact far from straightforward.

---

[104] Although it is obviously the case that it is evoked by the content of some individual poems.

[105] Arist. *Poet.* 1456a25–31 complains that the chorus is not sufficiently involved in Euripides' plays. Halliwell 1998: 243 suggests that the specification that the chorus must συναγωνίζεσθαι (literally to 'compete together'), should be taken as a requirement to be 'part of the whole', which stipulation, in view of the definition of 'the whole' in chapters 7–8 of the *Poetics*, must be understood as not just thematic pertinence but indispensable involvement in the action. Cf. similarly Peponi 2013: 24–5. On the general difficulty of interpreting this passage see Halliwell 1998: 242–52, Hunter 2017: 212–14.

[106] Perhaps most significantly Kranz 1933; see also Helg 1950: 53–7, Alt 1952, Pohlenz 1954: 440, Lesky 1971: 454, Panagl 1971. Cf. Csapo: 1999–2000: 407–8. On the issue of style specifically cf. Croiset 1891: 336–7, Delulle 1911: 25, Lesky 1971: 455, discussed by Barlow 1971 esp. 2–6.

[107] E.g. Parry 1963: 90–103, 147–72, Neitzel 1967, Segal 1971, Walsh 1974, Nordheider 1980: 21–6, 45–56, 82–7,93–104, Hose 1990–1. Cf. Csapo 1999–2000: 408.

[108] Csapo 1999–2000, who cites Knox 1985 as an example of this trend.

Recognising the inherently visual quality of Euripides' lyrics, by contrast, allows us to appreciate the full artistry of his aestheticism, rather than confining our understanding of it to the narrow criterion of relevance in the form of contribution, reaction or relation to the content or plot of the rest of the play. While blending is conceptually based it is, as I have argued, the way in which various concepts are blended together, rather than the concepts themselves, that gives rise to the fundamentally visual quality of his work. Form, it emerges, is a major consideration in late Euripidean lyric composition – sometimes operating in a manner substantially independent of content.

That Euripides' formalism should come to light through my investigation of the visuality of his lyric is unsurprising. A formal dimension is arguably part and parcel of the quality of visuality: for many objects of visual aesthetic beauty, such as buildings, abstract art or certain *objets d'art*, their beauty lies as much in their form as their meaning – indeed in some cases in their form alone.[109]

Euripides' visual, blend-based lyric constructs a fascinating intellectual landscape of novel, non-linear and polysemic nexuses of concepts, inviting us to dwell on the remarkable manner of their interconnection and mingling. He delights his audience by virtuosic manipulation of the mind's sensory apparatus through the form of his expression as much as, if not more than, the meaning expressed.

---

[109] On the enduring centrality, despite recent emphases on the associated problems, of formalist concerns to our understanding of Ancient Greek art see Neer 2002: 7, Neer 2010: 6–11. On the importance of the material and qualities such as variegation and ornamentation in Ancient Greek conceptions of art see Steiner 2014: 24–33. In Ellis 2022 I undertake a wider-ranging rehabilitation of late Euripidean lyric through foregrounding its aesthetic aspect, including a variety of formal features. For an alternative, politically oriented, understanding of form in Euripides cf. Wohl 2015.

# The Dynamics of Physical, Aesthetic and Cultural Taste in Aristophanes

*Afroditi Angelopoulou*

## Introduction

More than any other of the senses, taste is fraught with ambivalence. As a physical, gustatory sensation, it is disparaged by early thinkers, most notably by Plato, whose assessment of taste as non-philosophical and lacking in culture (primarily because of its link with the appetitive pleasures; see e.g. *Timaeus* 73a6), shaped to a great extent Western ideas concerning the hierarchy of the senses.[1] And yet in Western discourse taste came to designate the aesthetic faculty of discernment and to describe refined choice.[2] The equation between gustatory taste and aesthetic sensibility has been deemed problematic, for unlike the 'distal' and 'higher' senses of sight and hearing, this 'lower' sense abolishes the distance between the subject and the (incorporated) object of knowledge and is therefore epistemologically unreliable.[3] The close association of taste with the body (and we should note that taste involves the other carnal senses too, viz. touch and smell) has been a constant reminder of its equivocal nature, which is also reflected in its semantic paradox: 'it might seem that the very idea of "taste" to signify discernment is already flirting with distaste by invoking the "lower" senses … "Taste" is a perilous business. It is hedged in from all sides by the physical possibility of revulsion, disgust, and disdain'.[4]

The contradictions inherent in the semantics of taste are also at the heart of Old Comedy, a genre grounded in the dynamic tension between delight and disgust, the

---

[1]   See e.g. Korsmeyer 2002: 1–10; on taste in Graeco-Roman antiquity see Rudolph 2018a.

[2]   See Weiss 1997: 7 on the definition of taste: 'According to context, taste means: the sense by which we distinguish flavors; the flavors themselves; an appetite for such preferred flavors; the discriminative activity according to which an individual likes or dislikes certain sensations; the sublimation of such value judgments as they pertain to art, and ultimately to all experience; and by extension and ellipsis, taste implies good taste and style, established by means of an intuitive faculty of judgment'.

[3]   On the comparison between aesthetic taste and gustation see e.g. Hume 2017: 200, Gigante 2005: 10. But see the objections of e.g. Kant 2017.

[4]   Highmore 2010: 124.

sublime and the grotesque. More broadly, the use of the lower senses is typical of 'lowbrow' genres such as satire and iambic ('blame') poetry, which tend to subvert social and aesthetic as well as 'sensory hierarchies'.[5] Comic playwrights often provoke the senses and judgements of their audiences by integrating the multisensory experience of festivals, such as the Great Dionysia, into the stage.[6] Such practices anticipate contemporary theatre productions which activate various sensory channels (gustatory, olfactory, etc.) to evoke memories, create moods and trigger knee-jerk, visceral reactions within the attendants.[7] Indeed, we now know that sensory and perceptual information plays a significant role in human conceptual architecture, namely that it can affect (social and moral) cognition in profound ways.[8] Paying attention to the use of sensorial stimuli in performance, then, allows us to appreciate more deeply the role of the body as a powerful tool of communication and to discern how, through the excitation of the senses, theatrical events can 'create an in-between state of experience and awareness'.[9]

My discussion accordingly focuses on the role of gustatory experience in Aristophanic comedy, which offers some of the earliest evidence in extant Western literature of the creative interplay between physical, aesthetic and cultural taste. Consider how during *Frogs*' dramatic contest, the tragedian Aeschylus accuses the patron god of theatre (and judge of the contest) Dionysus of 'bad taste', proclaiming: 'Dionysus, the wine you drink does not smell of flowers' (1150). This comment, which draws from the sociocultural context of the symposium and associates intellectual with literal consumption,[10] illustrates the significance of olfaction and gustation as not only biological but also historical and social phenomena.[11] Indeed, taste is a '*par excellence* cultural sense' that

---

[5]  Telò 2013: 53.
[6]  See e.g. Bradley 2014: 202–4.
[7]  See e.g. Di Benedetto 2010: 113: 'Like information for smell, taste messages also end up in the limbic system. Arriving in the limbic system results in immediate preconscious associations that will trigger memories tied to places and times that the flavours have been experienced previously. Taste sensation can be a form of virtual time travel.' On the link between food, memory and emotion see Lupton 2017.
[8]  See e.g. Moll et al. 2005 on the impact of gustatory embodied experiences on cognition. See also Eskine, Kacinik and Prinz 2011, on how literal bad taste can influence moral judgement. More broadly, on the embodied nature of morality see e.g. Strejcek and Zhong 2014.
[9]  Di Benedetto 2010: 1.
[10]  See Lada Richards 1999: 139–41. On the function of the symposium in Aristophanic poetry more broadly see e.g. Bowie 1997. Cf. also Ar. fr. 688 on the analogy between different modes of dramatic reception and distinct wine-tasting sensations ('hard' and 'dry', versus 'sweet' and 'nectar-tasting'); see Biles 2014: 6–8 on the suggestion that Cratinus and Aristophanes may embody these two opposing gustatory experiences. Cf. Telò 2013 on Aristophanes' use of olfaction as a tool of aesthetic discernment against his rival Cratinus.
[11]  On Aristophanes' employment of the semiotics of smell to discriminate gendered bodies see Antonia Marie Reinke's chapter in this volume.

can convey social meaning;[12] according to Pierre Bourdieu, any analysis of cultural practices ought to reconnect 'the elaborated taste for the most refined objects' with 'the elementary taste for the flavours of food'.[13] Thus considering the way taste operates on the comic stage can enhance our understanding of the specific sociocultural practices, habits and ideas that shaped the exercise of this sense.[14] Such an endeavour also brings with it awareness of the complexity of this carnal sense, whose affective function renders it a potent rhetorical device within the context of the theatre – and elsewhere [15]

This chapter, then, seeks to revisit the status of taste in Aristophanes by examining how the playwright employs it as a physical sense, as well as *qua* concept and trope, to communicate his moral and aesthetic judgements, but also to promote his comedy as a highly sophisticated, novel and educational mode of entertainment – *dexiotēs* ('skilfulness', 'sophistication'), *sophia* ('subtlety') and *kainotēs* ('novelty') being the 'buzzwords for Aristophanes' preferred brand of comedy'.[16] For this purpose, I will consider passages from *Acharnians, Knights, Clouds, Frogs* and especially *Wasps*. As we will see, these narratives offer a systematic account of taste as an inclusive concept – that is, as appetitive pleasure, consumption, overindulgence and surfeit, as well as value judgement and aesthetic and cultural sensibility. I therefore suggest that a holistic approach to taste as a phenomenon correlated with the entire gustatory and alimentary experience sheds crucial light on the significance of this lower sense as a link between Aristophanic politics, ethics and aesthetics. And since aesthetics can be (and has been) understood as 'a form of moral improvement', 'aimed at sensation, sentiment, and perception',[17] it is useful to consider first the way physical taste is implicated in the problematics of pleasure – itself the 'core aesthetic experience'[18] – and simultaneously exists as a deeply ambivalent concept.

---

[12] Backhouse 1994: 13. However, as Korsmeyer 2017a: 2 observes concerning the variability of subjective experience: '[I]t is important not to exaggerate differences either; if we did not on the whole share coordinating sensory worlds, life would be a constant blunder'.

[13] Bourdieu 2017: 54; see also 56: 'Taste, a class culture turned into nature, that is, *embodied*, helps to shape the class body. It is an incorporated principle of classification which governs all forms of incorporation, choosing and modifying everything that the body ingests and digests and assimilates, physiologically and psychologically' (original emphasis).

[14] See e.g. *Vesp.* 493–5: one's preference for sea-perch, instead of sprats, can spark suspicions of 'buying *opson* ("delicacy") with a view to tyranny'. For the ideological dimensions of the *opson* see esp. Davidson 1997: 278–80.

[15] See esp. Citron and Goldberg 2014, who have shown that when concrete taste words are intended metaphorically, they can also evoke implicit emotional responses.

[16] Biles 2016: 120. More generally on Aristophanic (aesthetic) taste see e.g. Sommerstein 1992, Bremmer 1993.

[17] Highmore 2010: 122.

[18] Destrée 2015: 472. Cf. Gigante 2005: 2: 'modern [but also ancient] aesthetics as evolved from the concept of taste involves pleasure and pleasure is its own way of knowing'.

## The Role of Pleasure and Disgust in Shaping the Ethico-Aesthetics of Aristophanic Comedy

In his *Eudemian Ethics*, Aristotle remarks upon the difference between olfactory and gustatory pleasures by quoting Stratonicus, who maintained that 'the scent of flowers is beautiful (καλὸν ὄζειν), whereas that of things to eat and drink is pleasant (ἡδύ)'. Here, we can note the link – also present in Plato – between taste and *hēdonē*, a term frequently associated with the bodily pleasures of food, drink and sex.[19] Aristotle further observes that gustatory pleasures (περὶ τὸ γευστόν) that are not perceived by 'the tip of the tongue' but rather 'by the throat' (τῷ φάρυγγι) are the province of gourmandisers (ὀψοφάγοι); this is why 'they wish that they may have the gullet of a crane, instead of a long tongue, as is the case with Philoxenus, son of Eryxis' (1231a10–18). The passage is indicative of a broader tendency in Greek thought to disparage intemperance, especially with regard to the appetitive pleasures, with which the sense of taste is intimately linked.[20] And it is of course not coincidental that, to drive his point home, Aristotle employs some of comedy's stock characters – 'Mr. Hospitable', son of 'Mr. Belch' – as primary examples of gluttony,[21] since eating becomes in this genre 'a social stereotype'.[22]

In Aristophanic comedy, terms denoting immoderate consumption, both literal and metaphorical ('devour', 'quaff', etc.), crop up with remarkable frequency. Typically associated with this kind of inordinate activities are greedy politicians such as Cleon, who 'embodies the type of the voracious consumer ... ready to gobble up comestibles and citizens' lifeblood indiscriminately'.[23] In *Knights*, Cleon/Paphlagon is the embodiment of moral and aesthetic disgust, primarily because of his eating transgressions, which also chime in neatly with his menial, low-class profession (44: βυρσοδέψην Παφλαγόνα). In the opening scene, he is presented as a Cyclops-like monster who, 'having lapped up the confiscated goodies (ἐπίπαστα λείξας δημιόπραθ᾽), is now snoring, belly-up drunk on his hides' (104–3; 115–16). This comic ridicule is firmly located in the 'biocultural arena of disgust', taste's conceptual companion, which 'simultaneously invokes a form of sensual perception, an affective

---

[19]   See e.g. Destrée 2015: 472–3. On the primacy of gustation inherent in the semantics of *hēdonē* see Beekes 2010 s.v. ἡδύς ('sweet, tasteful, pleasant, pleasing'; IE * sueh2d-ú- 'sweet'); see also Mallory and Adams 2006: 236.

[20]   Cf. *Nub.* 1071–4, where the Worse Argument attacks the notion of temperance (σωφρονεῖν) as an excessive restraint on *hēdonai* (including the gustatory pleasures of *opsa* and *potoi*), echoing Simonides' sentiments that a life without pleasure is 'not worth living' (584 *PMG*).

[21]   See e.g. Wilkins 2000: 69–70 on gluttons as favourite targets of comic playwrights.

[22]   Hitch 2018: 39. She observes that during the classical period, the Athenian agora was flooded with different foods brought by the world market that had been created after the Persian Wars, so that moderate and immoderate eating 'began to be expressed in terms of personal choice of foods, that is, "taste"'.

[23]   Worman 2008: 62, 83.

register of shame and disdain, as well as bodily recoil'.[24] Paphlagon is a hideous creature that offends all the senses (cf. e.g. 125; 134; 137; 892), while the paradox of his appeal can be best captured by the 'taste' of his demagogy – the words coming out of his mouth are 'cow dung' (657), which the Council nevertheless 'ingests' with great pleasure (653). Through the sustained interplay between physical, aesthetic and cultural (dis)taste, the play seeks to influence its audience's judgement against one of Athens' most prominent politicians; for Cleon's 'disgustingness' is inextricable from his inappropriate gustatory habits, his driven-by-the-belly politics (280–1) and his lack of cultural taste (193: ἀμαθῆ καὶ βδελυρόν), itself a feature that undermines his social status and moral integrity (180–1,191–2; cf. *Wasps* 956–9, where the implication is that only someone deeply uncultured would engage in transgressive consumption).

And while the desire to obtain all kinds of gustatory pleasures is a condemnable trait for the (elite) leaders of the *dēmos*, it is certainly one of the signature features of the Aristophanic hero. It is worth considering in this context *Acharnians'* opening lines, which play on the assumption of Cleon's voracity to generate a delightfully 'disgusting' climax in the protagonist's pursuit of pleasure:[25]

ὅσα δὴ δέδηγμαι τὴν ἐμαυτοῦ καρδίαν,
**ἥσθην** δὲ βαιά· πάνυ δὲ βαιά· τέτταρα.
ἃ δ' ὠδυνήθην, ψαμμακοσιογάργαρα.
φέρ' ἴδω· τί δ' **ἥσθην** ἄξιον χαιρηδόνος;
ἐγᾦδ' ἐφ' ᾧ γε τὸ κέαρ **ηὐφράνθην** ἰδών,
τοῖς πέντε ταλάντοις οἷς Κλέων **ἐξήμεσεν**.
ταῦθ' ὡς **ἐγανώθην**, καὶ φιλῶ τοὺς ἱππέας
διὰ τοῦτο τοὔργον· ἄξιον γὰρ Ἑλλάδι. (1–8)

How many cares have torn my heart, and how few are my pleasures – just four. The things that caused me pain, sand-hundred heaps! Let me see; what pleasure could be worthy of joy? I know! My heart was full of delight to see the five talents that Cleon spewed out. That made me shine! I love the Knights for this deed – one 'worthy for Greece'!

[24]  Highmore 2010: 120; also 124: 'At its most extreme, distaste is revolt, physical nausea, vomiting, and retching. In ordinary circumstances distaste is signalled through a register of affects sliding from condescension to disdain to scorn and contempt'. On the ancient emotion of disgust see Lateiner and Spatharas 2016a.

[25]  The Greek text follows the edition of Olson 2002. Here and throughout, translations are my own unless otherwise noted.

Cleon is forced to 'vomit forth' the bribes he had, it is implied, 'gobbled up' (cf. *Knights* 258, 404–5, 1147–50). Paradoxically, this emetic spectacle proves to be the only source of delight for Dikaiopolis who, being deeply repelled by Athens' public life, decides to withdraw from it and secure a private truce with the Spartans (*Acharnians* 33; see esp. 599: ταῦτ' οὖν ἐγὼ βδελυττόμενος ἐσπεισάμην). In *Acharnians*, the sustained interplay between pleasure, and physical and moral disgust, maps primarily onto the opposition between peace and war, which warmongering politicians (like Cleon) and generals (like Lamachus) promote for their own profit. Such opposition is neatly illustrated by that moment when Dikaiopolis uses a feather from Lamachus' helmet to puke on his reversed shield (a vignette reminiscent of symposiastic, and thus leisurely and pleasurable life) because he is disgusted by the general's 'war costume' – his crests (585–6: τῆς κεφαλῆς νύν μου λαβοῦ | ἵν' ἐξεμέσω· βδελύττομαι γὰρ τοὺς λόφους).

Both here and elsewhere, the playwright combines taste attraction with aversion to highlight (among other things) the sharp contrast between corrupt politicians, with their unrestrained eating and self-indulgent appetites (see e.g. *Acharnians* 65–90), and the average citizen who, because of the formers' bad policies (in this instance, the decision to prolong the war with Sparta), is forced to either starve or 'nibble' on petty leftovers at best (see further below). *Acharnians* centres on a private citizen's decision to reverse one such bad policy and finally to savour the 'sweetness' of peace. Indeed, after having tasted the three treaties available (187: τρία γὲ ταυτὶ γεύματα), Dikaiopolis opts for, and 'drinks down', the 30-year peace treaty, which 'smells like nectar and ambrosia', and 'tells the palate, "go wherever you wish"' (195–200). This wish-fulfilment scenario materialises on stage, as we watch the protagonist enjoy all sorts of relishes, such as the Copaic eel, meat and birds, accompanied by delicious seasonings.[26] Here, Aristophanes employs gustation as a powerful memory device to engender feelings of nostalgia and thereby stimulate his audience's appetite (for the leisurely life), reminding them how good peace really 'tastes' and feels like – as Dikaiopolis puts it near the end of the play: 'Do you want to place a bet and let Lamachus decide which is tastier, locusts or thrushes (1115–16: πότερον ἀκρίδες ἥδιόν ἐστιν ἢ κίχλαι;)?'[27]

As the above-mentioned examples illustrate, Aristophanic comedy seeks to shape its audience's judgements and reasoning processes, purporting to serve a higher didactic purpose, through the sustained excitation of the lower senses – that is, by means of its fundamental appeal to sensorial life and affective experience. This strategy certainly

---

[26] See esp. *Ach.* 881–94 on Dikaiopolis' sexual and gastronomical desire for the Copaic eels (ὦ τερπνότατον σὺ τέμαχος … ποθουμένη … ποθεινή … ποθουμένην); 1003–17, 1037–47. On the alignment of eating and sexual intercourse see e.g. Rudolph 2018b: 16–18.

[27] See Olson 2002 ad loc.: 'Dikaiopolis' point is that only someone in dire straits (such as a hungry soldier in the field) would resort to [locusts] as food'.

implies the artful interlacing of body and mind as well as of cognition and sensation, on which the playwright regularly relies to invite a more reflective response. This is especially evinced in the Megarian scene (*Acharnians* 739–835), which builds on the double entendre of *choiros* (meaning 'pig' but also referring to female genitalia)[28] to convey a serious message – namely the devastating impact of war policies on the average Greek countryman: being in desperate straits, the Megarian trader decides to offer Dikaiopolis his young daughters disguised as piglets, whose meat, we are told, is 'delicious (ἅδιστον) when skewered on a spit' (795–6), in exchange for food (cf. also *Wasps* 571–3).[29] Charles Platter has further discussed how by the time of Aristophanes, Megarian comedy came to connote vulgar, physical (and thus lowbrow) humour, a style that the playwright would often affect to reject. Yet in this instance, such style becomes 'a convenient tool to excuse (while drawing attention to) one's own vulgarity'; for, 'by making [the Megarian scene's] author a Megarian himself, Aristophanes affects to show the typical behaviour of Megarians on stage, and rhetorically, to strike another blow for his comedy's higher calling'.[30] Physical taste is employed here as part of this scheme, which entails the imbrication of 'high' and 'low', of attraction and repulsion, of sensory and intellectual pleasure.[31]

Such practice therefore enables Aristophanes to provide (and promise) pleasure even while he criticises it.[32] On the one hand, the poet offers his artwork as both an aesthetic example and a moral lesson that underpins his promise to 'teach' (διδάξειν) his fellow citizens how to be truly happy (*Acharnians* 656: εὐδαίμονας εἶναι); for the pursuit of happiness certainly presupposes the obtainment of bodily pleasures, as Dikaiopolis' case makes clear.[33] At the same time, he claims to have 'stopped [his audience] from

---

[28]  See Henderson 1990: 131.

[29]  See Wilkins 2000: 36–8 on women as objects of consumption. See also Scott 2017 on the gendered politics of food and eating in Aristophanes' plays: 'since Old Comedy is a symbol of success, and can be used to mark the status of the eater and his power over others, it would appear that this specific aspect of comic power and success is denied to female characters who, even when their sexual appetites are met, are not seen indulging in appetite for food' (675).

[30]  Platter 2007: 88; 210 n. 16.

[31]  See also Edwards 1991 on how the dynamics of 'high' and 'low' shape Aristophanic poetics through the contradictory associations of τρύξ (as new wine but also dregs), the ambiguity of scatological humour and the tensions inherent in the σκῶμμα (as vulgar buffoonery and insult, but also as a valuable tool of 'serious' ethical and political criticism).

[32]  Wohl (2002: 106) has already underscored the implications of such a paradox in her analysis of *Knights*, arguing that Aristophanes 'seduces by warning against seduction and educates by gratifying. It proves harder than Plato suggested, then, to tell a doctor from a pastry chef or an Aristophanes from a Cleon, for the critique of pleasure – as Cleon's speech showed – is always implicated in the pleasure it critiques'.

[33]  See e.g. Henderson 1990: 309.

being too much taken in by foreigners' speeches, from taking pleasure in being flattered (ἥδεσθαι θωπευομένους), from being gaping citizens' (633–5).³⁴ What he has to offer instead does not consist in the empty pleasures of flattery and bribes – the province of demagogues like Cleon – but in 'teaching what is best' (657–8).

As it emerges then from these preliminary remarks, taste is considerably implicated in the politics and poetics of pleasure, which constitutes an important element of the playwright's ethico–aesthetic programme. Aristophanes' plays are replete with ideas about the role of the poet as an educator of the citizens, as well as on the function of poetry as both entertainment and a 'teaching' (*didaskalia*) – that is, as something that has the capacity to benefit and gratify at the same time (cf. e.g. *Frogs* 686–7).³⁵ Accordingly we will now turn to consider in greater detail the way physical taste also shapes the Aristophanic discourse on taste.

## Gustatory Aesthetics: Towards a Consumption Model for Aristophanic Art

Gustatory considerations underwrite *Frogs*' dramatisation of literary taste through the staged opposition between tragedians Euripides and Aeschylus. Early on in the play, Dionysus employs a gustatory analogy to convey his gluttonous desire – his 'lust' (πόθος) and 'longing' (ἵμερος) – for Euripides' plays: 'have you ever suddenly craved minestrone?' he asks his notoriously gluttonous brother, Heracles (who, unsurprisingly, responds, 'Say no more; I totally get your point'; 59–67). But when it eventually comes to choosing between the two poets, Dionysus is at a loss – 'for the one I consider to be *sophos*, yet the other pleases me', he exclaims (1413: τὸν μὲν γὰρ ἡγοῦμαι σοφόν, τῷ δ᾽ ἥδομαι). The text does not make clear which is which, but if the term *sophos* is meant here to designate Euripides' sophisticated subtlety (cf. e.g. *Clouds* 1370–1),³⁶ then Aeschylean tragedy would end up appropriating the property of *hēdonē* that Dionysus had originally attributed to Euripides' works.

---

³⁴ I treat the *hapax* χαυνοπολίτας as a synonym for κεχηνότας (cf. e.g. *Eq.* 1263: τῇ Κεχηναίων πόλει); see Beekes 2010 s.v. χάος, whose derivatives include χαόω ('to devour') and χαῦνος ('slack, porous, loose, bloated', etc.). Given the fact that *Acharnians* is one of those plays where, as Worman (2008: 84) notes, 'the pervasive metaphorical register is that of food and its preparation', the underlying imagery may also intimate a gluttonous, as well as fatuous, readiness to 'take in' demagogic speeches. On the 'gaping' imagery having 'more to do with public speaking than sexual activity' see again Worman 2008: 91; also n. 100.

³⁵ On the idea of poets as teachers, propagated principally by the poets themselves see Ford 2002: 197–201.

³⁶ See also *Ran.* 954–8, for which see Slater 1999: 367: 'Euripides has taught the spectators … by training actors in roles that model behaviour which the audience then imitates, but to Aeschylus' mind that teaching has corrupted the Athenian populace'. Cf. *Ach.* 447–8, 485 on how 'consuming' Euripidean tragedy can improve Dikaiopolis' self-presentation and speech-making abilities, bolstering his arguments for his *apologia* to the chorus.

Thus, there emerges a subtle opposition between the more 'base' pleasure (given its appetitive nature) that Euripidean tragedy elicits, and the potentially edifying pleasure of Aeschylean tragedy. The positive transvaluation of pleasure, as this is associated with Aeschylus, is further intimated by the crucial question of the poet's ability to educate the citizens which, to a considerable extent, determines the outcome of the contest (cf. *Frogs* 1007–10). For this task, the older tragedian is deemed more suitable, since his art can successfully combine *terpsis* (916) with moral improvement – a more advantageous kind of pleasure, to which Aristophanic comedy also aspires. It is also worth adding that Euripides is associated with the 'bad eater' who, as the case of the ascetic Socrates makes clear (*Clouds* 102–4 esp. 175–9), can be as suspicious and problematic as the glutton; Aeschylus' 'weighty' and 'meaty' – and thus more nutritious – *epē* ultimately outbalance the Euripidean 'slender' and 'vegetarian' Muse (*Frogs* 924, 940–4).[37] It turns out that neither the abstinent philosopher nor the – perhaps too 'thin' (λεπτός; *Frogs* 956) – tragedian can be the best educator; for, ultimately, they both render the citizens unhealthy, unfit, uncultured and apolitical.[38]

Aristophanes is working within a well-known tradition that draws analogies between food and literature as providers of nourishment. According to Matthew Wright, such an analogy has important implications for the social function of comedy, which 'may be seen as catering to the Athenians' essential bodily needs as well as to the political life of the community'.[39] Indeed, the sense of taste significantly shapes the discourse of spectatorship in part because, as Carolyn Korsmeyer has argued, 'the objects of taste are taken into one's own body; they *become* one. Because tasting and eating alter one's very constitution, their exercise requires trust'.[40] This notion is at the heart of *Knights*' staged contest between two demagogues who vie for the trust and belly of their audience (cf. 1207–8). This play presents an old and bloated Demos, overly habituated to indulging in the sweetness of Cleon's flattery and bribes. Cleon/

[37] Cf. *Old Age* frg. 128 on the 'taste' of Euripidean tragedy as 'non-meaty'. See also Wright 2012: 137–8, who suggests that the relationship between 'fat' and 'thin' may mirror the relationship between 'old' and 'new', adding that 'it is not at all easy to see which style (if either) is preferable. [ … ] On the other hand, almost all the other comic references to thinness are seemingly pejorative'.
[38] See *Ran.* 1069–73, 1085–98, 1491–9. On the association of Euripides with Socrates via the 'thin' style of their language see O' Sullivan 1992: 130–7 esp. 133: according to a fragment from the original *Clouds*, Socrates is reputed to have been the co-author of Euripides' 'clever tragedies' (fr. 392: τὰ σοφά; σοφός in this context could imply 'a clever but shallow, rather formalistic dexterity'. Cf. also *Ach.* 445.
[39] Wright 2012: 130. More broadly, on the representation of food in Greco-Roman literature see Gowers 1993.
[40] Korsmeyer 2002: 189 (original emphasis). It is in this significant respect (i.e. ingestion/digestion/alteration) that taste differs from its cousin smell which, as we saw in the examples mentioned above, forms an essential part of gustatory experience and can be used as an attractor (cf. *Ach.* 195–200) or 'repeller' (cf. *Ran.* 1150), but the results of its penetration into the body are, to a considerable extent, less consequential/permanent.

Paphlagon, we are told, continuously 'stuffs' his Master with 'tasty' money: 'Here, take this three-obol piece, savour it, gobble it down' (51: ἐνθοῦ ῥόφησον ἔντραγ᾽ ἔχε τριώβολον); the demagogue 'always keep[s] the people on [his] side by sweetening them with gourmet bons mots' (214–15: καὶ τὸν δῆμον ἀεὶ προσποιοῦ | ὑπογλυκαίνων ῥηματίοις μαγειρικοῖς).[41]

These analogies not only draw from the culinary arts but are inspired by the familiar practice of distributing snacks (as well as wine) to spectators in the theatre, designed to pander to the audience's needs and secure its goodwill (see e.g. *Peace* 962–7).[42] And while gustatory imagery is regularly employed by comic poets to refer to a literary work as an object of consumption, it is transferred here into the realm of politics to uncover the devious workings of Cleon's demagogy: by continuously 'feeding'/cajoling his audience with only 'titbits' of pleasure (such as the paltry jury pay; cf. *Knights* 804), he keeps them satisfied while withholding from them their true 'dainty' (*opson*; *Knights* 1031–2; cf. *Wasps* 666–79, 700–3).

And yet as the Sausage-seller affirms, if Demos were to savour the long-forgotten, 'crude' flavours of the countryside (i.e. porridge and olives; *Knights* 806), which can be obtained during peacetime, he would remember his true rustic (and *apragmōn*, 'quiet') self and would give up his current taste habits of the (*polupragmōn*, 'busy') city life;[43] thus coming to his senses, he would go after the detestable Paphlagon 'with the *drimus* ["sharp," "bitter"] temper of a farmer' (808). But as things stand, Demos is addicted to only one kind of flavour; what is needed, then, it is insinuated, is someone who can counteract the sweet yet noxious taste of Cleonian demagoguery and thus restore the constitution of the inflamed citizen body.

This idea is central to *Knights*' final scene. The Sausage-seller outdoes Paphlagon in their bid for (gustatory) pleasure, offering all sorts of 'sweeteners' (644–6, 678: ἡδύσματα) and delicacies, only to purge Demos' 'palate' from all the surfeit of toxic sweetness in the end – in other words, by implementing the law of *similia similibus*.[44] Having been 'purified' (1321, 1336; cf. *Wasps* 1043), the once old and swollen

---

[41] Trans Henderson 1998a. See Sommerstein 1981 ad loc.: 'the Greek could also with two slight changes mean "add the fat"; the whole sentence is ambiguous between politics and cookery'. See also Worman 2008: 87: 'As Aristophanes' wry vocabulary indicates, this sweet stuff constitutes serious argument. Like Socrates' assessment of sophists' fare in *Protagoras*, it is something "cooked up", aimed at seducing the tongue rather than nourishing the body'.

[42] See e.g. Wright 2012: 134 esp. n.122.

[43] On the town/country opposition in Aristophanes see Carter 1986: 82–7.

[44] See Wohl 2002: 105–6 on how this play dramatises the promise made in the parabasis of *Acharnians* to improve the *dēmos* (*Ach.* 657–8) by curing its 'inflammations': 'Like Socrates' doctor [in the *Gorgias*], he will cure a *dēmos* bloated on the delicious but unhealthy *opson* of Cleon's flattery and will teach it to resist such harmful overindulgence in the future. *Knights* would seem to be Aristophanes' delivery on that promise'.

Demos re-emerges on the stage as a handsome youth (and capable in his youthful malleability of being properly trained in the right kinds of taste). Importantly, the rejuvenated Demos has acquired starkly different eating habits: no longer indulging in excessive gustatory pleasures (to the point of cannibalism; cf. *Knights* 1135–40), the *kalos* (1321) Demos now looks like one of those 'messmates' of Miltiades and Aristides (1325: ξυνεσίτει). Implied in this verb is not only a communal (instead of a solitary/ transgressive) eating activity,[45] but also one that is more disciplined,[46] as well as more 'noble'.[47] Such then is the transformative potential of Aristophanic comedy, whose taste, unlike that of Cleon's demagoguery, can be both pleasurable and nourishing.[48]

We get a glimpse of the kind of consumption model Aristophanes has in mind for his own art from the parabasis speech of *Clouds*, which discusses the defeat of its original version at the Dionysia of 423 BC. Here, the poet relies on a gustatory term to designate the mode of aesthetic perception of his plays:[49]

ὦ θεώμενοι κατερῶ πρὸς ὑμᾶς ἐλευθέρως
τἀληθῆ, νὴ τὸν Διόνυσον τὸν ἐκθρέψαντά με.
οὕτω νικήσαιμί τ᾽ ἐγὼ καὶ νομιζοίμην σοφός
ὡς ὑμᾶς ἡγούμενος εἶναι θεατὰς δεξιοὺς
καὶ ταύτην σοφώτατ᾽ ἔχειν τῶν ἐμῶν κωμῳδιῶν
πρώτους ἠξίωσ᾽ **ἀναγεῦσ᾽** ὑμᾶς, ἣ παρέσχε μοι
ἔργον πλεῖστον· εἶτ᾽ ἀνεχώρουν ὑπ᾽ ἀνδρῶν φορτικῶν
ἡττηθεὶς οὐκ ἄξιος ὤν. ταῦτ᾽ οὖν μέμφομαι
τοῖς σοφοῖς, ὧν οὕνεκ᾽ ἐγὼ ἐπραγματευόμην.
ἀλλ᾽ οὐδ᾽ ὡς ὑμῶν ποθ᾽ ἑκὼν προδώσω τοὺς δεξιούς. (518–27)

Spectators, I will speak the truth to you freely, by Dionysus, who nourished me. So may I be victorious, and be thought *sophos*, I considered you to be intelligent

---

[45] See e.g. Wilkins 2000: 67: 'In both Greek and Roman society the man who ate alone transgressed the essential solidarity of commensality'.

[46] Such moderation accords with the image of a fully self-controlled Demos, noted by Slater 2002: 83; see also 84 on how 'the *Knights* enacts the cure of Demos, a cure that includes rejection of his role as spectator in a theatre of politics dominated by other actors and his assumption of centre stage in the drama of his own political existence'.

[47] For the antidemocratic politics of Demos' appearance (as *tyrannos*) in this final scene see e.g. Wohl 2002: 112–15.

[48] On the identification between the playwright and the Sausage-seller see Nelson 2014: 116.

[49] The Greek text follows the edition of Dover 1989.

spectators and this to be the cleverest of my comedies – this is why I deemed you worthy of being the first to taste it, a work of so much toil. Then I lost, defeated by vulgar men, though I did not deserve that. For these things I put the blame on you, the wise ones, for the sake of whom I laboured. But even so, I will never betray willingly the discerning ones among you.

The activity implied by the *hapax* term *anageusai* (523)[50] brings into sharp relief the qualitative dimension of spectating dramatic performances. As a compound of *geuomai* ('taste', 'savour', 'enjoy'),[51] the verb intimates the emotional and affective but also the intellectual experience of 'taking in' the poet's clever and sophisticated art (note the recurrence of *sophia* and *dexiotēs*-related terms). Around this term constellate various meanings that operate simultaneously, namely 'to savour', 'to test, sample', but also 'to choose', to which *geuomai* is etymologically related (cf. Dikaiopolis' selection process during his wine/treaty-tasting, his *geumata*, at *Acharnians* 187).[52] Implied in this last sense is the process of aesthetic discernment, attended by an equally refined aesthetic pleasure, proper to a *phusei sōphrōn* comedy (viz. one that is inherently wise by virtue of its moderation, *Clouds* 537), whose enjoyment (cf. 560: χαιρέτω; 561: εὐφραίνησθ᾽) is primarily achieved by the play's clever and innovative *epē* (544; cf. Dionysus' emetic reaction to the 'usual', worn-out jokes at *Frogs* 11, where 'bad taste' elicits literal distaste) – as opposed to the unreflective gratification provided by *phortikoi* ('vulgar') playwrights (*Clouds* 524). Set against the broader background of overconsumption, which pervades comic narratives, Aristophanes' choice of verb (of tasting, versus eating; cf. *trōgō*, *esthiō*, etc.) points towards a more selective gustatory/aesthetic activity, giving greater prominence to the perceptions of the tip of the tongue, as it were, rather than the throat. The playwright thus promotes an affective-*cum*-intellectual consumption, which he reserves especially for his own work as an edible object of delectation.[53]

We can now turn our attention to *Wasps*, which treats in a more systematic way and further illuminates the key ideas I have touched upon so far, while 'also represent[ing] the

[50] On the various possible meanings of the first compound (*ana-*), either as 'anew', 'for the second time', or in the sense of display, revelation see Dover 1989 ad loc.

[51] See Mallory and Adams 2006: 225–6: 'the concept of "taste" was closely bound to ideas of "enjoy, please" and there are two terms in Proto-Indo-European for this. The root *\*geus* is widespread and the semantics range from "taste" to "test" to "that which is pleasing."'

[52] See Hitch 2018: 23.

[53] Concerning the metapoetic dimension of this passage see esp. Hitch 2018: 40: 'The chorus leader, here a mouthpiece for the poet, describes himself as the provider of food, combining the Homeric role of the good king with that of the Muses, since his food is poetry. His audience will taste his play, with all of the transformative and possessive implications of this metaphor.'

climax of a series of plays that self-consciously reflect on and justify the essential features of Aristophanic comedy'.[54] In particular, the play revolves around the problematics of intellectual and aesthetic discernment (among others). My aim in this concluding section is to indicate how taste structures *Wasps*' narrative by bringing into sharp relief these central themes, but also by interweaving the two parts of the comic plot – that is, the courtroom and the symposium as complementary sites of taste.

## The Centrality of Gustation and Appetitive Imagery in *Wasps*' Deconstruction of Taste

The opposing tastes thematised by *Wasps* are reflected in the names of the two protagonists, Philocleon and Bdelycleon, which neatly illustrate the dynamics of attraction and repulsion – of taste and distaste – setting the story into motion. The old Philocleon has an obsessive attachment to Cleon (underscored by the prefix *phil-*) and an unhealthy (cf. *nosos*; 76, 80, 87) addiction to the juries (88: φιληλιαστής); in fact, he has a singular 'taste' for lawsuits:[55]

> ἐγὼ γὰρ οὐδ᾽ ἂν ὀρνίθων γάλα
> ἀντὶ τοῦ βίου λάβοιμ᾽ ἂν οὗ με νῦν ἀποστερεῖς.
> οὐδὲ χαίρω βατίσιν οὐδ᾽ ἐγχέλεσιν, ἀλλ᾽ ἥδιον ἂν
> δικίδιον σμικρὸν φάγοιμ᾽ ἂν ἐν λοπάδι πεπνιγμένον. (508–11)

> I wouldn't trade the life you now deprive me of not even for pigeon's milk! For I don't take pleasure in mullets and eels – a tiny little lawsuit baked in the pot would be more pleasant to eat.

Philocleon reacts against his son's offer to provide a 'noble lifestyle' (506: ζῆν βίον γενναῖον; see also 720–4) which, as the passage above indicates, is defined first and foremost by an educated palate, and entails savouring finer things – 'hare meat, all kinds of garlands and beestings and curdled goat-milk' (709–10; cf. 676–7) – than the three obol jury pay (609, 791).[56] This boorish old man, who has become addicted to such pleasures (512: εἰθίσθης γὰρ ἥδεσθαι τοιούτοις πράγμασιν),[57] has strong affinities to *Knights*' Master Demos, both with respect to their demagogic taste habits and insensitive palate, but also in terms of their difficult disposition, bilious anger and faulty sensorium

---
[54] Platter 2007: 85.
[55] The Greek text follows the edition of Biles and Douglas Olson 2015.
[56] See Worman 2008: 100.
[57] Cf. *Pax* 641–3 on an entire city's 'taste' for 'savoury' slander (ἄττα διαβάλοι τις αὐτῇ, ταῦτ᾽ ἂν ἥδιστα ἤσθιεν).

(cf. *Knights* 41–3: ἄγροικος ὀργὴν κυαμοτρὼξ ἀκράχολος, | Δῆμος πυκνίτης, δύσκολον γερόντιον | ὑπόκωφον = 'with a farmer's temper, bean chewer, extremely bilious, the Demos of the Pnyx, a difficult, half-deaf, little old man').[58] Crucially, both Philocleon and Master Demos seem to be fed by their own *drimutēs* (*Knights* 808; *Wasps* 146). *Wasps* dwells on this trait by emphasising the Athenian jurors' 'prickly' nature (cf. 225–6: κέντρον … ὀξύτατον), and in particular their emotional condition of acerbic bitterness, sustained by the ingestion of bitter, sharp and sour flavours, literal as well as metaphorical (cf. 462, 480; esp. 1082: θυμὸν ὀξίνην πεπωκότες = 'drunk with bitter spirits'), which further facilitate the release of their bilious response (χολήν; cf. 403). As the chorus leader proudly declares, such is 'the nature of men who are sharp-tempered and righteous and look [as bitter as] cress' (454–5: ἀνδρῶν τρόπος | ὀξυθύμων καὶ δικαίων καὶ βλεπόντων κάρδαμα).[59] Here, acidity is equated with Athenian-ness, so that, the more acidic the more (old school) Athenian (cf. 1075–90)[60] – and thus the more prone to irrationality which, *Wasps* seems to suggest, governs the Athenians' judgements and decision-making (in lawcourts, the Pnyx, as well as the theatre). Accordingly, the play explores what would happen if these tough, waspish Athenians were to take other than bitter substances into their body.

As in *Knights*, at stake here is the restoration of Philocleon's/the *dēmos'* constitution;[61] and while the old Master Demos ultimately changes his ways by being magically restored to youth, the (rather pessimistic) *Wasps* places centre stage the semi-failed attempt of a son to alter the deeply entrenched ways, the *tropoi* of his old-aged father by 're-educating' him (514: ἀναδιδάξειν).[62] As becomes apparent from both the private trial and the symposium scenes, this educational goal also involves the orchestration of perception and the senses. Such sensorial training is intimately related to the central question of sensibility and preference (in other words, Taste), which becomes prominent from the outset. Indeed, the playwright (via Xanthias) warns his audience to expect nothing too sophisticated (65: δεξιώτερον) – for the failure of the all-too-cerebral *Clouds* has taught him well – but also something more subtle (66: σοφώτερον) than lowbrow comedy,

---

[58] See Olson 1996, 137 on how both heroes function as 'an image of the Athenian δῆμος in the city'. See further Allen 2009 on how *orgē* can be seen in *Wasps* as 'a fundamental principle and constitutive component of democratic politics' (84).

[59] Cf. *Eq.* 631 for which see Clements 2013 esp. 87.

[60] See esp. Konstan 1985: 32–3.

[61] Cf. Bdelycleon's (futile) wish that the healing god Apollo instil sweet 'honey' in Philocleon's heart, ridding him of his 'bitter' and 'tough' (στρυφνὸν καὶ πρίνινον), as well as irrational, *ēthos* at *Vesp.* 877–8. See Biles and Olson ad loc. on the adjective *struphnos*, which is first attested here and in Hippocrates and 'is used of sour or bitter taste … and thus metaphorically of harsh temperament'. See further Taillardat 1965: 197–200.

[62] Cf. e.g. Hubbard 1991, who interprets the confrontation between Bdelycleon and Philocleon 'in terms of the sophistic opposition between *nomos* and *physis*'.

namely 'laughter stolen from Megara': 'for we don't have two slaves tossing nuts from a basket to the spectators, there's no Heracles being cheated of his dinner, no Euripides facing abuse once again' (57–61).

The examples of cheap laughter mentioned here are principally grounded in gustatory experience, as they target (either directly or indirectly) appetitive pleasure, through the representation of gluttony and condemnation of catering to the audience (cf. *Wealth* 797–9).[63] In Zachary Biles' words, these images tap into 'a more pervasive cultural association of the stomach and hunger with an abject human condition that is fundamentally opposed to and even constrains more dignified human behaviour, including reliance on faculties of thought and discernment'.[64] As Bdelycleon argues, this is precisely the condition in which Athens' political leaders aim at keeping their constituents; the current sociopolitical regime makes sure that his father stays hungry (*Wasps* 672–4; cf. 291–302), so that he can better recognise his 'tamer' (703–4). At the same time (as *Knights* also tells us), demagogues such as Cleon manage to seduce and persuade their constituents precisely by appealing to, and feeding, their appetitive part (to borrow Plato's register).[65]

*Wasps* sheds light on the workings of this irrational part by focusing on and caricaturing the Athenian court system, which is presented as another kind of sensational spectacle that satisfies the basest of pleasures (cf. esp. 565–75, 578–87).[66] Of special relevance are the various terms denoting gratification, which reoccur in Philocleon's vivid account of the advantages of jury life (cf. 572, 573, 606, 612), as he moves from the pleasures of the eyes and ears to the ones of touch, taste and smell (605–18) – the best kind, as he asserts (605: ἥδιστον τούτων … πάντων). Noticeably, the private courtroom scene highlights Philocleon's irrationality in part by drawing attention to the way he relies on these lower senses (viz. his bodily instinct, or 'gut' feelings) to determine the case. The inherently suspicious juror is convinced that one of the accused, (the dog) Labes, is indeed guilty of 'devouring all by himself the Sicilian cheese' (896–7) because 'just now, this disgusting man gave out a nasty cheesy belch!' (913–14); in fact, the defendant is as 'hot' as the soup (τῆς φακῆς) that Philocleon slurps (918; cf. 905: 'In the meantime, I'll pour myself some soup and gulp it').

---

[63] Cf. Aristotle's testimony that spectators will resort to eating 'especially when the contestants are bad' (*Eth. Nic.* 1175b12–14).

[64] Biles 2016: 120.

[65] According to Lupton 2017: 318, 'an appetite is an emotionally flavored hunger'. Cf. *Vesp.* 240–5; also 286–9 on how such hunger, unless properly alleviated, can lead to autophagy.

[66] See Biles 2016: 118 on how *Wasps* 'fuses its satire of the demagogue's manipulation of the law courts with an examination of audience tastes and critical judgment', as well as how this play 'systematically conflates the courtroom shenanigans that typify Philocleon's daily experience with the world of the theatre' (122).

At this juncture, we are reminded of Bdelycleon's earlier assurance that during the trial proceedings, his father would be able to sate his hunger and avoid any errors of judgement: 'if someone makes a long speech, you won't have to wait starving, biting yourself and the defendant' (776–9) Philocleon objects that eating food (780: μασώμενος) would incapacitate his discerning abilities (779: διαγιγνώσκειν καλῶς); and while his response sets up the joke that jurors can in fact determine whether a witness is lying by 'chewing it over' (783: ἀναμασώμενοι), it also anticipates the unintended effect of gustation on Philocleon's judgement. Bdelycleon ultimately fails to soften his father's attitude (and thus change his mind) through the pitiful spectacle of Labes' whelping puppies (cf. 973–81); for, as it turns out, the soup's tear-inducing qualities nearly cause Philocleon to 'cry away' his better judgement – 'and all this because I filled up on the soup!' (982–4).

The sustained focus on the way Philocleon interacts with his food implicitly points back to the appetitive images the playwright had rejected as evidence of bad taste (and judgement), while also intimating Bdelycleon's/the poet's failure to (re)shape his father's/audience's sensorium (cf. 1045).[67] Philocleon's soup functions as a constant reminder of his crude palate, thus setting up the symposium scene, which forges a link between, but also deconstructs, physical, aesthetic and cultural taste, ultimately subverting the plot's 'refining' progress from necessity to luxury. There, the old man's uncouthness is made manifest by his immoderate consumption of wine (παροινικώτατος) and 'fancy' food – 'like a little donkey feasting (εὐωχημένον) on roasted barley' – his boorish jokes, and his inappropriate stories (1299–321). Importantly, and in sharp contrast to *Knights*' rejuvenated Demos, Philocleon's (over)eating patterns remain problematic (cf. esp. *Wasps* 1304: ἐνέπλητο).

To be sure, the final scenes show how Philocleon's sensorial training, which involves the refinement of his palate, is at least partially successful. Indeed, Philocleon's gustatory experience alters his constitution to the extent that it changes his taste habits – he eventually becomes repelled by lawsuits (1338: ἰαιβοῖ αἰβοῖ).[68] But this new consumption model also unleashes Philocleon's drives and instincts, and eventually backfires on his son who, as a result of his father's lawless behaviour, faces the 'sweet' prospect of a 'vinegary lawsuit' (1366: ὡς ἡδέως φάγοις ἂν ἐξ ὄξους δίκην) – not unlike our poet who, in his effort to liberate his audience from their habitual appetites (for cheap art and Cleon's visceral demagogy), must face abuse in the form of unpalatable lawsuits (cf. 1014–45).

---

[67] For the association between Bdelycleon and the poet, see e.g. Biles and Olson 2015: xxxiii.

[68] See Levine 2016 on the interjection *aiboi* as an expression of disgust but also of laughter, whose 'self–contradictory nature reminds us that disgust and delight coexist on the same emotional spectrum' (87).

The exodos (1474–1537) further hints at the positive transformative potential of gustation, whereby the (destructive) drive to 'devour' defendants is transfigured into the (constructive) desire to 'feast on' literary opponents (1506): for the consumption of wine also liberates Philocleon's Dionysian energy, leading to a spectacular display of competing cultural and aesthetic, old and new tastes, as a rejuvenated Philocleon engages in dance competition with the sons of the tragedian Carcinus – an unconventional finale designed to appeal to the audience's preference for novelty (1536–7).[69]

We can therefore appreciate the centrality of gustatory experience in *Wasps*, which is deeply concerned with (controlling) its audience's (and, by implication, the *dēmos*') inward condition and the kind of substances (literal and figurative) they take into their body. The importance of taste is also evidenced by the sustained manner in which the playwright manipulates this lower sense (together with touch and smell) to invite self-reflection, bringing to awareness and thereby criticising his audience's appetitive (i.e. base) taste habits. *Wasps* thus constitutes a prime example of how Aristophanes relies on the body even as he attempts to undermine it through the construction of a series of implicit binary oppositions that, as we have seen, pervade many of his plays (e.g. affect/reason, appetitive/intellectual, body/mind, 'low'/'high').[70]

To sum up, this brief analysis has brought to light the significance of taste in Aristophanes' work, primarily through the close association of this sense with pleasure and appetite – concepts intimately related to ethical and aesthetic considerations that permeated the wider sociocultural context within which Old Comedy was produced. The Aristophanic corpus offers compelling evidence of how this bodily sense constitutes an ideal cognitive–affective tool to communicate ideas on aesthetic and moral values and is therefore a most valuable source for anyone interested more broadly in the role of embodied experience in knowledge and valuation. Far from being concerned with trivial subject matter, by resorting to the bodily senses, Aristophanic comedy offers a stark reminder of how aesthetic taste is firmly rooted in physical sensation.

---

[69] See Biles and Olson 2015: xxxvii: 'Philocleon's series of transformations culminates in more confident and none too subtle assertion of *Wasps'* place alongside – and by implication, above – the other comic performances at the Lenaea of 422 BC'.

[70] The importance of this strategy is evidenced also by the fact that it anticipates the agenda of one of the most adept literary artists, Plato, who would frequently enlist the senses – including taste – in support of his arguments against embodied experience. See e.g. Angelopoulou 2022 on the significance of taste as an inclusive concept in the philosopher's writings.

# PART II

## Senses and Power

# '"But not a word about me" (περὶ ἐμοῦ δ' οὐδεὶς λόγος): Sensing Xanthias in Aristophanes' *Frogs*'

## Zachary Case

'Human beings are tied together by a certain sensory fabric, a certain distribution of the sensible, which defines their way of being together; and politics is about the transformation of the sensory fabric of "being together"'.[1]

Xanthias plays a starring role in the first half of *Frogs*. And yet he is sometimes neglected, not only by scholars, who have tended to view him as a foil to the god-*cum*-citizen Dionysus, the protagonist onstage the entire play and said to unify its distinct halves,[2] but also by Dionysus and Heracles themselves in the opening scene, in which Xanthias thrice points out their failure to notice him: 'but not a word about me' (περὶ ἐμοῦ δ' οὐδεὶς λόγος, 87, 107, 115). So, let us spare him a word.

Susan Lape is one scholar who has close paid attention to Xanthias in her reading of the first half of the play, which explores the deconstruction of essentialist identities through Xanthias' cross-dressing and role-playing, and demonstrates that the slave succeeds in showing status distinctions conventionally thought to be natural to be in fact conventional.[3] Indeed, at times it is made to look as if Xanthias' position as a slave and Dionysus' as master are the wrong way around, Xanthias being rational and courageous and Dionysus silly and cowardly (285–308, 479–502, 590–604), their roles and costumes repeatedly swapped (494–502, 522–533, 579–89) and, ultimately, Aeacus failing to distinguish between the two in the torture scene (668–9). These drastic inversions of status testify to the performative dimension of civic identity and to the impossibility of distinguishing master from slave by physical appearance alone,

---

[1] Rancière 2009: 56
[2] Esp. Segal 1961.
[3] Lape 2013: 81–6.

something which democracy's critics such as the 'Old Oligarch' and Plato already liked to point out at Athens (Pseudo-Xenophon *Constitution of the Athenians* 1.10–12, Plato *Republic* 562b–3c).[4]

Yet the political implications of the first half of *Frogs* go beyond the (at times) visual indistinguishability of Xanthias and Dionysus. I am going to argue that Xanthias is not merely contingently indistinguishable from Dionysus in appearance and behaviour, but he is fundamentally indistinguishable from him as an embodied, sensing being, one who feels passion and especially pain. In other words, the two characters do not just *look* the same, but they also *feel* the same. What we see throughout the first half of the play, beginning with the prologue and culminating in the torture scene, is the reduction of the master–slave duo to an inexorable and status-defying condition of corporeality, vulnerability and precariousness.[5] This manifests a body of feminist theory that has been labelled 'corporeal humanism', which, as Ann Murphy has discussed in contradistinction with the set of ideologies typically embraced under the umbrella of humanism centred on disembodied ideals such as autonomy and freedom, is 'grounded in the ontological fact of vulnerability, dispossession and exposure' and offers 'a more expansive and inclusive paradigm'.[6] Reading the pain-filled scenes in *Frogs* from this feminist perspective helps to articulate a way in which fifth-century BC status distinctions can be undone by recognition of the body's capacity for sensation itself, contesting the unverifiable 'naturalness' of the slave-object and affirming the incontrovertible humanity of the slave-subject.[7] The re-humanisation of Xanthias in this way disturbs what Jacques Rancière calls the 'distribution of the sensible' (*la partage du sensible*), which is the name given to 'the system of self-evident facts of sense perception that simultaneously discloses the existence of something in common and the delimitations that define the respective

---

[4]   For less polemical accounts that take for granted the visual indistinguishability of masters and slaves see Arist. *Pol.* 1254b28–34, Aeschin. 1.10, 1.138–9, Dem. 47.61, 53.16. Discussing these and other evidence, including aspects of Athens' demography and cosmopolitanism that worked to blur citizen and non-citizen identities see Vlassopoulos 2007, 2009, 2010. See also Osborne 2016 for corroborating visual evidence. Connecting this cultural anxiety surrounding issues of appearance and social mobility to comic 'down-dressing' see Reinke 2019a: 70–4.

[5]   These categories are best associated with the work of Judith Butler: see Butler 2004, 2009, 2015, 2022. Other feminist thinkers engaging with them include Bergoffen 2001, Diprose 2002, Garland-Thomson 2002, Cavarero 2007, Murphy 2011, Oliver 2015.

[6]   Murphy 2011: 589. Murphy continues by adding the qualification that this paradigm is 'still attentive to the differences that mark bodies, and respectful of the radically different ways that vulnerability and dispossession are lived'.

[7]   On the status of the slave in ideological antithesis to the freeborn citizen as well as full human being in fifth-century Athens see DuBois 1991, 35–68, Cartledge 2002: 133–66, Osborne 2010: 85–103.

parts and positions within it' or, more simply put, the power structures predicated on a person's place, or non-place, in the sensory world.[8]

I will go on to contend that Xanthias may not be the only Aristophanic slave whom we might regard as a potential human 'self' with all the vulnerability that implies – as opposed to another non-human 'other' exploited for comic effect – even as the representation of comic slaves is typically read as confirming rather than subverting the most entrenched ontological hierarchy of Greek thought.[9] By way of conclusion, I will return to the ending of *Frogs* and consider the possibility of Xanthias' absent presence in the final scene, which may be understood as recapitulating his bid to be noticed at the start.

## Sensing Xanthias

I am not focalising Xanthias on a whim. This move might be justified by the play's Eleusinian dimension, which invites a more open perspective, since the Mysteries were accessible to (Greek-speaking) slaves and thereby offered a more egalitarian conception of community formation than, for instance, the Panathenaea, with the chorus of initiates including women as well as men (157, 445 with the scholia on *Knights* 589) and professing their righteousness towards all (457–9).[10] It might also be warranted by the play's Dionysiac dimension, Dionysus himself being an outsider to the traditional pantheon and a figure who incorporates otherness within himself, a view corroborated in *Frogs* (e.g. 156–7, 458–9).[11] It might even be in keeping with the play's paraenetic dimension, since the specific advice that the chorus gives in the *parabasis* to re-enfranchise the oligarchs rests upon the *dēmos* having already passed a decree to enfranchise the slaves who had fought at Arginousae (686–705), both being acts that include the excluded.[12] Yet the reason for paying close attention to Xanthias is not simply to do with the Eleusinian, Dionysiac or paraenetic frames, which come into focus only as the play unfolds. Xanthias, in fact, is front and centre from the play's opening line.

---

[8]   Rancière 2013: 3–42, quoted at 5, though Rancière's focus is on the capacity to speak and be seen rather than the capacity for mere sensation. For more thorough analysis of Aristophanic comedy through Rancière see Zumbrunnen 2012: 21–40, 60–80, Telò 2020b, Case 2021b: passim. See also Radcliffe in this volume.

[9]   For discussion of the representation of slaves in Aristophanes, usually regarded in terms of the structuralist-informed model of transgression and reaffirmation of the social hierarchy see the essays in Akrigg and Tordoff 2013. For a different approach, which is the basis for the one taken here see Case 2021b: 142–70.

[10]  For readings of the play which stress ritual openness in post-Arginousae Athens see Bowie 1993: 228–53, Edmonds 2004: 58, 111, Sells 2012. For the evidence that slaves could be initiated at Eleusis see Dem. 59.21; *IG* ii² 1672.207.

[11]  Lada-Richards 1999: 17–44, 258–60, with references to other Greek sources.

[12]  McGlew 2002: 163–70, Griffith 2013: 52.

The prologue of *Frogs* seems designed precisely to shine a spotlight on Xanthias. He is the centre of comic attention, the one who has the first word and initiates the dialogue with metatheatrical and comedic self-awareness by proposing to make jokes in the first place (1–2). Given that the plot does not strictly begin until the second scene when Dionysus arrives at Heracles' house and explains his personal quest to the underworld to revive his favourite poet Euripides, the function of this prologue, which reveals nothing about the plot – distinctly unlike other comic prologues featuring slaves (namely those of *Knights, Wasps, Peace* and *Wealth*) – is at least partly to draw attention to Xanthias. And Aristophanes is at pains to keep Xanthias in sight beyond the prologue through the following scene where Dionysus and Heracles converse, even when he is no longer the prime focus of the action. For Xanthias repeatedly complains in asides, a strategy designed to generate rapport with the audience in comedy,[13] that nobody is taking note of him and the load he is being forced to bear (87–8, 107, 115, 159).[14] He thereby articulates his own exclusion from the story of *Frogs*, and in doing so disavows that exclusion. Unlike the silent characters at the start of Aeschylus' tragedies as caricatured later on in this play (911–26),[15] Xanthias will not stand idly by. He will, of course, become much more prominent once the scene shifts to Hades itself, eventually earning the full admiration of the chorus (590–7), who admire Dionysus only ironically (534–40). Yet even when being entirely disregarded by Dionysus and Heracles, he is making himself known to the spectators, loud and clear.

Why all this focus on Xanthias, even when he is no longer the centre of comic attention? What is there to notice, apart from the fact that he can be quite amusing? One answer is simply that Xanthias acts as a representative of a certain kind of lowbrow, Old Comic humour bearing the 'load' of the joke-making as well as the baggage; indeed, σκεύη (12) is also a word for 'props', so Xanthias' early complaints might be understood as a metatheatrical comment about his role in facilitating the humorous costume changes that are coming up. A better answer, only briefly noted by Bruce Heiden, stems from the fact that the focus is acutely on his bodily suffering about which Dionysus pays no heed.[16] That seems a better observation in relation to Xanthias' specific choice of jokes at the start of the play, since jokes involving baggage-carrying routines need not be the only ones so repugnant to Dionysus; they are not actually mentioned in the

---

[13] Sommerstein 2009b: 146, Moodie 2012.
[14] These are not the only rapport-generating asides delivered by Xanthias, since he also plausibly speaks asides by making inflammatory, and characteristically humorous, remarks that otherwise mysteriously bypass the master at lines 33–4, 41, 308, and possibly at 51 and 311: see Dover 1993: 44–5.
[15] Taplin 1972.
[16] Heiden 1991: 107.

programmatic *parabaseis* of *Clouds* or *Peace* as a 'no-go' (while jokes about causing slaves to suffer *are* said to be in that category in the *parabasis* of *Peace*: see below). They may have been chosen, above all, to emphasise the suffering of a slave being 'squished' (πιέζομαι, 3), 'squashed' (θλίβομαι, 5), 'bearing a load' (ἄχθος ἐπ' ἐμαυτῷ φέρων, 9) and questioning why he needs to carry the baggage in the first place (τί δῆτ' ἔδει με ταῦτα τὰ σκεύη φέρειν, 12). The load is being shouldered 'quite unbearably' (βαρέως πάνυ, 26), the adverb βαρέως always being used in Aristophanes to denote misfortune.[17] At least there is the solace that he can joke about his 'triple-damned neck' (ὦ τρισκακοδαίμων ἄρ' ὁ τράχηλος οὑτοσί, 19) as it is being 'squashed' (ὅτι θλίβεται μέν, 20) – but wait, he 'can't say anything funny' (τὸ δὲ γέλοιον οὐκ ἐρεῖ, 20)! The effect, then, is that Xanthias is constantly being reduced to his suffering body all in the space of a few minutes of stage action. There is a sense of urgency to these jokes involving a man in pain, jokes which, as Mario Telò has argued, themselves trigger the desire to feel a masochistic 'pleasure in pain' in the spectator-figure Dionysus.[18] If we accept this, then Xanthias and Dionysus are already suffering together, albeit in different ways for now: the former suffering from the physical burden of the load he is carrying, the latter from the experience of laughter. Far from flagging the slave's distinctly servile nature as being 'fit for abuse', as has been argued of the representation of slaves' bodies in art,[19] it is Xanthias' and Dionysus' shared experience of pain that will be drawn out in the first half of *Frogs*, building up to the crucial torture scene.

Let us return to the prologue before we get there. Ignoring the plight of his slave, Dionysus condemns Xanthias' 'insolence and great luxuriance' (ὕβρις καὶ πολλὴ τρυφή, 21) for complaining, and claims that he has done his slave a favour to spare him from 'toiling and carrying a load' (ἵνα μὴ ταλαιπωροῖτο μηδ' ἄχθος φέροι, 24) by walking in front of the donkey carrying the slave carrying the baggage. This smacks of the 'Old Oligarch's' complaint about the τρυφή afforded to slaves at Athens (*Constitution of the Athenians* 1.11), except here Aristophanes may be showing how ridiculous that idea is in the face of the very real toiling of slaves and of the actual luxuriance of masters.[20] Confronted with Dionysus' quasi-sophistic denial that, in the face of empirical evidence to the contrary, he is carrying anything since he is being carried, Xanthias curses his luck and makes the play's first reference to the events after Arginousae, after which slaves who had served in the navy were awarded a special grant of citizenship:

---

[17] Cf. *Nub.* 716; *Vesp.* 114, 158, *Thesm.* 385, 474, *Ran.* 803, *Eccl.* 175.

[18] Telò 2020c: 54.

[19] Wrenhaven 2013: 63–74.

[20] On the negative connotations of τρυφή, a term associated with aristocratic luxuriance in democratic Athens see Kurke 1992: 102–6.

οἴμοι κακοδαίμων· τί γὰρ ἐγὼ οὐκ ἐναυμάχουν;
ἢ τἂν **σε** κωκύειν ἂν ἐκέλευον μακρά. (33–4)

Oh goddammit! Why didn't I fight at the naval battle?
Then I'd be ordering *you* to wail a different tune. [21]

If only Xanthias had served, he might be free; he was close to shedding his servile
status just like that. Indeed, it was only a matter of bad luck that on the day of the naval
battle Xanthias 'happened to have an eye problem' (ἔτυχον ὀφθαλμιῶν, 192; cf. οἴμοι
κακοδαίμων, τῷ ξυνέτυχον ἐξιών; 196) that prevented him from serving. However,
it is Xanthias' *not* serving that is stressed, a fact that is emphasised once more by the
unusually narrow-minded Charon shortly after, when he refuses to let the slave onto
his boat-cum-trireme for that reason (190–2).[22] Nevertheless, it is precisely because of
this, let me suggest, that *Frogs* is able to gesture towards a place where *even* slaves such
as Xanthias not included in the citizenship grant after Arginousae might have a claim to
political inclusion by the transformation of the 'sensory fabric' of the social order, to use
Rancière's phrase quoted in the epigraph at the start of this chapter. For if citizen identity
is determinately, if not solely, grounded on the inviolable body of the free person set
against the violable body of the slave (as in Demosthenes 22.55 and 24.167) – what has
been called the 'democratic body' in David Halperin's words[23] – then the naturalness of
that identity is challenged in a sequence of scenes showing the bodies of a citizen and a
slave in pain. After all, the experience of pain and suffering is a great leveller.

As we have seen, *Frogs* begins by emphasising Xanthias' body and the painful load
pressing upon his neck (τράχηλος, 19) and his shoulders (ὦμον, 87). It is a load that is
burdensome enough for Xanthias to throw it down (160) and for even an unnamed
corpse to refuse to carry it for anything less than two drachmas (172–8)! As the
play goes on, however, it is also and equally Dionysus' body which is subject to pain,
though the pain affects different regions of his body, each body being vulnerable in its
own way.[24] This is first of all made clear in the rowing scene where Dionysus learns to
row in 'competition' with the frog chorus (197–268), a scene that has been read as
legitimising the enfranchisement decree by the link between participation in a trireme
and participation in democracy.[25] Indeed, by serving in the naval battle, described by
Charon in an oddly corporeal image literally meaning the battle 'about the flesh' (τὴν

---

[21]   The Greek is taken from Wilson 2007 and the translations are my own.
[22]   Edmonds 2004 notes that 'Charon in other myths takes passengers indiscriminately from all ranks' (128).
[23]   Halperin 1990: 88–112 esp. 96–9. Cf. Hunter 1992.
[24]   Bergoffen 2001: 132–3, Murphy 2011: 578.
[25]   Dover 1993: 50, Clay 2002, Edmonds 2004: 126–35.

περὶ τῶν κρεῶν, 191),[26] the slaves were able to prove themselves equal to citizens simply by being able-bodied enough to row (and suffer in rowing); and if the fat, incompetent citizen-hoplite Dionysus 'son of Winejar' (υἱὸς Σταμνίου, 22) can do it (and suffer doing it), then so can anyone (197–268, esp. 203–5). As the pot-bellied (γάστρων, 200; cf. 663–4, 1095) god begins to row, he moans that his arse is hurting (ἐγὼ δέ γ' ἀλγεῖν ἄρχομαι | τὸν ὄρρον, 220–1) and, as Xanthias had complained about being neglected before by Dionysus and Heracles (87, 107, 115), that this is of no concern to the frogs who are providing the timing of the stroke (ὑμῖν δ' ἴσως οὐδὲν μέλει, 224). While Xanthias is strolling around the lake to meet Dionysus easily on the other side, a trip that involves the 'rest stops' (ἀναπαύλαις, 195) Dionysus had craved for his own comfort (113) – that really is the kind of τρυφή Dionysus had wrongly imputed to his slave earlier (21) – Dionysus is struggling to row across it. He continues to moan as the frogs gleefully croak away, this time irritated by blisters and a sweaty arsehole:

Δι. ἐγὼ δὲ φλυκταίνας γ᾽ ἔχω,
χὠ πρωκτὸς ἱδίει πάλαι,
κᾆτ᾽ αὐτίκ᾽ ἐκκύψας ἐρεῖ—
Χο. βρεκεκεκὲξ κοὰξ κοάξ. (236–8)

DIONYSUS. But I have blisters,
and my arsehole's been sweating,
and pretty soon it'll peep out and say –
CHORUS. Brekekekex koax koax.

Whilst Xanthias had grumbled that he (or rather his neck) could not 'say' (ἐρεῖ, 20) anything funny while being physically oppressed (though at least he got the joke out by *praeteritio*), Dionysus here cannot 'say' (ἐρεῖ, 238) anything at all, since he (or rather his arsehole) is immediately cut off by the frogs' croaky refrain. When Dionysus tells them to shut up (παύσασθε, 241), they respond by croaking all the louder (μᾶλλον μὲν οὖν | φθεγξόμεσθ᾽, 241–2), displaying a sort of Schadenfreude towards Dionysus' struggles that prefigures the feelings mutually displayed by Xanthias and Dionysus later on, as each takes disturbing pleasure in the violence inflicted upon the other (563–8, 606–12, 618–21). By the time we get to the *parodos*, then, the doubling of Xanthias and Dionysus is well under way, a doubling that is predicated most significantly on their mutual reduction to bodies that feel pain.

---

[26]  This reading seems preferable to the alternative reading περὶ τῶν νεκρῶν, which would (too) contentiously refer to the generals' failure to reclaim the corpses, on which see Dover 1993: ad 190. In either case, however, corporeality is at stake.

Attention then shifts to less earth(l)y matters in the *parodos*. The chorus give the sense of having transcended corporeality altogether, shedding their amphibian identity to become sacred initiates who pray to exist 'without toil' (ἄνευ πόνου, 402) and 'shake off the pains' (ἀποσείονται δὲ λύπας, 346) of old age. Yet once Dionysus and Xanthias reach Pluto's palace, their vulnerable bodies are put into increasingly sharp focus in the lead-up to the torture scene. Physical punishment is the order of the day when they are greeted by Aeacus, who threatens Dionysus in extremely visceral terms with retribution for Heracles' heroic exploits in stealing Cerberus (465–78): laceration of guts, grabbing of lungs and tearing asunder of bleeding balls and entrails. In fear of being completely mutilated, Dionysus shits himself (ἐγκέχοδα, 479; cf. 308) – a different kind of embodiment being shown there – and in doing so becomes the direct object of derision (ὦ καταγέλαστ', 480).[27] Master and slave are becoming increasingly hard to tell apart, a point dramatised by the frequent changes of costume, even as it is denied by Dionysus, who retrospectively maintains that 'Heraclo-Xanthias' (Ἡρακλειοξανθίαν, 499) is never really anything more than 'whip-fodder' (μαστιγίας, 500) and that their first costume swap was only a joke (522–5). It is said to be only a 'joke' (γέλοιον, 542) as well for the master to get hypothetically punched in the face without being able to retaliate (542–8); and it is presumably meant only as a joke when Dionysus invites Xanthias to take a swing at him for free (585), as a reward for swapping costumes for a third time in fear of further physical threats from an outraged innkeeper (572–5) – this time teeth–bashing, execution and disgorging of the windpipe. Dionysus is asking for it. The joke will be on Dionysus when he is actually 'to be whipped' (μαστιγωτέος, 633) in the torture scene, which is the key scene in re-humanising Xanthias' body, as it stages the reduction of Xanthias and Dionysus to conditions of embodied vulnerability together and at the same time.

There, the identities of Xanthias and Dionysus, both having stripped (641) to obscure identification by costume,[28] become fused together in pain. The result is that they become entirely indistinguishable, for at the end of it all, Aeacus cannot decide who is who (668). Yet what matters is not just that the 'test', which recalls and perverts the Athenian judicial procedure of 'evidentiary' torture (*basanos*),[29] completely and utterly fails. That much has already been observed: '[T]he test that is supposed to shore up the

---

[27]  Sommerstein 2009a writes that 'Xanthias is possibly going too far when he uses this form of address to his owner who is, moreover, a god' (110). Yet the point of this straight insult instead of a subversive aside is surely that the master and slave are interchangeable here.

[28]  On the stripping consisting in the removal of outer garments but not padded body suits see Sommerstein 1996 ad loc.

[29]  For different views on the *basanos* see Gagarin 1996 (invoked as a rhetorical strategy), Mirhady 1996 (used for privileged evidence), Thür 1996 (ideologically distinguishing the slave from the citizen).

difference between slave and god leads only to an emphasis on their underlying similarity … The *basanos'* inability to uncover a hidden, authentic identity suggests that there is no inner ground of being that truly separates Dionysus from Xanthias'.[30] As such, it is worth adding, the scene undoes the paradigmatic tale reported by Herodotus about the Scythian slaves' 'recognition' of their inherent servitude at the mere sight of the whip (4.1–4), ideological justification for 'natural' slavery like none other.[31] For Xanthias, unlike those Scythians, is animated rather submissive at the prospect of being beaten: 'bring it on!' is the sentiment of his responses (δίκαιος ὁ λόγος, 637; καλῶς λέγεις, 643). What matters more than the outcome of the *basanos*, however, is that its specific framing draws attention to the embodied experience of the vulnerable human being, who, as we have seen so far in *Frogs*, feels pain.

This is because there is a shift in emphasis in the scene, noted by Alan Sommerstein in his commentary on the play.[32] The *basanos* is initially proposed as a legal procedure to settle a dispute about Xanthias' (i.e. Heracles') innocence (615–17). Aristophanes might well have chosen to show how absurd the use of torture to validate evidence given by a slave would have been, if it were ever actually followed through, as it seems not to have been in reality. Indeed, one can easily imagine an alternative comic scenario where Dionysus and Xanthias say absolutely anything to make the torture stop, an argument that could be deployed to discredit the evidence gained by torture, as advised for instance by Aristotle (*Rhetoric* 1376b–77a). Yet the *basanos* ends up raising an ontological issue about which of Xanthias and Dionysus is a god, on the (evidently disputable) grounds that gods do not feel pain (634). That shift is extremely telling. It implies that what is at stake is not whether the testimony of a slave can be trusted, but rather whether the objects of torture are human at all. The joke is that the god, who is a free quasi-citizen too, is just as vulnerable as the human. Xanthias, described at one point by Aeacus during the torture as a 'sanctified *human*' (**ἄνθρωπος** ἱερός, 652; cf. 299), just happens to be a slave.

Try as Dionysus and Xanthias may to mask the fact that they have sensation (αἰσθήσεται, 634) and are concerned about their welfare (προτιμήσαντά, 638, προτιμᾷς, 654; οὐδέν μοι μέλει, 655), and to deny the fact that torture causes them to feel pain (ὠδυνήθης, 650; ἤλγησεν, 660, 664) and wail (κλαύσαντα, 638, κλάεις, 654), neither is anaesthetised to the lash of the whip.[33] Each manifests his precariousness in the sense of 'a primary vulnerability to others, one which we cannot will away without ceasing to be

---

[30]  Lape 2013: 84–5.
[31]  Finley 1980: 118–19.
[32]  Sommerstein 1996: ad 634.
[33]  For a unique slave's complaint about the grim reality of being whipped see Agora Inv. IL 1702, discussed by Harris 2004.

human', and fails to uphold the 'fantasy of mastery' that denies human vulnerability.[34] This is shown, above all, when at various points each utters an ineffable cry (ἀτταταῖ, 649; ἰοὺ ἰού, 653; οἴμοι, 657) which, as Elaine Scarry influentially argued, is the outward sign of the body in pain.[35] Naomi Weiss has considered Scarry's analysis in relation to the complexities of staging of pain in tragedy, focusing on its 'intercorporeal' effect on the audience,[36] though pain's resistance to expression in language is germane to comic representation too (as is the audience's 'feeling' of the characters' suffering, though the phenomenological dynamics of theatre and the spectators' own bodily responses are not my primary concern here, as they are in Weiss's chapter in this volume). The more Xanthias and Dionysus try to explain away their cries by turning them into jokes – taking up and exceeding Xanthias' earlier inability to say anything funny when in pain (20) – the more brutal the lashings become. At one point, Xanthias lets his vulnerability slip when he says that he exclaimed οἴμοι because he was taking a painful thorn out of his foot (656). After several rounds of 'blow for blow' (πληγὴν παρὰ πληγήν, 643), Aeacus becomes frustrated with the lack of progress and, upon Xanthias' prod that Dionysus is 'breaking' (659), goes on to whip Dionysus even more cruelly on the front (662–3). This prompts Dionysus to respond with even more intensity: whereas he started off explaining away his pain by referencing mundane incidents (646–7, 653–5), he ends up reciting a passage of tragic verse (664–7 = Sophocles fragment 371), thus also implicitly giving the game away.

    None of this proves anything for Aeacus, of course. His indecision must be the consequence of both characters' conspicuously failing the test to prove who is a god, rather than of both demonstrating their divine anaesthesia. The whole exercise, in any case, has been in vain, as Dionysus protests too late, since he claims the gods of the underworld will immediately recognise their divine relative (670–3) – also an echo of courtroom procedure in cases of disputed identity where nothing more than who is willing to vouch for you is key.[37] The gods could have easily distinguished the god from the human, it may be retrospectively admitted, but could they have distinguished the slave from the free, or at least a slave body from a free body? The answer the play gives is a resounding no.

    The effect of this scene, nevertheless, is typically said not only to generate laughter, but also to normalise the use of torture against slaves and to reinforce their legal status as violable, a point often made about the comic abuse of slaves more generally.[38] Unlike in

---

[34]  The quotes are from Butler 2004: xiv, 29.
[35]  Scarry 1985. As Scarry writes, pain 'does not simply resist language but actively destroys it, bringing about an immediate reversion to a state anterior to language, to the sounds and cries a human being makes before language is learned' (4).
[36]  Weiss 2023a: 122–61. See also Weiss's chapter in this volume.
[37]  Vlassopoulos 2009.
[38]  See e.g. DuBois 1991: 33–4, Osborne 2010: 99.

scenes of tragic suffering where the feelings of the sufferer are typically thought to meld with those of the spectator, the comic suffering is said to work in the manner of Brechtian *Verfremdung*, prompting 'not empathy but alienation, not infectious grief but disengaged, self-conscious laughter'.[39] It is worth adding that even advocates of 'corporeal humanism' hesitate when pronouncing the vulnerable body to be an incentive for ethical obligation, since the perception of vulnerability might in other cases inspire violence or abuse – or perhaps, as in this case, *Schadenfreude* (606–12, 618–25).

Yet the violence staged in the torture scene of *Frogs* is so gratuitous and so extraordinary on the ancient stage that the mutual feelings of pain felt by Xanthias and Dionysus should not be dismissed as comic trivia – not to mention, at least potentially, the real feelings of the actors playing those characters, as one may wonder how violently and realistically this scene would have been staged, and how much pain the actors in padded body suits (after stripping off their outer costumes) would have felt in performance, given comedy's proclivity to break down the boundaries between fantasy and reality.[40] After all, this is the most viscerally and uncompromisingly pain-filled scene staged in Greek comedy (if not in all of Greek drama, excepting the beginning of the Aeschylean *Prometheus Bound* (1–81) and one scene from Aeschylus' *Suppliant Women* (825–907)),[41] in which the sadistic parody of the procedure for offering a slave up for torture and the enactment of a form of torture seemingly never followed through in Athenian courts turns out to be entirely unnecessary to advance the plot. If laughter is what Aristophanes is aiming to elicit, it is laughter of an awfully discomforting, alienating, self-conscious type indeed.[42] This is especially because Dionysus and Xanthias take so much pleasure in each other's pain, mimicking the pleasure of the audience and re-enacting the pleasure of Dionysus at the start, even as pain is equally inflicted upon themselves and their own bodies – bodies that collapse any inalienable distinction between inviolable 'self' and violable 'other'. Given how easily status distinctions can be reversed with a mere change of costume in this play, which was after all produced in a context where the prospect of mass enslavement by losing the Peloponnesian War might have been felt to be very real (Xenophon *Hellenica* 2.2.3), the joke may ultimately be on those Athenians who, like Dionysus, think themselves to be inviolable, invulnerable and, above all, indifferent to pain.

---

[39] Lada-Richards 1999: 117.

[40] Slater 2002 goes so far as to see the *actors'* pain as constituting a 'significant part of the audience's enjoyment' (190).

[41] On the ubiquity of the infliction of bodily violence in comedy, though with nothing else quite as prolonged or extreme as in this scene see Kaimio et al. 1990.

[42] On this aspect of laughter in Aristophanes see Case 2021b: 22–39, 57–60.

## Sensing Other Slaves

With this in mind, we may go even further and argue that Xanthias is not the only slave in Aristophanes' plays whose human vulnerability is sensible in moments of corporeal anguish and whose violent abuse is problematised as a result.[43]

Consider the following: his namesake Xanthias in *Wasps* (1292–1325), the unnamed slaves in *Lysistrata* (1216–24) and 'Manes' in *Birds* (1313–36), which are the three examples cited by Kenneth Dover to attest to the 'extraction of humour from the mistreatment of slaves'.[44] In each case, however, Aristophanes seems to be at pains *not* to allow the comic slapstick to overshadow the painful plight of the slave.[45] Xanthias' envy of tortoises with their protective shells (*Wasps* 1292–6; cf. 429) and intention to get out of his violent master's way (*Wasps* 1325) is an admission of his own vulnerability, even as his violability is asserted by the chorus. Adopting the kind of perverse logic of the Unjust argument followed by Pheidippides in *Clouds*, the wasp chorus say that it is right to call anyone who takes a beating, including an old man, a 'slave' (παῖς, 1297–8) (also and primarily meaning 'child', ironically applied here). Yet that comment, enacted by Philocleon during the symposium as he beats up his slave to the refrain of παῖ παῖ (*Wasps* 1307), becomes rather awkward in the light of the protagonist's hyper-aggressive behaviour, which includes beating up citizens who legitimately threaten legal recourse (*Wasps* 1332–4, 1388–91). This is exactly what Xanthias does in *Frogs* by calling the people around to witness that he is being assaulted by Dionysus (ταῦτ' ἐγὼ μαρτύρομαι, 528), his alleged crime being clothes-stealing (*lōpodusia*), and thereby performing a legal right denied to slaves in reality but which plenty of Aristophanic characters – in all other instances citizens – express when they too are being flagrantly assaulted by rowdy protagonists.[46] As for 'Manes' in *Birds*, he might not complain about the beating he is dealt by Peisetairos for being

---

[43] Though that is not to say that this is true of every slave across the Aristophanic corpus, as some slaves get a 'rougher' treatment than others: mute, nude females and Scythian archers, for instance, on which see, respectively, Zweig 1992 and Hall 2006: 225–54.

[44] Dover 1972: 206. Further examples are cited in Dover 1993: 43–4, in which one of the prime functions of slaves is said to be to 'elicit laughter by being hurt, threatened, or frightened'.

[45] Some scholars have already made gestures towards this position: see Kaimio et al. 1990: 66–8, Ruffell 2013: 248–54. See also Sommerstein 2009b: 140–4, observing that slaves are not solely victims but are sometimes the ones perpetrating the violence against citizens and that, whereas comic heroes who are violent against fellow citizens are usually triumphant, comic heroes who are violent against slaves are usually the ones to come off badly.

[46] Sommerstein 1996: ad 528. For a more charitable view, which regards the 'criminal' actions of the comic heroes as legitimate see Spatharas 2008.

too slow to follow his orders, even as he may be running around as fast as he can,[47] but the bossy tyrant of Cloud-cuckoo-land is hardly slow to beat up citizens who threaten legal recourse as well (*Birds* 1397, 1462–9). In none of these cases is the assault of slaves merely tolerable, slaves being covered by the law on *hubris* after all, a point grudgingly ceded by the 'Old Oligarch' (*Constitution of the Athenains* 1.10; cf. Demosthenes 21.47–50; Aeschines 1.15) – unless you believe assaulting citizens is tolerable too.

The *Lysistrata* example is more disturbing: the Athenian delegate knocks over the doorkeeper and then callously threatens to set the slaves' hair on fire, in a plainly gratuitous act of abuse designed to make them wail. However, even in that case the action is being performed only reluctantly in order to gratify the audience. It is just not on, the Athenian protests: 'I won't do it. But if it must be done at all, we'll persevere and indulge you' (οὐκ ἂν ποιήσαιμ'. εἰ δὲ πάνυ δεῖ τοῦτο δρᾶν, | ὑμῖν χαρίσασθαι, προσταλαιπωρήσομεν, *Lysistrata* 1219–20). Even if there is comic irony in the feigned hesitation here, there is enough of a glimpse of resistance to the superfluous violence. What is more, the action is described as a 'vulgar routine' (φορτικὸν τὸ χωρίον, *Lysistrata* 1218), exactly the kind of thing which is often said to represent *bad* taste on the comic stage; and yet it is almost immediately restaged when the slaves reappear only a few lines later as 'whip fodder' (μαστιγίαι) to be chased away once more (*Lysistrata* 1239–40). The gag seems designedly unfunny, not least in contradicting the 'Aristophanic' standards of sophisticated humour as programmatically laid out in the *parabasis* of *Clouds* and elsewhere (esp. *Clouds* 518–44).

The most direct example of comic bad taste relating directly to slaves' abuse comes from the *parabasis* of *Peace*, in which the chorus boast that one feature of Aristophanes' plays is that he does not 'do' scenes involving slaves getting a beating and being mocked for it:

> καὶ τοὺς δούλους παρέλυσεν
> τοὺς φεύγοντας κἀξαπατῶντας καὶ τυπτομένους ἐπίτηδες
> ἵν' ὁ σύνδουλος σκώψας αὐτοῦ τὰς πληγὰς εἶτ' ἀνέροιτο·
> "ὦ κακόδαιμον, τί τὸ δέρμ' ἔπαθες; μῶν ὑστριχὶς εἰσέβαλέν σοι
> εἰς τὰς πλευρὰς πολλῇ στρατιᾷ κἀδενδροτόμησε τὸ νῶτον;" (742–7)

---

[47] Dunbar 1995: ad 1317 suggests that the scene is more 'dramatically effective' if [Peisetairos] becomes impatient and annoyed at 1324–5 *despite* the obvious speed with which the slave is running out and in'. For other slaves who complain about abuse against them see *Eq.* 4–5, 64–70, *Nub.* 58, *Plut.* 1144.

And he got rid of slaves
who run away and are deceitful and fittingly get a beating,
just so that a fellow slave could mock his blows and then ask:
'poor fellow, what happened to your skin? Surely the lash hasn't assaulted
your sides with a great force and laid waste to your back?'

That kind of gag, as the chorus go on to say, is a terrible 'vulgarity' (φόρτον, *Peace* 748) and a form of 'lowbrow buffoonery' (βωμολοχεύματ' ἀγεννῆ, *Peace* 748) said to be entirely out of keeping with Aristophanes' 'high art' (τέχνην μεγάλην, *Peace* 749). Of course, Aristophanes is being disingenuous, as usual in his parabatic professions; *Peace* itself is the play involving a blatant use of violence by a (divine) master against a (divine) slave, in this case Polemos against Kudoimos (*Peace* 255–62). Nevertheless, it is revealing that he would even suggest that mockery (σκώψας, *Peace* 745) combined with the violent abuse of slaves, including the use of the bristle-whip (cf. *Frogs* 619) and the beating of the sides and back (cf. *Wasps* 1295), represents the opposite of what Aristophanic comedy is said to stand for. When Aristophanes does employ (twists on) those very gags, then it might well be thought that he is deliberately aiming to prompt discomfort as much as derisive laughter or vicarious pleasure in the audience. In the end, Dionysus at the start of *Frogs* may actually have a point about jokes involving baggage-carrying slaves: perhaps their comic abuse for no other reason than that they are conventionally slaves is an emetic after all (μὴ δῆθ᾿, ἱκετεύω, πλήν γ᾿ ὅταν μέλλω 'ξεμεῖν, 11).

## Sensing Xanthias Again

What I have been arguing is that Aristophanes' representation of slaves, above all of Xanthias throughout the first half of *Frogs*, anticipates a kind of 'politics of the vulnerable body', to adopt the phrase used by Debra Bergoffen to call for recognising vulnerability as the grounds for a more humane ethics.[48] The more Xanthias is sensed – and is sensed sensing – the more he can be regarded as a vulnerable human and not merely a violable slave.

It remains to address the fact that Xanthias disappears from the action in the second half of the play following a scene where he exchanges in 'slavish' (δουλικόν, 743) conversation with a fellow slave. This turn of events is usually interpreted as signifying the restoration of the 'proper' order of things, for instance with Charles Segal writing that

---

[48] Bergoffen 2001. For Bergoffen, however, it is the violation of consent rather than the infliction of pain that is the key expression of vulnerability and constituent of a so-called crime against humanity: 'In adopting the standards of pain and suffering, we have set the bar too low' (120).

'the proper separation is made between τὸ χρηστόν, and τὸ δουλικόν, and each element is to go its own way: the slave element disappears after Dionysus' proper attainment of his true divinity and his appointment as judge'.[49] What that reading fails to take into account is that it is not necessarily the end of Xanthias. As some scholars have suggested, he may in fact return to the stage as a silent extra, if it is *he* who is asked to carry the death-harbouring objects that Pluto is gifting to allegedly dangerous Athenian politicians like Cleophon (1504–13).[50]

This would make sense in terms of the comic convention of having slaves bear such loads to accompany their triumphant masters, a slave called Xanthias performing this role for Dicaeopolis celebrating a rural Dionysia in *Acharnians* (241–79), for instance. Moreover, having Xanthias return would make sense in terms of the dynamics of *Frogs*, which opened precisely with him as a baggage-carrying slave who represented the distilled essence of comedy and whose role was essential in progressing the plot. As Xanthias himself had anticipated earlier, here is another time when he may be needed (ἐμοῦ δεηθείης ἄν, εἰ θεὸς θέλοι, 533), the slave without whom Dionysus would never have made it so far in the first place.[51] Above all, Pluto makes several explicit references to conventional punishments of slaves, now reserved for certain politicians: tattooing, binding with fetters and sending them to a harsher place of work (1510–14).[52] And so, with a baggage-carrier present and the category of the slave back on the agenda, we end close to where we began, quite possibly with Xanthias back onstage as well. Here, however, the slave is nothing more than a rhetorical construct used to threaten those politicians who will not hurry down to Hades.[53] Xanthias (or whoever is carrying the items) may be playing a slave role but, tellingly, there is no 'slave' addressed as such by Pluto. The slave seems to have shed the tag. If it is specifically and distinctively Xanthias, then the focus may once again be on him.

If it is not, however, the effect may be even more pronounced. We might ask who *is* carrying the items: it could be an anonymous slave, or it could rather awkwardly (and uncharacteristically in comic endings) mean that Dionysus or Aeschylus would have to carry the objects along with their torches – and so now *they* would be playing the

---

[49]   Segal 1961: 216. For a more extended version of my alternative approach to the second part of the play, and the implicit resurfacing of egalitarian energies see Case 2021b: 162–70.

[50]   Sommerstein 1996: ad 1500–27, Griffith 2013: 209–12. Of course, his return could have been made into a bigger deal in performance than the text alone allows us to know.

[51]   Cf. Griffith 2013: 'Xanthias provides indispensable service and support, both practical and moral, without which his cowardly and bumbling master would never have succeeded in his quest' (210).

[52]   Sommerstein 1996 ad loc.

[53]   On the tag of slave as a rhetorical insult that could be used against politicians in lawcourt speeches see Vlassopoulos 2009: 355–6.

role of the slave, the baggage-carrier being a 'comic signifier of slave status',[54] thereby resurrecting the trope of role reversal once again. Considerations of staging aside, there is an even more pointed effect of an absent Xanthias here. For that takes us directly back to the start of the play and his repeated protest that he is not being noticed: 'but not a word about me' (περὶ ἐμοῦ δ' οὐδεὶς λόγος). What remains in this case is an absent presence – a kind of Aeschylean silence, if you will. If Xanthias is not included in what Rancière (quoted in this chapter's epigraph) labels the 'distribution of the sensible' of 'our city' (πόλιν τὴν ἡμετέραν, 1501), the one that Pluto bids Aeschylus to save upon his revival, it is a scandal. After all, as we saw, the first half of Frogs, culminating in the torture scene, had positioned Xanthias as an embodied, sensing human being, no different in this regard to Dionysus in his capacity as a citizen – or to any other citizen for that matter. At the end of the play, then, it is left to the audience to notice him as such without his needing to protest.

[54] Compton–Engle 2015: 105.

# Smell, Sex and Gender in Aristophanes' *Lysistrata*

*Antonia Marie Reinke*

'Don't wash. I'm returning and will be back in eight days'.[1] Napoleon's famous instructions to his wife Josephine are highly suggestive about the links between sex, smell and gender. The scent of the woman is the aphrodisiac of the man. More specifically, Napoleon implies a distinction between different kinds of female odour: the external scent of bathing, cosmetics and perfuming, on the one hand, and the intrinsic, physical smell of the female body, on the other. Even with eight days to go, Napoleon clearly prefers the latter: it captures the special aroma of his own wife, undiluted in its appeal. What happens if we trace the ingredients of this olfactory anecdote – gender, smell and sex – to the ancient Greek world and, more specifically, to the comedies of Aristophanes?

Unlike the love letters of Napoleon, Aristophanic comedies are dramatic performances. They are enacted through the bodies of actors and encountered, in real time, by an ancient Greek audience. Even beyond this apparent embodiment, the Aristophanic world is an exceptionally physical one: staged with grotesque bodily costuming, including padded stomachs, buttocks and oversized leather *phalloi*,[2] it abounds in culinary delights, sexual pursuits and jokes about defecation and constipation. This emphasis on the body heightens the 'embodied cognitive relationship between performer and spectator'[3] that underpins the dramatic genre. It speaks to the audience as sensory beings that may relate, also on a physical level, to the comic performance on stage. The dramatic activation of the senses and sensory perception are crucial to comedy's embodied capacity. While the genre is rich in visual and auditory clues, it shows a special pre-occupation with the so-called 'lower senses',[4] the senses of touch, taste and smell. Often accorded a less privileged position in ancient and modern hierarchies of

---

[1]  'Ne te lave pas, j'accours et dans huit jours je suis là' (Tulard 1981: 155).
[2]  See Stone 1981: 18, Green 1991: 24–6, Foley 2000: 281–2, Hughes 2006: 41–2, Csapo 2014: 57, Compton-Engle 2015: 17–18, 23–4.
[3]  Meineck 2012: 4, Lather 2018: 35.
[4]  Howes 2005: 10.

the senses,⁵ they are central to Aristophanic comedy.⁶ Indeed, as Afroditi Angelopoulou argues in this volume about the sense of taste, they may be key instruments in the comedian's positioning of his own art between carnality and sophistication.

This chapter will approach Aristophanes' employment of the 'lower senses' from a different angle: focusing on their olfactory aspect, it will explore the significance of the sense of smell for Aristophanes' dramatisation of gender identities, especially in his *Lysistrata*. As I will argue, the two levels of female smell that we encounter in Napoleon's words above – women's use of perfume and their own bodily odour – are central to the shifting Aristophanic framing of gendered smell. The comic osphresiology persistently moves between models of surface and essence, and so does its portrayal of gender. The opposition between the sexes in *Lysistrata* and the notable artificiality of their staging will provide particularly fruitful grounds for this study. In the tensions between men and women, sweet fragrances and pungent smells, theoretical concepts and stage props, the complexity of Aristophanes' poetics of gender becomes particularly apparent.

Beyond the small, but growing body of Classical scholarship on the senses, and the sense of smell in particular,⁷ this chapter is especially indebted to Pascal Thiercy's foundational exploration of odours in Aristophanes and the stimulating recent studies by Rob Tordoff on Aristophanes' *Peace* and Mario Telò on *Knights*.⁸ Both scholars tease out the intriguing antagonistic significance of Aristophanes' osphresiology with particular clarity – between the protagonist and his comic adversaries in the former and the poetic smell-scapes of Aristophanes and his rival Cratinus in the latter. As we will see, the battle of the sexes in Aristophanes' *Lysistrata* allows the play to share in the same competitiveness of comic odours and to speak to the discriminatory potential often associated with olfactory markers: as sociologists note, smell is used, with particular frequency, to distinguish between different social groups and identities.⁹ This chapter will illustrate how it serves as a prime vehicle for contemplating gender distinctions in Aristophanes.

⁵ Cf. Classen, Howes and Synnott 1994: 3–5,15–36, Harris 2007: 468, Butler and Purves 2013: 2–3, Bradley 2015: 8, Mueller 2016: 1.
⁶ Cf. Telò 2013: 53.
⁷ See in particular Lilja 1972, Thiercy 1993, Classen, Howes and Synnott 1994: 13–50, Tordoff 2011, Telò 2013, Bradley 2015 and the contributions in Lather 2018.
⁸ Thiercy 1993, Tordoff 2011, Telò 2013.
⁹ See Largey and Watson 1972. Cf. Classen, Howes and Synnott 1994: 33, Telò 2013: 53–4, Bradley 2015: 10.

## Sex, Smell and Aristophanes' *Lysistrata*

Pascal Thiercy quips about the Greeks' understanding of the link between sex and smell that it almost appears as if the Greeks made love with their noses: 'C'est avec leur nez qu'ils font l'amour'.[10] Female scent, in particular, they associated with a strong aphrodisiac force.[11] Thus, the early Greek lyric poet Archilochus observes that a well-scented woman can strike with desire even the most feeble old man (fragment 48.5). A few centuries later, Plutarch's Gryllus puts a more satirical spin on the matter: Greek men, he asserts, refuse to sleep even with their own wives unless they come to bed 'infused in the scent of perfume and scented powders', μύρων ὀδωδυῖαι καὶ | διαπασμάτων (Plutarch *Moralia* 990b–c). The well-scented female is an enticement, even a pre-condition, to the sexual act. It comes as no surprise, then, that she takes a prominent role in the sex-strike of Aristophanes' *Lysistrata*. The comedy tells the story of the refusal of the Greek women, led by the Athenian Lysistrata, to sleep with their husbands until they agree to make peace and end the Peloponnesian War out of desperation for sexual fulfilment. Scent is a crucial tool in the women's arsenal. In the words of the female protagonist:

> ταῦτ' αὐτὰ γάρ τοι κἄσθ' ἃ σώσειν προσδοκῶ,
> τὰ κροκωτίδια καὶ τὰ μύρα χαί περιβαρίδες
> χἤγχουσα καὶ τὰ διαφανῆ χιτώνια. (46–8)

That's exactly what I think will rescue Greece:
Our fancy little dresses, our perfumes [τὰ μύρα] and slippers,
our rouge and see-through underwear![12]

As I will propose in the present chapter, this is only the beginning of a far more complex Aristophanic engagement with the intricate relationship between odour and gender in the play. When we read *Lysistrata* nose first, we may detect an olfactory poetics of gender that evolves in a perpetual tension between smell as an external artifice that evaporates as quickly as a trace of perfume or the laughter in a comic performance and the idea of an essential and olfactorily marked gender identity that may linger persistently. Activated in the comedy's battle of the sexes, the meaning of smell and olfactory perception is always contested, refracted and re-claimed – and so is, I will argue, the play's understanding of gender itself.

---

[10]  Thiercy 1993: 515.
[11]  On the erotic force of a positive female scent and perfuming see Thiercy 1993: 514–17, Henderson 1991: 52, Detienne 1994: 50–62, Sommerstein 1998 ad *Eccl.* 524.
[12]  Greek quotes are taken from the most recent *OCT* or Teubner editions; translations are my own or, in the case of Aristophanes, based (with small adaptations) on Henderson 2000 and 2002.

## Scenting the Sex-Strike

Let us begin from Lysistrata's utterance above. The first trace we catch of the comedy's gendered osphresiology features a very specific kind of female-associated odour: μύρον, 'perfume' (67). A man-made concoction of fragrant herbs, flowers and oils, it is applied to a woman's body from the outside. Only in young women – such as Myrrhine, whom we will meet below – may its aphrodisiac sweetness reside naturally. In the words of Aristophanes' *Assemblywomen*, 'softness blossoms on their juicy breasts', τὸ τρυφερὸν ... ἐπὶ τοῖς μήλοις ἐπανθεῖ (901–4). The line captures a sense of youthful beauty in an intermingling of haptic, visual and olfactory-gustatory clues derived from the natural world. More often, however, perfume is explicitly mentioned as a facilitator of scented femininity. As such, it is so integral a marker of the comic female that it appears in the long list of tell-tale feminine equipment in the fragmentary *Women at the Thesmophoria II* (fragment 320.4) and fits seamlessly between their fancy little dresses and slippers in Lysistrata's account.

As indicated above, women's perfumes fulfil an important aphrodisiac function and enhance, or even enable, male sexual delight. However, their external application immediately suggests a more ambiguous quality. They are open to deceptive exploitation. And women are notoriously deceptive in the Greek imagination.[13] Thus, feminine scents are often presented as serving their female owners rather more than their ostensible male beneficiaries. A prime motive for women's olfactory deception is their stereotypical promiscuity, which is a rich source of humour in Aristophanes' comedies. His female characters use perfumes to spice-up their extra-marital relations and chew garlic to throw their husbands quite literally off their scent (*Women at the Thesmophoria* 493–6). Praxagora, the heroine of *Assemblywomen*, even claims that her lack of perfume proves her fidelity (524). When her husband asks in incredulity, 'can't a woman get fucked even without perfume?' (525: οὐχὶ βινεῖται γυνὴ κἄνευ μύρου), she emphatically denies. Older Aristophanic women resort to other olfactory stratagems: characteristically marked by ugliness and excessively libido,[14] they attempt olfactory beautification to attract younger lovers. Once again, *Assemblywomen* offers a case in point. σαπρά, 'rotten one', is a favourite insult levelled against the play's old women.[15] It links their odour with the stench of decay, even while they are ridiculed as 'plastered' and 'rubbed' with beauty products (878: καταπεπλασμένη, 904: ἐντέτριψαι). But women's olfactory deceptions

---

[13]  Indeed, Pandora, the very first woman, is marked by a 'deceitful nature' (*Op.* 67: ἐπίκλοπον ἦθος).

[14]  See *Eccl.* 877–1111, *Plut.* 959–1096. Cf. Henderson 1987a: 117–20, Robson 2013: 46. See Gerber 1978, Lee 2015: 100, on their perceived lack of erotic attraction in wider Greek culture.

[15]  *Eccl.* 884, 926, 1098. Cf. *Lys.* 378, *Thesm.* 1025, Hermippus: fr. 10.1, *Art.* fr. 2.1, Plato Com.: *Kle.*, fr. 1. On the olfactory force of σαπρός see *Vesp.* 38.

may, of course, also pursue less mundane motives. Already in Homer's *Iliad*, perfume becomes complicit in Hera's crafty distraction of Zeus's attention from the Trojan War. Set to seduce her husband with an array of female allurements, 'she first cleansed from her lovely body every stain, and anointed herself richly with oil, ambrosial, soft and fragrant' (14.170–2).

The role Lysistrata ascribes to feminine scent at the beginning of the comic sex-strike clearly draws on this tradition of aphrodisiac, yet deceptive female fragrance. Indeed, we might consider *Lysistrata* as one extended deception along these lines – a deception that infuses the female with a superficial and suspiciously sweet scent. As a first step in elucidating Aristophanes' poetics of gender and gendered odours in the play, this takes us to a surface level: female scent belongs to the external performance of female gender.

## A Whiff of Female Tyranny

As the comedy progresses, this superficial model of scented identity construction undergoes significant shifts – most prominently, in the confrontation between the play's two half-choruses of male and female oldsters. In the transition from younger to older characters and individuals to collectives, the role of smell becomes more visceral and is framed in a language of revelation rather than deception.

While the younger, married women are central to the fragrant allurements of the sex-strike itself, the older women of the chorus seize control of the Athenian war funds on the Acropolis. As we will see, their openly antagonistic stance receives a different olfactory gendering. When the male choreuts attempt to overcome the female resistance, their encounter soon turns physical. Thus, in *Lysistrata* 615, the men's leader exhorts them to strip, ἀλλ᾽ ἐπαποδυώμεθ᾽, and tackle the matter head-on. Without their jackets, according to the most common scholarly explanation, the men are free to engage in more vigorous bodily activity.[16] And indeed, violent threats of beatings (635–6), kicks (656–7), headlocks (680–1) and even enforced genital depilation (683–6) are soon exchanged between the two choruses. At the same time, the comedy advances to a more intense contemplation of gendered odours through this act of stripping. It is as if the chorus' greater degree of bodily exposure has somehow activated a more sensory register in the play. Once stripped of their cloaks, the male choreuts comment on the women's acts as follows:

---

[16]  On choral stripping as allowing greater 'freedom of movement' see Sifakis 1971: 104. Cf. Ketterer 1980 on *Ach.* 627, Stone 1981: 428, Sommerstein 1990 ad *Lys.* 615. Choruses remove their outer garments also in other plays (*Thesm.* 655–6, *Vesp.* 408–9). Cf. Austin and Olson 2004 ad *Thesm.* 656, Biles and Olson 2015 ad *Vesp.* 408–10. Individuals remove their garments before vigorous movement in *Thesm.* 568 and also in other genres: see, for instance, Lysias' *Against Simon* 3.12.

ἤδη γὰρ ὄζειν ταδὶ πλειόνων
καὶ μειζόνων πραγμάτων μοι δοκεῖ,
καὶ μάλιστ᾽ ὀσφραίνομαι τῆς Ἱππίου τυραννίδος· (616–19)

I think this business smells of much
greater trouble,
I definitely catch a whiff of Hippias' tyranny!

Despite the repetition of olfactory verbs in these lines (616: ὄζειν, 618/19: ὀσφραίνομαι),[17] the ideas they suggest are not, in fact, smellable. Both use the sense of smell primarily metaphorically, as a shorthand for a vague cognitive assessment.[18] And yet, ὄζειν, 'to smell of', much like the English 'to smack of', still connotes the unpleasantness of the sensory perception – of a repelling smell rather than taste, in the Greek case. Thus, the women's capture of the Acropolis is associated with the stench of a deeply undemocratic endeavour,[19] the rule of Athens' famous last tyrant. If we follow Jeffrey Henderson,[20] the resemblance between the tyrant's name, Hippias, and the Greek word for horse, ἵππος, suggests furthermore the equestrian position in sexual intercourse: women on top. The olfactory metaphor slides into a visual analogy, where the political and the sexual overlap. Sex is fundamentally hierarchical in the ancient Greek world and a subservient position to the female to be strictly avoided, at least in the public perception.[21] Not incidentally, the choral leader had exhorted 'every free man' (614: ὅστις ἔστ᾽ ἐλεύθερος) to join their stripping above – an exhortation that now gains a meaning both political and sexual. The men's battle is to assert their dominance in both fields.

That the women's dual threat to the men's position should be imagined, at least metaphorically, as the intrusion of an unpleasant smell, a tyrannical whiff emanating from the female chorus, is intriguing. It differs notably from the idea of feminine odours introduced at the beginning of the play. While the scent of the perfumed young wives is meant to attract and arouse their husbands into compliance, the unpleasant odour associated with the old women of the chorus has the opposite effect: it repels and provokes. As such, it also marks a difference to the olfactory trickeries that the old women of *Assemblywomen* employ. Rather than a grotesque and deceptive mirror image

---

[17] LSJ s.v. ὄζω: 'I smell/stink of', ὀσφραίνομαι: 'I smell/catch a scent of' (c. gen.).
[18] Especially ὄζειν is commonly used metaphorically elsewhere (cf. Henderson 1987 ad *Lys.* 616–24) and, according to Lilja, Aristophanes has a special affinity to metaphors 'taken from the sphere of odour' (Lilja 1972: 222).
[19] Note the Spartan intrigue the choreuts suspect in the immediately subsequent lines (*Lys.* 620–5).
[20] Henderson 2000: 355 n. 57
[21] On the threat of a woman in equestrian position see *Lys.* 676–8, 772–3.

of their younger fragrant counterparts, the female choreuts of *Lysistrata* are linked to a new brand of gendered osphresiology.

## Smelling Gendered Essence
The new strand in the comedy's conceptualisation of gendered odours is developed more fully as the altercation between the two choruses continues to escalate. In *Lysistrata* 637, the women copy the men's behaviour and remove their outer garments (θώμεσθ᾽, ὦ φίλαι γρᾶες, ταδὶ πρῶτον χαμαί). When they furthermore claim a stake in the city's affairs, including the right to counsel for peace (638–56), and threaten the male chorus with physical violence (636, 656–7), the men step up their game:

ἀλλ᾽ ἀμυντέον τὸ πρᾶγμ᾽, ὅστις γ᾽ ἐνόρχης ἔστ᾽ ἀνήρ.
ἀλλὰ τὴν ἐξωμίδ᾽ ἐκδυώμεθ᾽, ὡς τὸν ἄνδρα δεῖ
ἀνδρὸς ὄζειν εὐθύς, ἀλλ᾽ οὐκ ἐντεθριῶσθαι πρέπει. (661–3)

Every man with any balls must stand up to this threat!
Let's doff our shirts, because a man's got to smell like a man
straight away, and shouldn't be wrapped up like a souvlaki.

Calling to action anyone with balls,[22] the male chorus strips of their undergarments as well. This 'bold and apparently unprecedented move' in Greek drama[23] leaves the chorus 'theatrically naked', displaying their *phalloi* and bulging physiques to full view.[24] Yet again, the women follow suit:[25]

ἀλλὰ χἠμεῖς, ὦ γυναῖκες, θᾶττον ἐκδυώμεθα,
ὡς ἂν ὄζωμεν γυναικῶν αὐτοδὰξ ὠργισμένων. (686–7)

Quickly, women, let's strip off too, because we've
got to smell like women angry enough to bite!

[22] On the virility associated with testicles see Henderson 1987 ad loc. and the parallelism to *Lys.* 598.
[23] Compton-Engle 2015: 54.
[24] See Sommerstein 1990 ad *Lys.* 662.
[25] This is an even more striking move than the male chorus' continued undress. As Sommerstein observes ad loc., public stripping was 'something as unheard-of for a respectable Athenian matron as it was commonplace in the case of men (and hetaerae)'. On the respectable dress expected for Greek women see Cairns 1993: 120–5, 185–8, 305–40. Cf. Zweig 1992: 84.

As in the first round of stripping, the choruses' acts of visual, physical exposure introduce into their contest a sensory, more specifically olfactory, focus. This time, it exceeds a primarily metaphorical sense, levelled at a vexing opponent of the other sex. Instead, we encounter the notion of a smellable gendered self, forcefully claimed by each of the two choruses in turn. Thus, the men intend to strip, 'because a man's got to | smell like a man straight away' (663). Likewise, the women undress in order to smell like women, more precisely, like women angry to the point of biting (687). Surely, the significance of these claims for the comedy's exploration of smell is more significant than Pascal Thiercy allows when he observes that, at a time of limited personal hygiene, 'il est normal de sentir l'homme (ly 662 sq) ou la femme (ly 687)'. But what are we to make of the gendered 'smellability' they each evoke?

The nature and unparalleled extent of the chorus' self-exposure is instructive here. As indicated above, facilitation of movement is often considered the prime rationale for dramatic stripping. At the same time, scholars like Thomas Hubbard or Kenneth Reckford have postulated a sense of 'symbolic "unmasking"'[26] for comic choruses undressing themselves before the so-called *parabasis*, a choral song mid-comedy in which the audience is directly addressed and the comic poet often appears to speak *in propria persona*. The belief in an outright dropping of the chorus' dramatic role in the *parabasis*, let alone a full and consistent identification between chorus and poet, is certainly problematic.[27] However, the idea of the chorus' symbolic stripping, not least in a choral altercation that replaces the conventional *parabasis* in *Lysistrata*,[28] remains useful: in the present scene, the choruses' continued and antagonistic self-exposure suggests a rivalling play with the concept of self-revelation. The choruses compete in asserting to their opponents and the Athenian audience – arguably, their primary *parabatic* addressees – who they really are. The olfactory culmination of this process constitutes an intriguing twist: the sense of smell is activated as an even more immediate identifier of gendered essence than the vision to which they expose their bodies. In a reversal of traditional sense hierarchies,[29] smell trumps sight. The audience is invited to lean in and catch a proper sniff of the gendered choral selves presented to them. Yet, as they do, they smell … what exactly?

---

[26]  Hubbard 1991: 18, Reckford 1987: 188. Cf. Biles 2011: 44.
[27]  See Sifakis 1971: 106–8, Stone 1981: 425–8, Olson 2002 ad *Ach.* 627, Compton-Engle 2015: 127, for important counterarguments to such claims.
[28]  See Henderson 1987 ad *Lys.* 614–705.
[29]  See footnotes 4 and 5 above.

## A Woman Angry Enough to Bite

What *does* a man or woman smell like? The immediate dramatic context and the comedy as a whole supply particularly limited clues about characteristically male odours. Other plays immerse male figures, and the olfactory imagination of their audiences, in smells as diverse as Peisetaerus' ambrosial, quasi-divine scent in *Birds*, the thundering farts of rustic Strepsiades in *Clouds*, or the stink of the politician Cleon, whom Aristophanes attributes, in both *Peace* and *Wasps*, with 'the stench of a seal, the unwashed balls of Lamia and the arse of a camel' (*Peace* 758 = *Wasps* 1035).[30] Admittedly, none of these descriptors is particularly precise. Aristophanes' activations of smell are often caught in a slippage between different sensory markers (the sound of Strepsiades' flatulence, for instance, vies for prominence with its stink) and they tend to provide, at best, a series of prompts that open up a plethora of possible associations, multiplied by the olfactory histories of the audience members.[31] This is, of course, to an extent germane to all communication about smell. As Jonathan Harris astutely notes, 'the words we use to represent smell tend not to be nominal, but comparative – an object smells *like* something. Smell, therefore, has a tendency to slide referentially'.[32] Yet, as even this brief sketch of examples may indicate, Aristophanes likes to push olfactory referentiality to an extreme. His tendency to use odours metaphorically fits this picture perfectly. All the more notable is the olfactory self-revelation claimed by the male chorus in Aristophanes' *Lysistrata*: in referential circularity, a man's got to smell like a man. Any wider olfactory links remain, at least verbally, underexplored.[33]

Instead, the play's olfactory attention lies, once again, on the female. While taking up the play's earlier focus on female odours, this also gestures to the greater porosity of

---

[30] See *Av.* 1715–16: ὀσμὴ δ' ἀνωνόμαστος εἰς βάθος κύκλου | χωρεῖ, καλὸν θέαμα; *Nub.* 385–94 esp., 388–91: Στ. νὴ τὸν Ἀπόλλω, καὶ δεινὰ ποιεῖ γ' εὐθύς μοι καὶ τετάρακται, | χὤσπερ βροντὴ τὸ ζωμίδιον παταγεῖ καὶ δεινὰ κέκραγεν· | ἀτρέμας πρῶτον 'παππὰξ παππάξ', κἄπειτ' ἐπάγει 'παπαπαππάξ', | χὤταν χέζω, κομιδῇ βροντᾷ 'παπαπαππάξ', ὥσπερ ἐκεῖναι; *Pax* 758 = *Vesp.* 1035: [εἶχεν] φώκης δ' ὀσμήν, Λαμίας δ' ὄρχεις ἀπλύτους, πρωκτὸν δὲ καμήλου. See Olson 1998 ad *Pax* 758, on the monstrous Lamia.

[31] Particularly vivid examples are the smells of personified Holiday in *Peace* (523–6, 859–69) or the bouquets of the 'peace-treaties' symbolised by different kinds of wine in *Acharnians* (186–96).

[32] Harris 2007: 469 (emphasis in the original). Cf. Classen, Howes and Synnott 1994: 3.

[33] There are loose associations to other olfactory fields. Immediately after he urges the men to strip 'because a man's got to smell like a man', the male leader adds, '… and shouldn't be all wrapped up like a *thrion* [translated as "souvlaki" above]', οὐκ ἐντεθριῶσθαι πρέπει. The *thrion* is a popular food item wrapped in a fig leaf (Cf. Sommerstein 1990, Henderson 1987 ad *Lys.* 663). This may evoke ideas of culinary delights attracting/distracting the female opponent. In addition, the references to rejuvenation and military prowess in *Lys.* 664–70 might recall the celebrated 'masculine sweat' (ἀνδρικὸς ἱδρώς) of Marathon fighters in *Ach.* 696 or the delightful scent of the rejuvenated Demos in *Eq.* 1325–32 (~ Trygaeus in *Pax* 861–2). But none of this is made explicit.

women's bodies in the ancient imagination. Considered more prone to a 'leakiness'[34] of fluids and their accompanying odours, female bodies may well invite a more elaborate exploration of their particular smells. Of course, when the women encourage themselves in *Lysistrata* 686–7 to quickly strip off as well because they've 'got to smell like women' (ὡς ἂν ὄζωμεν γυναικῶν), this desire too shares in a certain self-referentiality. Unlike their male counterparts, however, the women expand on the comparison further: 'like women angry enough to bite', γυναικῶν αὐτοδὰξ ὠργισμένων (687). This phrase attests, no doubt, to the striking and, at times, obscure referential sliding of Aristophanic descriptions of smell. Yet, the play's other evocations of female odours may help to elucidate its significance. Thus, it clearly widens the opposition, which we already noted for the women's 'tyrannical whiff' above, between the alluring female perfumes of the sex-strike and the Aristophanic osphresiology of the choral women mid-play. In its biting hostility, the older women's odour differs notably from the aphrodisiac force of the earlier fragrance. It also follows an inverse trajectory: rather than embellishing women's external performance with a deceptively sweet scent, from the outside in, the female choreuts' undressing claims to lay bare the smell of their own bodies, from the inside out. They seek revelation, rather than deception – and, as we will see, repulsion rather than attraction. This recalls the effect of their earlier 'tyrannical whiff'. This time, however, the antagonising force of the women's smell follows their own intent.

Central to a deeper examination of the women's olfactory self-revelation is the adverb αὐτοδάξ, 'with the very teeth, even to biting' (687).[35] It takes up the bestial imagery that is applied to them earlier in the play, by the men and by themselves: in *Lysistrata* 367, the women threaten to tear out the men's organs with their fangs and they are metaphorically likened to wild beasts in *Lysistrata* 369, 468 and 477 (θρέμματα, θηρία and κνώδαλα, respectively). The female choreuts use this bestiality in order to express a more sexual antagonism in the lines immediately preceding their self-exposure:

εἰ νὴ τὼ θεώ με ζωπυρήσεις, λύσω
τὴν ἐμαυτῆς ὗν ἐγὼ δή, καὶ ποιήσω
τήμερον τοὺς δημότας βωστρεῖν σ' ἐγὼ πεκτούμενον. (682–5/6)

By the Two Goddesses, if you fire me up,
I'll unleash my wild sow and clip you bare,
and this very day you'll go bleating to your friends for help.

[34] Carson 1999: 87, Bradley, Leonard and Totelin 2021: 5.
[35] LSJ s.v. αὐτοδάξ. Cf. *Pax* 607.

The biting fury of the women's odour is here prepared in an image of reversed gender hierarchy. As they threaten to set loose their own ferocity, the women promise to 'shear' and domesticise the men. While the latter suggests the men's emasculating depilation,[36] the image of the wild sow is linked in Greek thought to unbridled wrath as well as the female vagina.[37] Both combine aptly in the present scene. As Froma Zeitlin observes, in the ancient imagination, women's genital exposure could provide a terrifying, apotropaic gesture against 'the opposite sex (the outsider) and the enemy (potential or actual)'.[38] Plutarch tells of a number of instances, in which women ward off male enemies, or scare their own men into bravery, by exposing their genitals to them.[39] The *Lysistrata* scene may well offer an early comic reflex of the same gesture: as the women literally expose themselves to their male opponents and aggressively evoke the idea of their 'wild sow/vagina', they draw on the antagonistic force of female genital display.

The idea of the women's repelling vaginal exposure is infused with an equally repelling odour, if we trace the meaning of αὐτοδάξ (687: 'with the very teeth, even to biting') yet a bit further. Richard P. Martin has intriguingly suggested that the 'biting' of the female smell refers back to the pungent 'bite' of the smoke that torments the male chorus earlier in the play (298: [ὁ καπνός] δάκνει, 301: ὀδὰξ ἔβρυκε).[40] The appearance of the rare ὀδάξ in *Lysistrata* 301, a shortened version of the even rarer αὐτοδάξ, is marked;[41] and, just like the women, the smoke is cast in bestial terms: it attacks 'like a bitch' (298: ὥσπερ κύων) and 'devours' the men's eyes (301). In addition, immediately before the women's self-exposure, they cast their altercation in the language of fire, πῦρ (682: ζω-πυρ-ήσεις: 'you will fire me up'). Martin draws attention to the fact that the smoke in the earlier passage is said to derive from 'a Lemnian fire (300: Λήμνιον τὸ πῦρ)'.[42] Following the ancient commentators on *Lysistrata*, he argues that this calls to the audience's mind the

---

[36] Note the male chorus' pride in their pubic bushiness little later in the play (*Lys.* 800) and comedy's treatment of depilation as a tell-tale feminine trait: *Lys.* 89, 151, 825–8, *Eccl.* 12–13, 65–7, *Thesm.* 216–17, *Ran.* 516.

[37] On ὗς, or 'wild sow', as a metaphor for anger see Sommerstein 1990 ad *Lys.* On its capacity as a slang term for vagina see Taillardat 1965: § 108 (ὁ χοῖρος), Maxwell-Stuart 1972: 216, Henderson 1991: 132 n. 130.

[38] Zeitlin 1982: 145. Between women, *anasyrma* could serve a prostropaic function. Thus, Baubo's self-exposure delights the grieving Demeter (Zeitlin 1982: 144–5, Olender 1990: 99–113).

[39] See *Mor.* 241b, 246a and 248b. Cf. Zeitlin 1982: 145, Bassi 1998: 136 n. 84.

[40] Martin 1987: 78.

[41] There are only four occurrences of ὀδάξ in Aristophanes (*Vesp.* 164, 943, *Lys.* 301, *Plut.* 690) and only two of αὐτοδάξ (*Pax* 607, *Lys.* 687).

[42] *Lys.* 300: κἄστιν γε Λήμνιον τὸ πῦρ τοῦτο πάσῃ μηχανῇ.

myth of the Lemnian women[43] – a myth drenched in repulsive odours. The *Lemniai* are best known for the killing of their husbands. Thus, they feature as female monstrosities *par excellence* in Greek literature, for instance in Aeschylus' *Oresteia* (*Libation Bearers* 631–4).[44] The initial cause of their massacre, however, lies in the stench that the goddess Aphrodite had imposed upon the women of Lesbos for neglecting her worship.[45] Shunned in bed by their disgusted husbands, the ill-smelling *Lemniai* resort to murder. The murderous stench of the Lemnian women enters the olfactory self-revelation of the female choreuts in *Lysistrata* in the biting fury they share with the oppressive smoke of the 'Lemnian fire' that pervaded the earlier scene.

   Thus, when the women of the chorus expose their bodies in order to smell 'like a woman angry enough to bite' in *Lysistrata* 687, they initiate a potent chain of sexually unsettling visual and olfactory associations, symbolically captured in the sight and smell of their vagina. This adds an important deeper layer to the play's olfactory poetics of gender: the scene introduces the sense of an underlying and more essential female sexual identity which is deeply threatening to the male other – or, taking the perspective of ancient comedy's target audience, the male self. Not incidentally, this odorous femininity is situated beneath the external trappings of culture and civilisation and imagined as exuding from the female body itself, rooted in a primarily physical and bestial aspect.

### A Return to the Deceptively Scented Female

The threatening visceral odour of the choral opposition does not linger – at least not ultimately. Soon, the comedy's olfactory poetics of gender changes track once more and returns to the superficial world of the perfumed gender performances of the younger women's sex-strike. The encounter between Myrrhine and Cinesias offers the key passage. Intriguingly, it almost re-writes, or perhaps more accurately re-scents, the earlier scene. Here too, we find a woman's self-stripping and a rich olfactory focus, but

---

[43]  Martin 1987: 78–80. Cf. Sommerstein 1990 ad Lys. 299–300. This reading is already suggested in the scholia (Σ[L] 298, referenced according to Stein 1891: 14). Aeschylus' fragmentary *Hypsipyle* and Sophocles' and Aristophanes' *Lemnian Women* suggest that contemporary audiences would have been familiar with the myth. Cf. Jackson 1990: 83. On Aristophanes' *Lemnian Women*, in particular, see Martin 1987: 101–5, and on ancient sources for the *dysosmia* in the Lemnian myth see Jackson 1990: 79–81. Alternative readings link the 'Lemnian fire' to volcanic activities that may have existed on the island of Lesbos in antiquity (for discussion see Martin 1987: 78–9 and especially the bibliography in his n. 4).

[44]  Cf. Zeitlin 1978: 155. Note also the proverbial Λήμνιον κακόν referred to in Σ[L] 298. Cf. Hdt. 6.138.4 on Λήμνια ἔργα.

[45]  Cf. Jackson 1990, Martin 1987: 81 esp. n. 13. Detienne 1994: 90–8 analyses the 'olfactory code' of the myth of the Lemnian women and traces its links to a later annual ritual of separation between the sexes observed on Lesbos and the ritual pollution associated with female menstruation.

the men's hostility is turned to desire, the women's threat to playful teasing and their olfactory tensions are mediated by bottled perfume. Once more, scented deceptions, rather than odorous revelations, take centre stage.

As the sex-starved Cinesias finally seems to have persuaded his young wife Myrrhine to sleep with him despite the strike, she stalls him in various ways – only to take off just before the act itself. Perfume is crucial to her delay tactics. And that is what we might expect, given that her very name, μυρρίνη or 'myrtle', is a fragrant plant closely associated by the Greeks with the worship of Aphrodite.[46] In the middle of undressing, she suddenly asks if Cinesias wants her to perfume him (938: βούλει μυρίσω σε;), which he emphatically declines. No scented arousal needed. Myrrhine presses on nonetheless: 'but I will, so help me Aphrodite, whether you want to or not' (939: νὴ τὴν Ἀφροδίτην, ἤν τε βούλῃ γ' ἤν τε μή). Here, she not only challenges conventional hierarchies of consent,[47] but also marks the central olfactory joke of the scene: celebrated as a male aphrodisiac elsewhere, perfume becomes an obstacle to sexual fulfilment in the hands of Myrrhine who, ironically, herself personifies alluring scent by name. Thus, she not only inverts the conventional, erotic function of perfume, she also changes the gendered directionality of its application. Cinesias is being perfumed in order to enhance *her* pleasure (cf. 941).[48] Again, the comedy briefly contemplates, through an olfactory theme, the idea of women on top (remember the 'whiff of *Hippias'* tyranny' above). But Myrrhine's pleasure is neither an erotic one – it is laughter at her husband's expense – nor does the perfume bring sensory delight, least of all to Cinesias. As he observes in *Lysistrata* 942–3, it does not smell sweet or of conjugal love at all, οὐχ ἡδὺ τὸ μύρον … οὐκ ὄζον γάμων.[49] In an olfactory self-fulfilling prophecy, the perfume's un-sexy smell anticipates the sexual frustration that he will experience little later, when Myrrhine disappears for good.

The smell also recalls, in a bottled version as it were, the sexual repulsion that we saw so closely associated with the older women's olfactory self in the choral encounter. At this point, however, it has become a mere prop – humorously employed, to be sure, in

---

[46]   See Martin 1987: 87, Elderkin 1990: 394, Detienne 1994: 63.

[47]   Note that the same phrase is used to stress lack of male sexual agency in *Assemblywomen* (*Eccl.* 981 = *Lys.* 939). See also *Lys.* 1036 and *Eccl.* 1097.

[48]   While the anointment of men with scented oils appears as a divine grace in Homer (cf. *Od.* 6.227–37, 23.152–63), its perception changes over time. On male perfuming treated as a token of excessive luxury, effeminacy and subservience see Xen. *Symp.* 2.3–4: 'For just as one kind of dress looks well on a woman and another kind on a man, so the odours appropriate to men and to women are diverse. No man, surely, ever uses perfume for a man's sake. Indeed, so far as perfume is concerned, when once a man has anointed himself with it, the scent forthwith is all one whether he be slave or free'. Cf. Plut. *Mor.* 990b.

[49]   The scent is further described as διατριπτικόν (*Lys.* 943): 'punning on two meanings' (Henderson 1978b ad loc.), this means either 'prepared by pounding' or 'causing delay'. Cf. Sommerstein 1990 ad loc.

the final stretches of the play's battle between the sexes, but deprived of its essentialising, visceral quality. Indeed, it is now worn by a man and, if we are to trust Myrrhine, only appears on stage at all because she ('Silly me!') picked the wrong scent by mistake (944).

## Smell and the Comic Artifice of Gender – A Conclusion

As the comedy's olfactory poetics of gender appears to shift from perfumed surface to essential odour and back, Myrrhine's ill-scented prop draws us to an important final question: is the Aristophanic idea of a 'smellable' gender, indeed of gender distinctions themselves, ever more than a comic prop, an artificial construct in the dramatic universe? The staging suggests otherwise, especially for the female. Precisely as the two half-choruses claim self-revelation and call the audience to believe in a gender distinction so real that it is smellable, the theatrical challenge to any such claims would have been blatant. In particular, the choruses' undressing to stage nakedness undermines the notion of self-revelation, olfactory or otherwise. As the choreuts take off their garments, they also strip off a significant part of their costumes.[50] The mask worn by all comic actors provides continued clues for identification, but the removal of dress blurs the lines, especially between male and female figures. As scholars have convincingly argued, from the neck down, the longer, feminine dress is a primary marker of comic females: without it, their bodies likely looked precisely like those of comic males, *phallus* and all.[51] In addition, the visible artificiality and grotesque hyperbole of the comic stage-naked body – loose woollen tights, oversized leather *phallus* and enormous padded buttocks and stomach[52] – undercut any sense of true self-revelation. In other words, the very attention drawn to the gendered smell of the stage-naked choreuts, especially to the women's aggressive odour, highlights the comic absurdity of their claim. Indeed, if there is such a thing as a characteristic smell of gender, the choreuts ought to all smell the same. After all, the members of the dramatic chorus were exclusively male; and we may wonder how much the effort of vigorous singing, dancing and self-stripping would have brought to the audience' attention precisely their sweaty, odorous bodies performing in the orchestra at this point.

Thus, the tensions we noticed in the play's olfactory poetics of gender, caught as they are between perfume and body odour, deception and revelation, surface and essence, find a refracted expression in the notable artifice of the comic staging of male and female

---

[50]   Cf. Sommerstein 1990: 662: at this point, they 'wear [ … ] only the leotard and tights (with phallus attached) worn by all comic performers under their character costumes'.

[51]   See Foley 2000: 291, Hughes 2006: 42, Csapo 2014: 57, Compton-Engle 2015: 28.

[52]   See Stone 1981: 18, Green 1991: 24–6, Foley 2000: 281–2, Hughes 2006: 41–2, Csapo 2014: 57, Compton-Engle 2015: 17–18, 23–4.

figures. So, where does this ultimately leave our exploration of smell and gender in Aristophanes? That the comic staging challenges especially female olfactory identities might suggest a possible response: as Lauren Taaffe has argued, Aristophanic comedy is characterised, at least to a point, by an 'illusion of gender disguise' that ultimately preserves the male subject even beneath a female exterior.[53] A man's got to smell like a man … In this light, the comic battle between the sexes is also an opposition between essential masculinity and feminine superficiality. And yet, as we have seen, there are tensions within the olfactory framing of female being: artificial as they may be, the old women of the chorus are linked to a more substantial odour than their younger counterparts, and not quite so easily confined to surface scents. Nor are the olfactory identities of men safe from comedy's unsettling force. Thus, the hyper-masculine phallic drive of Cinesias may find itself drenched in female-associated, sexually repulsive smells. And we find an even more striking counterexample in Agathon, the cross-dressing male poet of Aristophanes' *Women at the Thesmophoria*, a play staged in the very same year as *Lysistrata*. Linked to masculine odours only by the fact that his feminine dresses 'smell sweetly of a small penis' (254: ἡδύ γ᾽ ὄζει ποσθίου),[54] the tragedian vocalises choral lyrics – his most celebrated skill – that sound attractively θηλυδριῶδες, 'female-scented' through and through (131).[55] The odours that adorn the poet and his synesthetic creations blur the lines between male and female, surface and essence, and unsettle any notion of a smellable, stable male being. Clearly, much rather than offering simple answers to the crux of gender, Aristophanes' olfactory poetics raises compelling questions about it.

But does it do more than that? Aristophanic treatments of smell clearly acknowledge, even highlight, the complexity of gender – but to what end (if any)? Such ends have been postulated for other sensory fields in this volume. Thus, Angelopoulou argues that there is a poetological drive in Aristophanes' dramatisations of gustatory experience. In the oscillation of taste between a carnal sense of culinary delight and a metaphor of sophisticated discernment, she identifies a self-reflexive characterisation of the poet's own art. Zachary Case makes a more political point: in his view, Aristophanes stages the shared sensory perceptiveness between slaves and their masters also to showcase their shared humanity. The end that I would like to propose in conclusion of this chapter is also a political one, albeit one with poetological undertones. As we saw in the blatant artificiality of the comic stage body, Aristophanes' poetry is an artform that persistently highlights its own artificial status. But it also highlights the artificiality of the world surrounding it. To argue that Aristophanes' olfactory blurring of gender distinctions is

---

[53]  Taaffe 1993, Taaffe 1995: 9.
[54]  Cf. Henderson 1991: 109, Austin and Olson 2004 ad *Thesm.* 254.
[55]  Cf. de la Fuente 2002, Willi 2003: 44, Austin and Olson 2004 ad *Thesm.*131.

breaking a proto-feminist lance is perhaps slightly anachronistic;[56] but Judith Butler's notion of a 'gender reality' that is 'real only to the extent that it is performed'[57] still rings intriguingly true for Aristophanic comedy. All social reality in Aristophanes is fundamentally performed, and self-consciously so. Indeed, I would argue that the staging of the artificiality and performative nature of social boundaries – be it between men and women or between masters and slaves – lies at the very heart of Aristophanes' political project (if there is such a thing).[58] Perhaps especially in a society as reliant on performance as fifth-century Athens,[59] the layers of identity, olfactory or otherwise, that a person may apply defy clear-cut distinctions. Likewise, in Aristophanes' comedy, hopes of uncovering true personal essence always fail.[60] The plays' treatments of smell and gender give ample support to this argument.

[56] Case 2021b: 101–21 makes in interesting argument about *Lysistrata* along these lines elsewhere.
[57] Butler 1988: 527.
[58] Cf. Reinke 2019a: 159–162.
[59] See Goldhill and Osborne 1999, Rehm 2002a: 3–12, Pelling 2005.
[60] Cf. Reinke 2019b.

# PART III

## Senses and Vitality

# Seeing in Euripides' *Alcestis* and Shakespeare's *The Winter's Tale*

## Katharine A. Craik

Euripides' *Alcestis* (438 BC) and Shakespeare's *The Winter's Tale* (c. 1611) are plays about who, what and how we see. Both are centrally preoccupied with the relationship between reality and illusion, and both explore this relationship through an epistemology of seeing. The denouement of both plays centres around the obstacles experienced by men (Admetus and Leontes) in looking clearly at their chastely conjugal wives (Alcestis and Hermione). While each play concludes with a return to clear-sightedness, and to the prospect of life overcoming death, neither simply dramatises recovery, redemption or resurrection. Instead *Alcestis* and *The Winter's Tale* deal with the difficulties of seeing people accurately within families, also raising questions about how we recognise and attend to others more generally – especially the difficulties involved in seeing, and differentiating, the living and the dead. Shakespeare's indebtedness to Euripides lies in his development of the themes of resurrection and substitution, and in his elaboration of tragicomedy as a distinct dramatic genre. Both plays explore the complex dynamics raised by looking at others, and both use a tragicomic frame to consider how death renders starkly apparent the limitations of the sense of sight. *Alcestis* and *The Winter's Tale* each experiment with the possibility that lost people may be re-presenced through representation, including through visual art such as statuary. As a dramatic genre, tragicomedy tends to heighten spectacle, but also to work intensely with music and song. In these plays it is indeed the senses of touch and hearing which eventually promise more lasting reunion.[1] Addressing the transhistorical co-ordinates of the embodied senses across Greek and early modern drama reveals tragicomedy's unique capacity to explore the boundaries between what can be perceived and what cannot. It also sheds new light on the shared ways in which sensory processes were central to the unfolding of dramatic action, as well as the affective experience of audiences in ancient and Renaissance theatres.

---

[1] It is important to note that the term 'tragicomedy' does not strictly apply to Classical drama. As many critics have observed, the generic status of *Alcestis* is particularly problematic since it was originally performed as the final part of a tragic trilogy in the slot usually reserved for the satyr play.

The importance of *Alcestis* as Shakespeare's principal source for *The Winter's Tale* is well established, but scholars have not explored these plays' shared interest in the sense of sight, nor the connections they both draw between seeing, living and dying. The prologue of *Alcestis* revolves around the contrast between light and darkness, and between seeing and unseeing, as Apollo god of light and the sun appears in conversation with Thanatos or Death. Apollo explains that Admetus is permitted to escape death if he can find a substitute 'who would consent | to die for him, and not see daylight any more' (17–18).[2] Only his wife, Alcestis, is willing to take Admetus' place. To be in the light, but also to witness the light, is to remain alive; and the Chorus will later return to this same phrase to lament that the dying Alcestis scarcely 'still look[s] | on daylight' (82–3). Throughout *Alcestis*, in fact, it is the ability to see or to look at light which expresses aliveness. In *The Winter's Tale*, too, aliveness and vitality is signalled by sunlight – as when, for example, the first servant affirms that 'the sun shone bright' on the long-lost Perdita (5.1.94). But the difference between life and death is not so easily determined in the tragicomic landscape of either play. While the unreliability of the sense of sight is often highlighted in Classical and Shakespearean tragedies, many of which explore the relationship between reality and various kinds of illusion or delusion, the generic hybridity of *Alcestis* or *The Winter's Tale* further raises the dramatic stakes.[3] Here it is the boundaries between the living and the dead which are stretched as Euripides and Shakespeare dramatise the ways in which death distorts acts of seeing among those who are dying, and among those who are left behind. Of particular interest are the uneven ways in which, in the closing scenes, Alcestis and Hermione appear recognisably alive in their own eyes, in the eyes of their husbands and in the eyes of those who encounter them. Attending closely to the senses, particularly the sense of sight, reveals new points of connection and difference between these two plays, especially around the events which onstage and offstage audiences see and do not see.

Scholars have found strong evidence of the influence of Greek drama in Shakespeare's late plays. *The Winter's Tale* makes extensive use of ancient myth and the oracle's verdict, delivered from the temple of Apollo, provides one of the play's pivotal scenes. Shakespeare also alludes at various points to the stories of Persephone, Orpheus and Asclepius.[4] Another version of the Alcestis story is found in Shakespeare's earlier comedy *Much Ado About Nothing* (1598–9) which also deals with a woman's false death and restoration. The specific indebtedness of *The Winter's Tale* to *Alcestis* is

[2]   All *Alcestis* translations are adapted from Grene and Lattimore 1955, and the Greek text is as in Diggle 1984.
[3]   On the partial knowledge of the world offered by the senses see Wright 2005: 268; and, on concealment and recognition more widely, 270–97. For a parallel discussion of Shakespearean drama's demonstration 'that we cannot achieve certainty in our knowledge of existence on the basis of the senses alone' see Cavell 2003: 4.
[4]   Louden 2007: 8.

clear. An engraving of Garrick's 1780 production of *The Winter's Tale* registers Euripides as an important source, depicting Hermione next to a pedestal showing scenes from *Alcestis*.[5] While earlier generations of scholars emphasised Shakespeare's adaptation of the Pygmalion story from Ovid's *Metamorphoses*, which he knew in both the original Latin and in Arthur Golding's 1567 English translation, and to Petrarch's *Rime Sparse*, critics have more recently identified thematic, generic and dramaturgical parallels with *Alcestis*.[6] For example, both plays emphasise the importance of hospitality: Admetus welcomes Heracles into his household in *Alcestis* while, at the start of *The Winter's Tale*, Leontes has played host for nine months to Polixenes (whose name comes from *poluxenos*, meaning 'having many guests').[7] Although no English translations were available to him, Shakespeare may have encountered Euripides' play in George Buchanan's 1539 Latin translation, or in the short story *Admetus and Alcest* by the Elizabethan writer George Pettie.[8] He also knew Greek tragedy through his extensive work with Plutarch's *Lives*, the main source for several of his Roman plays.[9] As Pollard 2017 has argued, Shakespeare inherited from Euripides a particular fascination with 'staging women's apparent deaths and uncanny revivals'. When Shakespeare revived Euripides' tragicomic story of a dead woman being returned to a grieving man, he was also reviving Greek tragic theatre more generally.[10] This chapter traces the legacy for early modern theatricality of two particular aspects of Hellenic drama: the ways that people express or encounter aliveness through the sense of sight, and the ways that they look at art. While the Alcestis story is transformed in important ways by Shakespeare's early modern Christian context, in which death loses some of its sting, other aspects of Greek tragicomedy continue to have traction. Shakespeare draws from Euripides an appreciation of how the sense of sight can determine only imperfectly the difference between life and death, or living and dying, experimenting with the already flexible co-ordinates of tragicomedy in order to put pressure, through sensory experience, on the technology of early modern theatricality.

While both *Alcestis* and *The Winter's Tale* give sustained attention to the difficulties involved in seeing other people, they also dramatise the difficulties involved in looking

---

[5]  The image is widely reproduced, including in Orgel 1996: 66. All quotations are from this edition.

[6]  There are particularly clear links between *The Winter's Tale* Act 5 Scene 3, and *Alcestis* lines 1006–1158. For close textual discussion see Dewar-Watson 2009: 78–9. On Shakespeare's use of Ovid and Petrarch see Enterline 1997: 29.

[7]  Louden 2007: 12.

[8]  See Pitcher 2010: 98. Buchanan's translation can be found in Sharratt and Walsh 1983: 209–44. All quotations are from this edition.

[9]  See Braden 2017: 110.

[10]  Pollard 2017: 194; see also Pollard 2013.

at art. Alcestis and Hermione turn (or are turned) into realistic artworks which come to life in the imagination of other characters, as well as before spectators in the theatre. At the end of *Alcestis*, Heracles brings a veiled woman to Admetus' household. Admetus' determined and lengthy resistance to touching or even looking at this woman, who is eventually revealed to be Alcestis herself, takes up around one tenth of the entire play.[11] As Chiara Blanco argues in her chapter in the current volume, Admetus' reluctance is an expression of his awareness that it is he, rather than Alcestis, who was destined to die; and that he has circumvented death only by virtue of his wife's sacrifice. Earlier in the play, Admetus had created in his mind's eye several lifelike images of his wife: first as a statue, and then as a dream. Shakespeare, too, devotes sustained attention to what happens when people turn, or are turned, into images; and it is argued here that this is one important element he took from his Euripidean source. In the opening two acts of *The Winter's Tale*, Leontes' jealous rage causes him to fashion in his imagination an elaborately counterfeit vision of Hermione whom he suspects of adultery. Falsely accused and then publicly humiliated, Hermione collapses and seemingly dies. Like Alcestis, she subsequently returns – this time to Antigonus – in the form of a dream-vision. And in the play's final scene, Hermione is returned to her family, and to life, as a statue 'as like Hermione as her picture' (5.1.74) which miraculously awakens. Both Alcestis and Hermione are veiled (in Hermione's case, by a curtain); both are re-introduced through an intermediary (Heracles in *Alcestis*, Paulina in *The Winter's Tale*); and both, significantly, are silent before their husbands on their return. While the denouement of both plays hinges on the difficulty men experience in seeing women clearly, this difficulty is dramatised as a series of disturbing encounters with visual art which involve diminishment for the people who are looking. Euripides and Shakespeare explore aliveness through different but related dramaturgical strategies, blending life with the representation of life in stylised conclusions which rely on spectatorship. Considering the sense of sight in *Alcestis* reveals new aspects of Shakespeare's interest in his main source. Since both plays develop an ontological uncertainty between seeing and being seen, it seems fitting that this process also works in the opposite direction: exploring how sight works in *The Winter's Tale* nuances our understanding of seeing in *Alcestis*. Both plays heighten theatre's intense engagement of the senses, destabilising the borders between life and death, and putting pressure on our assumptions about what, or who, is 'really there'.

[11] Slater 2013: 62.

# 1

Aliveness is clearly signalled in *Alcestis* by the ability to see. Towards the start of the play, in lines which anticipate the concluding scene, the chorus mentions Apollo's son, Asclepius, who has the power to bring mortals back to life. Had Asclepius himself remained alive, he might have been able to save Alcestis:

> εἰ φῶς τόδ' ἦν
> ὄμμασιν δεδορκὼς
> Φοίβου παῖς, προλιποῦσ'
> ἦλθ' ἂν ἕδρας σκοτίους
> Ἅιδα τε πύλας· (122–6)

> If the eyes
> of Phoebus' son were opened
> still, if he could have come
> and left the dark chambers,
> the gates of Hades.

Cast down by Zeus, Asclepius may however no longer resurrect 'those who were stricken' (127). Death's unequivocalness appears close at hand, in accordance with the absolute, polluting presence of Thanatos, and the ensuing dramatisation of Alcestis' departure is a description of fading or darkening. Only just still breathing, she 'wants to look once more upon the life of the sun ... | She must see the sun's shining circle yet one more time' (206–8). The different circumstances of Alcestis and Admetus are expressed through different dramatic registers. Alcestis uses emotional language with complex metrical patterning when she sings to the 'Sun, and light of the day'. Admetus responds in matter-of-fact language with simple iambic trimeters, using the regular verse of tragic speech: 'The sun sees you and me, two people suffering' (244–6). A darker vision of Charon then materialises in Alcestis' mind's eye: 'I see him there at the oars of his little boat in the lake, | the ferryman of the dead' (252–3) until, finally, 'darkness creeps over my eyes' (269). Now Alcestis turns to her children: 'Daylight is yours, | my children. Look on it and be happy' (271–2). Daylight is bestowed by the dying upon the living when Alcestis tells Admetus that it is through her death that he will 'live and see the daylight'. Alcestis once more feels her 'eyes darken' (385) while her son recognises that his mother is 'not here with us | in the sunshine any more' (395). Admetus, too, notes that the dying Alcestis 'does not see' (404). The choral lyric which follows, a long praise of Alcestis, describes the 'sunless chambers of Hades' (436), an idea later echoed in

Heracles' description of the underworld with 'the sunless homes | of those below' (852–3) where he will travel to demand Alcestis' return. The widowed Admetus laments that he may no longer take 'pleasure in the sunshine' (868), and his resistance to seeing or feeling the light suggests his reluctance to keep living. Euripides' stark imagery therefore repeatedly links death to darkness, and life to sunlight; or seeing to living and to pleasure, and unseeing to dying and despair. The two states seem emphatically separate since, as the Chorus puts it, 'How could a person both be dead and live and see?' (142)[12]

While the ability to see is associated with aliveness, the capacity to be recognised by others as alive seems more complex. Difficulties emerge when people look at Alcestis and try to determine whether or not she still lives:

Χο. εἰ δ᾽ ἔτ᾽ ἐστὶν ἔμψυχος γυνὴ,
εἴτ᾽ οὖν ὄλωλεν εἰδέναι βουλοίμεθ᾽ ἄν.
Θε. καὶ ζῶσαν εἰπεῖν καὶ θανοῦσαν ἔστι σοι. (139–41)

CHORUS. We should like to know
whether the queen is dead or if she is still alive.
MAID. I could tell you that she is still alive or that she is dead.

Even when Alcestis dies onstage, the dividing line between life and death remains in doubt. While any onstage death lies beyond dramatic representation, as the actor's living body must intimate the character's dead one, Alcestis' death seems especially indeterminate.[13] Admetus implores her to stay, and to keep looking at her children, but she declares 'There is no use | in talking to me any more. I am not there' (386–7). The following line is shared, but it is Admetus who seems to disappear at the end of it, rather than his wife:

Αδ. τί δρᾷς; προλείπεις; Αλ. χαῖρ᾽. Αδ. ἀπωλόμην τάλας. (391)

ADMETUS.     Are you really leaving us?
ALCESTIS.                              Goodbye.
ADMETUS.                                          Oh, I am lost.

---

[12] For a detailed analysis of the metaphor of 'death as removal from light' in Homer and Euripides, among other ancient writers see Giannakis 2001:128. See also the discussion of 'the sense of sight being used to define what it meant to be a sentient, subjective being' in the introduction to Squire 2015: 10.

[13] For an account of Alcestis' embodiment see Bassi 2018.

As Blanco argues in this volume, Admetus appears at various points in *Alcestis* as not quite a living being. He is enduring a half-life in which he regards himself, with Alcestis, as more or less already dead. Living looks like dying, and dying looks like living – despite the Chorus' clear statement that Alcestis' 'fate shows | steep and near' (118–19). As Susanne Turner puts it in her study of sight and death in the ancient world, the dead have a tendency not only to disappear and resist being seen, but also to 'take on new forms of visibility'.[14] Alcestis seems both present and absent, both seeable and unseeable.

New and unfamiliar forms of visibility become especially prominent in the play's closing scene when Heracles brings a veiled woman whom he asks Admetus to take into his household. This scene does not revolve around the question of identity since the audience already knows that Alcestis will return. Apollo had warned Death at the start of the play that a man, Heracles, 'shall be entertained here in Admetus' house | and he shall take the woman away from you by force' (68–9). Instead the scene revolves around the problem of recognition. When Heracles claims, disingenuously, that he wishes he could 'bring your wife back from the chambered deep | into the light' (1073–4), Admetus replies that there is 'no way for the dead to come back to the light' (1076). It is the spectacle of the veiled woman, specifically, which he wishes to be spared: 'Oh, for God's pity, take this woman away | out of my sight' (1064–5). The reason for his forceful resistance lies in her resemblance to Alcestis:

> σὺ δ', ὦ γύναι,
> ἥτις ποτ' εἶ σύ, ταῦτ' ἔχουσ' Ἀλκήστιδι
> μορφῆς μέτρ' ἴσθι· καὶ προσήιξαι δέμας. (1061–3)

> You, lady,
> whoever you are, I tell you that you have the form
> of my Alcestis; all your body is like hers.

So close is the resemblance that 'as I look on her … I see | my wife' (1066–7). In Buchanan's version, the phrase 'modo et statura corporis simillima' (1139) emphasises the striking similarity to Alcestis of the veiled woman's appearance or demeanour.[15] Ted Hughes' 1999 translation also presses this same point. Here Admetus finds the veiled woman 'too like Alcestis' before remarking:

---

[14] Turner 2016: 143.
[15] Shakespeare may also have particularly noted the word *statura* in Buchanan's translation; see Sharratt and Walsh 1983 ad 1137–9 and Dewar-Watson 2009: 79.

I know the eyes of bereavement
Fixed in their focus on what's missing
Find it everywhere.[16]

Hughes captures the emotional burden of loss, its disconcerting effects on what one sees
(or cannot see), and the strain involved in keeping one's eyes literally and metaphorically
open at moments of heightened vulnerability. Heracles challenges Admetus' insistence
that the veiled woman should depart: 'First look. See if she should' (1105). He keeps
urging Admetus to look, and to look squarely at the likeness: 'look at her. See if she does not
seem most like | your wife' (1121–2). But if the veiled woman's resemblance to Alcestis
makes it difficult for Admetus to register her presence, the resemblance also – and more
strangely – makes it difficult for him to recognise her as his wife. Even when and perhaps
because Admetus is encountering a perfect simulacrum, he cannot see Alcestis clearly. All
that remains traumatically visible in Admetus' gaze is likeness itself. His protracted struggle
to look at the veiled woman is akin to the difficulty of looking directly at death which – as
the play's opening scene has made clear – both demands our attention and repels us. In a
scene which puts the viability of the sense of sight under intense scrutiny, death arrives as
life's disturbing facsimile rather than its opposite or counterpart.

    So long as Admetus relies on the sense of sight, the veiled woman looks like a
disconcerting approximation rather than the real thing. Even though Heracles insists
'This is your own wife you see. She is here', Admetus still regards the spectacle as a mirage:

Ἀδ. ὦ θεοί, τί λέξω; θαῦμ' ἀνέλπιστον τόδε·
    γυναῖκα λεύσσω τὴν ἐμὴν ἐτητύμως,
    ἢ κέρτομός μ' ἐκ θεοῦ τις ἐκπλήσσει χαρά;
Ηρ. οὐκ ἔστιν, ἀλλὰ τήνδ' ὁρᾷς δάμαρτα σήν.
Ἀδ. ὅρα γε μή τι φάσμα νερτέρων τόδ' ἦ. (1123–7)

ADMETUS. Gods, what shall I think! Amazement beyond hope, as I
look on this woman, this wife. Is she really mine,
or some sweet mockery for God to stun me with?
HERACLES. Not so. This is your own wife you see. She is here.
ADMETUS Be careful she is not some phantom from the depths.

At this key moment, when Admetus does not know what he is seeing, Euripides uses
three different verbs to express his confusion: 'look at her' (βλέπω, 1121); 'in seeing this

¹⁶  Hughes 1999: 75.

woman' (λεύσσω, 1124); 'you *see* your wife' (ὁράω, 1126). The verb ὁράω returns at 1127: 'See lest she is some phantom from the depths'; and again at 1129 in the compound form εἰσοράω: 'do I *see* (*look upon*) my wife, whom I was burying?' Admetus fears that his wife's ghost (φάσμα; or the more specifically spectral *larva* in Buchanan's Latin translation) has been sent to confound his capacity to see. Here it is the vulnerability of the senses which registers the threat posed to psychic integrity by death's difficult truths. Admetus' reluctance makes for a highly stylized, tragicomic moment which unsettles one of the fundamental conventions of dramatic representation: theatre's portrayal of the world's visible realities. In dramatising Admetus' disbelief as he stands face to face with his wife's double, Euripides collapses the mimetic technology on which theatre depends. Plays usually make actors look more or less approximate to people in the offstage world. But this new, almost-alive Alcestis rivals reality rather than mirroring it, proffering a new version of aliveness that looks like a mockery of Alcestis' own – and therefore of Admetus' too. Shakespeare experiments similarly with the radical possibilities of tragicomedy at the conclusion of *The Winter's Tale*. In Act 5, Paulina advises Leontes, who is readying himself to view Hermione's stony likeness, to 'prepare | To see the life as lively mocked' (5.3.17–18). In accordance with early modern tragicomedy's absolvitory drive, Shakespeare holds out the possibility that Leontes might eventually recover, thanks to Hermione's forgiveness. The prospect of any such restoration remains remote in *Alcestis*, however, where his wife's φάσμα brings Admetus only cold comfort. Euripides offers no cathartic return to equilibrium, and the alarming spectacle of Alcestis' double does not restore but instead further challenges Admetus' view of the fixed contours of reality.

The only way to break through this *mise-en-abyme* is to introduce a new and different mode of perception. Admetus eventually completes 'the slow process by which he is brought, with his eyes almost comically averted, to take his new ward by the hand'.[17] At first he will not touch her, and there is an uneasy humour of sorts in his assumption of the role of a reluctant bride.[18] Heracles insists 'Reach out your hand and take the stranger's' (1117) and then, unusually, line 1119 passes from Heracles to Admetus, and then back to Heracles, in a formal expression of Admetus' tentativeness. In performance, this is the moment when Alcestis is finally unveiled. Admetus notes once more, in wonderment, that he had 'never thought to see' (1133) his wife again, and marvels that Heracles has somehow contrived to 'bring her back from down there to the light' (1139). Light continues to signal aliveness and recovery, and yet the sense of sight remains inadequate to clinch the recognition. Only through touch is Admetus finally able to grasp Alcestis,

---

[17] Dyson 1988: 23.

[18] This moment is reversed in *The Winter's Tale* where Leontes reflects waspishly on Hermione's protracted resistance to his courtship: 'Three crabbed months had soured themselves to death | Ere I could make thee open thy white hand' (1.2.101–2).

both physically and psychologically. Here the reciprocity involved in touching, which remains unavailable to the audience in the theatre, functions more reliably than seeing or hearing as an expression of the difference between life and death.

This resolution is long delayed, and the protracted tension of this final scene reprises Admetus' earlier encounter with a coldly mocking copy of his wife. When Admetus remarks to the veiled woman 'you have the form | of my Alcestis; all your body is like hers' (1062–3), the noun δέμας (body) recalls a much-discussed episode earlier in the play. Here, with the still-living Alcestis visibly present onstage, Admetus had conjured up his wife's likeness in his mind's eye in the form of a statue:

> σοφῇ δὲ χειρὶ τεκτόνων δέμας τὸ σὸν
> εἰκασθὲν ἐν λέκτροισιν ἐκταθήσεται,
> ᾧ προσπεσοῦμαι καὶ περιπτύσσων χέρας
> ὄνομα καλῶν σὸν τὴν φίλην ἐν ἀγκάλαις
> δόξω γυναῖκα καίπερ οὐκ ἔχων ἔχειν·
> ψυχρὰν μέν, οἶμαι, τέρψιν, ἀλλ᾽ ὅμως βάρος
> ψυχῆς ἀπαντλοίην ἄν. (348–53)

> I shall have the skilled hand of an artificer
> make me an image of you to set in my room,
> pay my devotions to it, hold it in my arms
> and speak your name, and clasp it close against my heart,
> and think I hold my wife again, though I do not,
> cold consolation, I know it, and yet even so
> I might drain the weight of sorrow.

The dying Alcestis is transformed, in Admetus' imagination, into an accurate but static replica of herself. Once more the limits of the sense of sight are registered as Admetus imagines throwing his arms around the cold, hard stone.[19] Perhaps Euripides had in mind a similar myth, set (like *Alcestis*) in Thessaly, in which the bereaved Laodameia fashions an image of her late husband, Protesilaus, and keeps it in her bedchamber. Charles Segal (1993) has argued that Admetus' imagined Alcestis resembles a *kolossos*, or funerary statue; and that this fantasy suggests the powerful effects of mimetic art, including theatre.[20] More striking, however, is this episode's exposure of the constraints rather than the effectiveness of mimesis. The conjured image comes only precariously to

---

[19]  Here however 'sight proves surprisingly tactile' according to Turner 2016: 156.
[20]  Segal 1993: 37–50. Segal's interpretation builds on Vernant 1985: 325–38.

life since Admetus knows that he is envisioning vainly, and that his fantasy can bring only 'cold consolation'. The imagined statue does not satisfactorily resemble life, and indeed looks distressingly fixed and unresponsive – like Alcestis' senseless corpse to which her child Eumelus will soon helplessly call even though, as Admetus laments, 'she does not hear you' (404). While representative art may promise relief from trauma, or even from the finality of death itself, the statue's cold lifelikeness again seems more like a riposte than a solace. It poses a barrier to feeling rather than an opportunity for engagement, triggering only an endless and repetitive seeking for life. The unresponsiveness of stone, and the sheer awfulness of its lifelessness, is registered again – albeit in reverse – when, at the end of the play, Admetus reluctantly stretches out his hand, feeling 'like Perseus killing the gorgon' (1118).[21] Now the act of looking involves the risk of petrification not so much for the one who has died, but for the one who is left to live. If Euripides is interested in how the sense of sight conveys complex feeling, he is also interested in how stalled, frustrated, or forbidden acts of looking express profound emotional experience.

The imagined statue of Alcestis raises the problem that visual art cannot satisfactorily encompass either the still-living or the dead. It also suggests the constraining limits of the sense of sight as a way of truly seeing others. When Admetus finally recognises Alcestis, he resolves (in Lattimore's translation) 'we shall make our life again, and it will be | a better one' (1156–7). Euripides uses the verb μεθαρμόζω and Admetus' line is perhaps more accurately translated as 'now we tune our life to a different key'.[22] Cold, plastic representation has been superseded, finally, by a more harmonious, durational and kinetic model of art. In *The Winter's Tale*, too, Hermione's awakening is kindled through a process of harmony when Paulina instructs the musicians as follows: 'Music; awake her – strike!' (5.3.98). As in Shakespeare and George Wilkins' play *Pericles* (*c.* 1608), another tragicomedy written around three years before *The Winter's Tale*, music signals the prospect of new life. Here it is the healer Cerimon who helps Pericles' wife Thaisa, who is thought to have died in childbirth, 'To blow into life's flower again' (3.2.94) after her coffin has washed ashore at Ephesus. At the conclusion of *Pericles*, as at the end of *The Winter's Tale*, 'heavenly music' (5.1.220) accompanies Pericles' return from his death-like trance into new affective relationship, and into a future in which the living may turn more attentively to one another.[23]

This shift away from the constraints of the sense of sight, and towards the warmer and more restorative sense of hearing, features however in both plays only as a promise. In the closing lines of *Alcestis*, Admetus finally recognises the 'eyes | and body of my

---

[21]  For further discussion of this moment see Pollard 2017: 193.
[22]  This insight is gratefully drawn from Dr Nathaniel Hess's response to an earlier draft of this chapter.
[23]  Gossett 2014.

dearest wife' (1132–3). Death had removed a lock of Alcestis' hair at line 76, and this terrible consecration seems at last to be voided: Euripides' verb ἀφαγνίζεσθαι, used in the infinitive, means to de-sanctify, while Buchanan chooses *expiare* (1225). And yet despite Admetus' desire to talk to his newly restored wife, he cannot hear her voice. As Heracles reminds him:

οὔπω θέμις σοι τῆσδε προσφωνημάτων
κλύειν, πρὶν ἂν θεοῖσι τοῖσι νερτέροις
ἀφαγνίσηται καὶ τρίτον μόλῃ φάος. (1144–6)

You are not allowed to hear her speak to you until
her obligations to the gods who live below
are washed away. Until the third morning comes.

Alcestis must stay silent during the following three-day lustration period, remaining in a death-like state 'Until the third morning comes' (1146) – or, literally, until three days of light have passed. There are restrictions, then, to the capacities of sensorial or affective process to redeem human loss. The same provisionality marks the end of *The Winter's Tale*. Here, the visibly resurrected Hermione addresses her daughter Perdita directly as 'mine own' (5.3.123) but remains uncomfortably silent before her husband. As the Third Gentleman says of the statue's sculptor, Giulio Romano, 'He so near to Hermione hath done Hermione that they say one would speak to her and stand in hope of answer' (5.2.98–100). Even when she awakens, however, this hope of answer remains unfulfilled – and Hermione's nearness remains exactly that. The remarkable intensity of this tragicomic resolution suggests the persistent human difficulties involved in achieving lasting, meaningful communication with others – whether through seeing, hearing or touching them. As Mukherji and Lyne have argued, early modern tragicomedy enables expression of 'the integral relation between the law of genre and the structure of experience'.[24] As the editors of this volume argue in the Introduction, however, the complexities of sensory process tend to challenge the boundaries implied by laws and structures – including generic ones. In both *Alcestis* and *The Winter's Tale*, the indeterminacy of perception resists conventional tragic or comic resolution, whilst demonstrating the limits of the embodied senses as a way of framing or shaping reality.

[24] Mukherji and Lyne 2007: 8.

## 2

The visual experience of the audiences who attended theatres in London was changing rapidly at the time of *The Winter's Tale*'s first performances. Surviving records confirm that the play was staged at the Globe in May 1611, but also at court – probably in the Banqueting House – in November 1611, and again in 1612/13.[25] Indoor stage technologies were becoming increasingly complex, particularly their use of light and shadow. These allowed for more sophisticated manipulation of sight lines, and the development of newly flexible spaces which blurred the boundaries between what was seen or unseen. Early modern tragicomedies, including Shakespeare's, proved particularly well suited to these new spaces, perhaps because their action tends to blend familiar with irrational, inexplicable or unnatural events. One important feature of tragicomedy is indeed that it does not seek accurately to represent reality. As Driver (1960) writes: 'The whole structure crumbles when taken too seriously or when compared too closely (that is, too immediately) to life outside the theatre'.[26] *Alcestis* and *The Winter's Tale* not only refuse such close comparisons, but also disturb the assumption that life outside the theatre, or indeed life itself, are stable enough categories to be represented in visual art. Instead both plays use aesthetic representation to unsettle the relationship between those whom we see, and those whom we think we see. Both plays question the conventionally recognised separation between the living and the dead, bringing these two seemingly separate categories into disorienting proximity through attending to the approximations involved in sensory process.

To Leontes, the living Hermione is more vividly and persuasively present as a picture in his mind's eye than as a 'real person'. His imaginative construction of Hermione's lurid likeness indeed precipitates the play's major events since, as Douglas Wilson has written, 'the play begins by projecting the image of an adulteress'.[27] Leontes' psychological crisis is triggered by the monstrous counterfeit he evokes of the 'free face' (1.2.111) Hermione makes with his childhood friend Polixenes. Leontes ruminates obsessively over this vividly imagined Hermione 'making practised smiles', leaning cheek-to-cheek, meeting noses, and kissing Polixenes' inside lip. It is this projection which persuades Leontes that his wife has exchanged more than 'holy looks' (5.3.148) with his friend. The imagined Hermione, who exists only in Leontes' mind, proves more effectively and persistently

---

[25]  Orgel 1996: 80.
[26]  Driver 1960: 168.
[27]  Wilson 1984: 352.

agential than Hermione who cannot make herself seen or heard when it matters most.[28] So catastrophically convincing is this mental picture, indeed, that it triggers Leontes' madness which gives rise in turn to a series of further calamities: the trial of Hermione, the loss of Mamillius, the abandonment of Perdita, and the death of Antigonus. As Hermione knows, the stakes of Leontes' deluded vision could scarcely be higher: 'My life stands in the level of your dreams' (3.2.79).[29] The theatrical stakes are also heightened as the audience is made privy to Leontes' increasingly vivid descriptions of Hermione-as-adulteress, several of which he delivers to the audience in asides. When Leontes describes the contorted workings of his own imagination – 'With what's unreal thou co-active art, | And fellow'st nothing' (1.2.140–1) – he is also describing more generally how quickly and destructively the mind's eye can construct something (or someone) out of thin air. The onstage audience is sceptical, and Camillo in particular 'cannot | Believe this crack' (1.2.318–9), or flaw, exists in Hermione's character. But the play's opening scenes dramatise how easily we may come to misperceive the living, as well as the dead, and the play's offstage audiences in the theatre sometimes find themselves – like Leontes – mistakenly regarding Hermione in a new, unsympathetic light.

Part of the problem lies in the unevenness of sight as a register of the truth. It is the spectacle of Hermione's late pregnancy which initially triggers Leontes' groundless suspicions: ''Tis Polixenes | Has made thee swell thus' (2.1.61–2). The sense of sight is nevertheless repeatedly invoked in *The Winter's Tale* as a guarantee, particularly within families where children bear a striking resemblance to their parents. Perdita is remarkably like Hermione, according to the Third Gentleman, who notes 'the majesty of the creature in resemblance of the mother' (5.2.35). And Florizel closely resembles Polixenes: 'Your father's image is so hit in you, | His very air' (5.1.126–7). But to Leontes, the visible resemblance between himself and his children is, inexplicably, further evidence of Hermione's duplicity rather than her married chastity. Even as he notes that the nose of his young son, Mamillius, 'is a copy out of mine' (1.2.128), he remains unconvinced that this likeness is meaningful: 'women say so, | That will say anything' (129–30). It falls to Mamillius to reassure his own father of his legitimacy: 'I am like you, they say' (206). Meanwhile Leontes is enraged when Paulina insists that his daughter Perdita resembles him:

---

[28]  See Enterline 1997: 21: 'terrible consequences attend Hermione's speaking'. Compare Hamlet's description of his late father 'in my mind's eye' (1.2.186). Old Hamlet becomes highly effective and agential, propelling the play's action. Like *The Winter's Tale*, *Hamlet* is steeped in Greek tragedy; see for example Hamlet's speech which begins 'What's Hecuba to him, or he to Hecuba, | That he should weep for her?' (2.2.371–2).

[29]  Enterline 1997: 26.

Although the print be little, the whole matter
And copy of the father – eye, nose, lip,
The trick of's frown, his forehead …
And thou good goddess Nature, which hast made it
So like to him that got it (3.1.98–104)

The vocabulary of printing and copying suggests the material fact of Leontes' reproducibility, but he remains more persuaded by the imaginary tainted child he has constructed in his mind's eye: 'it is the issue of Polixenes' (2.3.92). Later in the play, the oracle will register with unassailable clarity that 'Hermione is chaste' and Perdita an 'innocent babe truly begotten' (3.2.123). To Leontes, however, it is Apollo's verdict which seems Apolline, or dreamlike, 'produced by the inner world of fantasy'.[30] Shakespeare often registers children's resemblance to their fathers as proof that their mothers have been 'true to wedlock' (5.1.123), and also writes about children who must scrutinise themselves for evidence of their own legitimacy.[31] But in *The Winter's Tale*, Leontes is perversely incensed not by reproductive inexactness but instead by reproductive precision. Just as Admetus is disturbed in *Alcestis* by the accuracy of the simulacrum offered by the veiled woman, Leontes is repelled not because his children are imperfect copies of his own 'mould and frame' (2.3.102) but because they are too much like him. As Paulina bluntly points out, Perdita's resemblance to her deluded father is precisely the problem: 'So like you, 'tis the worse' (2.3.97). The play's other vitiated father, Antigonus, expresses the same unjust fury when he threatens violence against his own young daughters to prevent them from bearing children: 'I'll geld 'em all – fourteen they shall not see | To bring false generations' (2.1.147–8). Once more, familial reproducibility confirms rather than dispels a father's unjust suspicions against his innocent family, showing how risky it is to rely upon the sense of sight as a way of registering likeness – particularly when such likeness is linked to a person's right to remain alive.

In fact *The Winter's Tale* is full of visibly false generations through which the contours of reality, or what Perdita calls 'great creating nature' (4.4.88), are adjusted, supplemented or overturned. Contemplating the abandonment of the baby Perdita, for example, Antigonus describes his vision of Hermione 'in pure white robes, | like very sanctity'. So powerfully present did she seem, Antigonus claims, that 'ne'er was dream | So like a waking' (3.3.17–18). Once more the limits of representation are put to the test as Antigonus struggles to differentiate a vivid image, formed in his mind's eye, from Hermione's literal presence. The

---

[30] Nietzsche 1999: 16.
[31] See for example Sonnets 2 and 3 which deal with acts of legitimate self-copying; and compare the bastard Edmund's claim, in *King Lear*, that he has a 'shape as true, | As honest madam's issue' (1.2.8–9).

vividness of this dream, and the exceptionality of Hermione, recall the moment in *Alcestis* when Admetus invites his wife into his subconscious:

ἐν δ’ ὀνείρασιν
φοιτῶσά μ’ εὐφραίνοις ἄν· ἡδὺ γὰρ φίλους
κἂν νυκτὶ λεύσσειν, ὅντιν’ ἂν παρῇ χρόνον. (354–6)

    You could come
    to see me in my dreams and comfort me. For they
    who love find a time’s sweetness in the visions of night.

Stony likenesses may seem cold and fixed, but dream-images are flexible and dynamic enough to bring comfort. Euripides uses the verb λεύσσω since, in Greek, one sees rather than has dreams. The corresponding section of Buchanan’s translation seems particularly to have interested Shakespeare: *umbra me per somnia | utinam reversa oblectet* (‘would that your ghost might delight me, returning in my dreams’). Perhaps it was Buchanan’s ‘ghost’ or ‘shade’ (*umbra*) which inspired the later exchange between Paulina and Leontes about Hermione’s ghost in *The Winter’s Tale*. Here Leontes pledges – on Paulina’s insistence – never to love again, lest his re-marriage cause Hermione’s ‘sainted spirit | Again [to] possess her corpse’ (5.1.57-8). In the strange speech which follows, Paulina imagines not only seeing the re-animated corpse of Hermione but actually inhabiting it. In Paulina’s personation, however, Hermione’s spirit seems less than saintly. At the sight of Leontes’ second wife, ‘I’d shriek’ (5.1.65), she threatens, and ‘I’d bid you mark | Her eye, and tell me for what dull part in’t | You chose her’ (5.1.63–5). Just as the memory of Alcestis is worse than death for Admetus, so this uncannily re-personated Hermione will torment Leontes until he promises that, from now on, he will see only ‘dead coals’ (5.1.67) where the beautiful eyes of other women should be. Leontes’ experience of the partially re-animated Hermione is the opposite of cathartic. He ends up assuming a withdrawn and bloodless ‘saint-like sorrow’ (5.1.2), a death-like state in which other people bring as little comfort as burnt-out stones.

    And yet, as the final scenes of *The Winter’s Tale* make clear, it is all a matter of how one looks. Now that the lost Perdita is emphatically re-presenced in Sicilia, Paulina states bluntly (in another imagined exchange with Hermione) that the invisible dead must cede place to the visible living: ‘so must thy grave | Give way to what’s seen now’ (5.1.97–8). The play’s denouement, in which Leontes and Perdita are re-united with the resurrected Hermione, is preceded by an exchange between three unnamed gentlemen who have seen too much. Witnesses to an earlier re-union (between Leontes, Polixenes and Camillo) the three gentlemen talk, appropriately enough, about the difficulty of translating into words the experience of beholding miraculous spectacle. In order to preserve dramatic tension for the play's final reveal, this earlier reunion is described through 'relation' (5.2.2) rather than brought literally before the eyes of the audience. The three gentlemen strain to match their words to the enormity of the sights they have seen. As the First Gentleman puts it, 'I make a broken delivery of the business' (5.2.9). To recover the spectacle in words is impossible: those who did not witness the reunion 'have lost a sight which was to be seen, cannot be spoken of' (5.2.42–3), being so remarkable that it 'undoes description' (5.2.57). As befits the illogicality of tragicomedy, this scene of recovery – which no one actually sees – looks like both a calamity and a jubilation. Even 'the wisest beholder that knew no more but seeing' (5.2.16–17) would be unable to say which it was, for even as the old friends embraced, 'They seemed almost with staring on one another to tear the cases of their eyes' (5.2.12–13). The sense of sight remains an unreliable indicator of truth and feeling for those who see, and also for those who are seen. This equivocation is further complicated by the fact that the audience witnesses this important episode only in their imagination. Shakespeare places intense pressure upon the boundary between theatrical spectacle on the one hand, and the kind of seeing which takes place in the mind's eye on the other. The realities revealed by the sense of sight seem fractional and incomplete, in keeping with tragicomedy's 'edgy certainties'.[32]

All of this is however only a preamble to the play's final scene which revolves around the spell-binding spectacle of Hermione's return. Visually stunning in performance, this scene has been re-imagined countless times by artists and painters. The denouement is designed to make an intense appeal to the audience's gaze, but Shakespeare nevertheless continues to explore what Webb calls 'the intimate connections that existed between the visual and the verbal'.[33] How to capture, in language, the feeling of witnessing a miracle? At first Leontes is so pained by the spectacle of Hermione's statue, through which he finds his own 'evils conjured to remembrance' (5.3.40), that Paulina offers almost immediately to hide it again:

If I had thought the sight of my poor image
Would thus have wrought you – for the stone is mine –
I'd not have showed it. (5.3.57–9)

Since viewers are shaped, for better or for worse, by what they see, the image risks harming the already fragile Leontes. It is specifically the statue's likeness to Hermione, and to real life, which is shocking. This exquisite piece of art is so realistic that it seems to move and

---

[32]　McMullan and Hope 1992: 6.
[33]　Webb 2016: 205.

breathe. Like Pygmalion's statue of Galatea, Hermione's statue not only reflects reality but exceeds it.[34] Art can be 'livelier than life', as the poet reminds the painter in *Timon of Athens*, another play sometimes described as a tragicomedy; and indeed, to Leontes, the statue's 'dead likeness ... | Excels whatever yet you looked upon'.[35] Paulina's strange phrase 'dead likeness' suggests both precision and mortality. No one is sure whether or not the statue is alive, including Camillo who wonders 'If she pertain to life' (5.3.113). In one of Shakespeare's other sources, Pettie's *Admetus and Alcest*, Proserpine clearly 'put life into his wife againe, and *with* speed sent her unto him'.[36] But Shakespeare, like Euripides, brings the states of death and aliveness into disorienting proximity. For those who care to look, the sight of the statue is neither comforting nor restorative. Leontes frets that his wife's statue might 'rebuke me | For being more stone than it' (5.3.37–8), just as Admetus fears he will be turned to stone if he looks directly at the veiled woman. The sense of sight risks not simply turning Leontes into stone – but, worse, exposing him as a cold and unresponsive person.[37] As long as Leontes is a mere 'looker-on' (5.3.85) he remains shamefully stone-like. While the act of looking is necessary in order to determine the statue's truth, this same act risks turning Leontes into a spectacle of his own deathlikeness.

Perhaps it is unsurprising that the sense of sight proves so risky in *The Winter's Tale* since the visible presence of death itself was one of the major innovations of Shakespeare's principal source. Unusually in Greek theatre, Death (Thanatos) appears in *Alcestis* as an embodied character carrying a sword and initiating a stand-off with the god of light. As Apollo makes abundantly clear, 'here is Death himself' (24). Death has come to lead Alcestis in place of her husband to Hades, and enters the palace where Alcestis lies dying. But rather than staging the ensuing conversation between Death and Alcestis, Euripides instead puts Death's next entrance in Alcestis' mind's eye. Death becomes such a vividly lifelike presence in Alcestis' imagination that she is bewildered no one else can see him. He has the same wings and glowing eyes which the audience has just literally witnessed onstage:

ἄγει μ' ἄγει τις, ἄγει μέ τις (οὐχ
ὁρᾷς;) νεκύων ἐς αὐλάν,
ὑπ' ὀφρύσι κυαναυγέσι
βλέπων πτερωτὸς Ἅιδας. (259–62)

[34] For a discussion of the influence of Ovid's Pygmalion on *The Winter's Tale* see Enterline 1997: 25.
[35] Shakespeare, *Timon of Athens*, 1.1.139; *The Winter's Tale*, 5.3.15–16.
[36] Hartman 1938: 138.
[37] Compare the myths in which Niobe is turned to stone, and in which Poseidon petrifies the Phaeacians' ship, both discussed in Louden 2007: 22.

I feel a hand grasping my hand,
Leading me – don't you see him? – leading me
To the home of the dead. He has wings;
His eyes glow dark under his frowning brow.[38]

Death takes Alcestis' hand, just as Admetus will do in the play's final scene. Casting into doubt what (and who) can be reliably seen, even when they appear before us, Euripides dramatises the difficulty of looking at death – but also the fact that death fractures what and how we see. Many have commented that *Alcestis* deals in 'doubling and opposition, both thematically and structurally'.[39] While this is undoubtedly true, the play also resists thematic and structural oppositions by blurring the difference between light and darkness, reality and unreality, presence and absence, the quick and the dead. To blend these categories, usually construed as opposites, is to follow the logic of tragicomedy which works through 'the coming together, the collision even' of two seemingly separate and distinct dramatic modes.[40] It is also to follow through on the affective power of the senses to merge what the audience witnesses, through theatrical spectacle, with those sights which are visible only in the imagination.

Both *The Winter's Tale* and *Alcestis* test the boundaries between what is seen and what is unseen. As Hamlet reminds the players, as he prepares to present *The Murder of Gonzago* in the third act of *Hamlet*, live theatre is uniquely capable of holding 'the mirror up to nature, to show virtue her own feature, scorn her own image, and the very age and body of time his form'.[41] Euripides and Shakespeare, however, challenge any straightforward understanding of theatrical representation as a way of making things visible and therefore comprehensible. Both plays disturb the fixed realism implied by mimesis by showing how representation can fix both the living and the dead in ways which make them harder rather than easier to see. While both Admetus and Leontes eventually achieve a sharper vision of sorts, this sharpness never really clarifies the difference between 'real life' and art, nor between life and death. Since the sense of sight keeps obscuring rather than clarifying engagement with others, both plays eventually turn away from the perceptive limits of visual art and towards the more profound resolution offered by music and sound. In the predominantly Christian landscape of

---

[38] Death is vanquished at the end of the play and returns only in the briefest description by Heracles: 'I sprang and caught him in my hands' (1142).

[39] See for example Slater 2013: 56. Enterline correspondingly suggests that *The Winter's Tale* is a drama of opposites which deals with 'the difference between speech and silence – or … between agency and impotence, male and female'. See Enterline 1997: 18.

[40] Dillon 2010: 169.

[41] *Hamlet*, 3.2.3–5.

*The Winter's Tale*, prospective awakening is a matter of spiritual commitment since, as Pauline tells Leontes, 'It is required | You do awake your faith' (5.3.94–5). The necessary faith is suggested by a Christian God, but also by the technologies of theatre. While visual art such as painting and statuary allow for near-perfect replication, their representative simulacra prove unsatisfactory and indeed diminishing for those who encounter them. Only theatre, where sight and sound achieve temporary synthesis, promises meaningful inter-relational understanding – even if this resolution remains nothing more or less than a tantalising prospect.[42]

[42] The author would like to thank Gary Browning, Elizabeth Craik, Nathaniel Hess, Tanya Pollard and the editors of this volume for their helpful comments during the writing and revising of this essay.

# Touching Death in Euripides' *Alcestis*

*Chiara Blanco*

One of the most prominent senses in ancient Greece, touch has pride of place in emotional accounts of Greek literature, with particular regard to those taking place on stage. Interactions between tragic characters, Euripidean in particular, rely considerably on the haptic sense, with touch being used as a vehicle to convey a plethora of different emotions: from sexual predatory attitude to empathy and consolation.[1] This chapter sets out to explore the relation between touch and human emotions in Euripides, by focusing on *Alcestis* as a case study. I aim to show that by exploiting the act of touching, Euripides succeeds in increasing the already palpable ambiguity of the play, capitalising essentially on contemporary funerary motifs in order to create an ending that is as familiar to his audience as it is grotesquely bizarre.

Rich in pathetic and intensely moving scenes, Euripides' *Alcestis* deals with the story of Admetus' wife, who decides to die on her husband's behalf, as per Apollo's concession. In the first part of the chapter, I investigate the use of touch and how it is employed in the tragedy to express the emotional and cognitive spheres of the characters. By exploring the different uses of touch in critical scenes of the play, I show that Euripides exploits the haptic sense not just to convey dramatically relevant emotions but, most importantly, to characterise the main personages on stage, Alcestis in particular. In the second part of the chapter, I focus on the role of touch in the *anagnōrisis* which takes place at the end of the play. I argue that the recognition scene purposefully recreates a common motif

---

[1] See for instance Eur. *Bacch.* 1117–18, where Pentheus touches Agave's cheeks in his last attempt to let his mother recognise him so that she might spare his life, *Ion* 1439–44, where the eponymous character encounters his mother, and Helen's encounter with Menelaos at *Hel.* 627–35. See also *Phoen.* 1693–4 and 1700–1, where blind Oedipus recognises his dead mother and wife Jocasta, and his dead sons, respectively, by touching them. A similar case is found at the end of Soph. *OT*, Euripides' 1480–3 where, as suggested by Worman (2020: 30), 'touch is a physical act and a sign with multiplying significances', which generates among Oedipus and his daughters a sense of belonging. Another interesting case is provided by the encounter between Orestes and Electra in Euripides' Eur. *El.*, 223–4. On touch used to express predatory behaviour see e.g. [Aesch.] *PV.* 848–9. On the role of touch in Greek tragedy see Worman 2020; on touch in ancient literature see Purves 2017.

of classical Attic funerary art: that of touching the departed, also known as *dexiōsis*. The importance of touch in Greek funerary reliefs has recently been brought up to attention, highlighting the prominent role of gestures in stimulating emotional responses from the spectators.[2] I argue that Euripides intentionally deploys this device in the climactic scene of the play: the muteness and immobility of Alcestis recreate the staticity of the funerary motif, which is further evoked by the physical contact between the two spouses.

## 1. Touching Emotions in the House of Admetus

Touch is used metaphorically throughout *Alcestis* to refer to human emotions. More specifically, the intense effects of emotions on individuals can be represented through the act of touching their inner organs, thus affecting them on a visceral level. The first metaphorical mention of touch in a deeply emotional sense comes from the leader of chorus A, at line 108: to express his emotional involvement in their masters' loathsome destiny, he replies to the chorus by using the expression: ἔθιγες ψυχῆς, ἔθιγες δὲ φρενῶν ('you have touched my heart, you have touched my soul').[3] Here the verb θιγγάνω is used to express the deep affection of the character, and his personal participation in the tragic events taking place in the play.[4] This expression appears to be idiomatic in Euripides, and is found both in *Trojan Women* and *Suppliants*: in both instances, there is no mention of the ψυχή, and only the φρένες are said to be touched as a manifestation of utter grief due to a loss. In *Trojan Women* 1217–19 the Chorus, speaking to Hecuba, lament the death of baby Astyanax (ἒ ἔ, φρενῶν | ἔθιγες ἔθιγες· ὦ μέγας ἐμοί ποτ᾽ ἂν | ἀνάκτωρ πόλεως), whereas in *Suppliants* 1161–2 the children of the slain chieftains express their grief for the loss of their fathers (ἔκλαυσα τόδε κλύων ἔπος | στυγνότατον· ἔθιγέ μου φρενῶν). Likewise, in *Hippolytus* 312, when Phaedra hears the name of Theseus' son, she is asked by the nurse whether she is touched by it: the verb used is, again, θιγγάνω (θιγγάνει σέθεν τόδε;).

Another interesting occurrence of the use of touch employed in a figurative sense is found at line 964: the chorus are wondering about the unbearable grief which befell the house of Admetus. While pondering the different scenarios, they say to have touched 'many

---

[2] Arrington 2018: 7–27. See also Davies 1985: 627–40, Spencer 1995: 126–8.
[3] All translations of Euripides' *Alcestis* are from Kovacs 2002.
[4] Interestingly, a similar expression is also found in Aesch. *Ag.* 432, when the Chorus describe the grief of the Greeks whose loved ones had died at Troy: the organ which is figuratively touched is, in this case, the liver (πολλὰ γοῦν θιγγάνει πρὸς ἧπαρ). Likewise, the figurative use of ἅπτω concerning emotions, and grief in particular, is not rare: a case in point is provided by Eur. *Rhes.* 915–16, where the Muse addresses Thamyris by claiming that he has touched her (φρήν. ἦ πολλὰ μὲν ζῶν, πολλὰ δ᾽ εἰς Ἅιδου μολών, | Φιλάμμονος παῖ, τῆς ἐμῆς ἧψω φρενός). On touch and emotions in antiquity see also Purves 2017: 1–20, 14 in particular, and Worman 2017: 34–49.

thoughts' (πλείστων ἀψάμενος λόγων). Here the sense of touch is employed from a different perspective: the act of thinking puts the chorus in a more active role, as opposed to the chorus leader, who is victim of the emotions which he experiences. Likewise, a similar use of ἅπτω is found in Euripides' *Hecuba* 674–5, where the maidservant claims that the queen, unaware of the death of her son Polydorus, does not 'touch' her sorrows: ἥδ᾽ οὐδὲν οἶδεν, ἀλλά μοι Πολυξένην | θρηνεῖ, νέων δὲ πημάτων οὐχ ἅπτεται. Here, too, ἅπτω is used to express Hecuba's figurative grasp, thus representing an extension of their cognitive capacity.

In Euripides, the connection between touch and the emotional and cognitive sphere of the individuals presupposes their direct involvement in the process, which moves from an emotion which affects their vital organs, to the active action of grasping conceptual objects like thoughts, and this also applies to *Alcestis*. Interestingly, though, haptic interactions in the play, as I will show below, have the function of highlighting the detachment of the eponymous character from the events taking place around her, thus failing to show any emotional or cognitive involvement on her side. A clear case in point is found when Admetus seeks consolation for his wife's sacrifice, and claims that, being dead, she will not be touched by any sorrow. The verb chosen by Euripides in this case is ἅπτω:

τῆς μὲν γὰρ οὐδὲν ἄλγος ἅψεταί ποτε … (937)

for she will never be touched by any grief …

This expression closely resonates with the one found in a fragment ascribed to Aeschylus' *Philoctetes* 255, namely: ἄλγος δ᾽ οὐδὲν ἅπτεται νεκροῦ. For both Alcestis and Philoctetes death seems to be a consolation as it relieves mortals from suffering.

Whereas the example above takes place after her funeral procession, Alcestis is represented as a liminal character throughout the play already before her death, as is also shown by her haptic interactions. That Alcestis in Euripides' homonymous tragedy is characterised as a borderline figure, being suspended between the realm of the dead and that of the living, has been adequately discussed.[5] As per Admetus' own admission, his

---

[5]   See e.g. line 141. See for instance Buxton 2013: 205, who argues that 'virtually the whole of the play, Alcestis herself is presented as being between life and death', and further supports this claim by positing that Alcestis' actions in the play show that she is in the process of dying even before being dead. Markantonatos 2013: 24 focuses on 'the bestial images clustered around Alcestis' and argues that 'the death-doomed woman is constantly pictured as a mere animal ready to be slaughtered'. Parker 2007: ad loc. argues that Alcestis, who bathes and dresses herself elegantly, already 'treats herself as a corpse'. Of the same opinion is also Bassi 2018: 47, who argues that 'Alcestis' likeness thus occupies a point on a continuum somewhere between her living body and her inanimate corpse'. See also Worman 2020: 43, who notices how, differently from other dying tragic characters, Alcestis is striking for her 'absence of expression of pain'. On Alcestis' liminal status with specific reference to the act of seeing see Craik in this volume.

wife 'is and is no more' (521), since 'one who is doomed to die is dead already' (527). Even before her death, Alcestis' behaviour does not seem to comply to that of the living, and strongly reminds the audience of her imminent death. Thus, for instance, when the maidservant describes the sombre atmosphere pervading the palace at the opening of the tragedy, she also specifies that Admetus holds Alcestis in his arms on the bed: the audience at this point would expect the interactions between the spouses to stir intense emotions or tenderness at the very least. Their anticipation, however, is soon disappointed: Admetus is said to hold his wife like a pitiful burden, and Alcestis' almost total lack of mobility and rigidity have a somewhat unnatural connotation since her very first appearance:

κλαίει γ᾽ ἄκοιτιν ἐν χεροῖν φίλην ἔχων
καὶ μὴ προδοῦναι λίσσεται, τἀμήχανα
ζητῶν· φθίνει γὰρ καὶ μαραίνεται νόσῳ.
παρειμένη δέ, χειρὸς ἄθλιον βάρος,
<κεῖται, τὸ σῶμα δ᾽ οὐκέτ᾽ ὀρθῶσαι σθένει.> (201–4)

Yes, he weeps, holding his beloved wife in his arms, and he begs her not to abandon him, asking for the impossible. For she is waning and wasting with her malady. And now, her body limp, a pitiful burden in his arms, <she lies unable to raise herself up>.

Devastated by the disease, Alcestis' body is not able to move naturally anymore.[6] As the maid explains, little is left of the woman, but what Euripides calls a 'pitiful burden' (ἄθλιον βάρος): Alcestis lies immobile in her bed, and asks Admetus not to remarry after her death, fearing for their children and how their prospective stepmother might treat them. The reaction of Admetus is singular, as he expresses his wish to commission a simulacrum of Alcestis, after her departure, to position on their marriage bed, so that by embracing the statue he will be reminded of his spouse:

σοφῇ δὲ χειρὶ τεκτόνων δέμας τὸ σὸν
εἰκασθὲν ἐν λέκτροισιν ἐκταθήσεται,
ᾧ προσπεσοῦμαι καὶ περιπτύσσων χέρας
ὄνομα καλῶν σὸν τὴν φίλην ἐν ἀγκάλαις

---

[6]    As Worman 2020: 44 argues, Alcestis' formal handing over of the children to Admetus (375: ἐπὶ τοῖσδε παῖδας χειρὸς ἐξ ἐμῆς δέχου) 'may not involve actual touching, although it does serve to settle Alcestis more firmly in her family circle'.

δόξω γυναῖκα καίπερ οὐκ ἔχων ἔχειν·
ψυχρὰν μέν, οἶμαι, τέρψιν, ἀλλ᾽ ὅμως βάρος
ψυχῆς ἀπαντλοίην ἄν. (348–54)

An image of you shaped by the hand of skilled craftsmen shall be laid out in my bed. I shall fall into its arms, and as I embrace it and call your name I shall imagine, though I have her not, that I hold my dear wife in my arms, a cold pleasure, to be sure, but thus I shall lighten my soul's heaviness.

When Admetus' wish is revealed to the audience however, one realises that his desire is already taking place on stage: the imaginary interactions between Admetus and Alcestis' simulacrum do not differ much from the dynamics between husband and wife (201–4). Once again touch is of primary importance: just like living Alcestis, her simulacrum will be the object of manipulations performed by male hands, those of the artisan who will forge it *in primis* (348–9). More importantly, while referring to the joy that he could get from interacting with the statue, Admetus uses an apparently ambiguous expression which primarily refers to the sphere of perception, namely, 'cold pleasure' (353: ψυχρὰν τέρψιν). Whereas the coldness would *prima facie* refer to the passive reaction which Admetus would get from the artifact as opposed to that of his wife, one is left to wonder whether the original and still living Alcestis has ever shown a more proactive attitude in the play.[7] The cold contact with the statue evokes both the materiality of the artifact and the coldness of a corpse, into which Alcestis is slowly turning.[8] In either case, Admetus' touch is not destined to be requited. It would appear that Euripides' intention is precisely to muddy the waters between Alcestis' human self and her artificial reproduction, in order to prepare the audience for the final recognition scene, a point to which I will return below. Although Alcestis' interactions do involve touch, she is consistently represented as the passive receiver. Furthermore, differently from other characters, Alcestis' touch does not represent a window into her cognitive sphere: whereas, as discussed above, the emotions of the chorus leader are stirred by figuratively touching his innermost parts, thus trespassing the permeable barrier of his skin, Alcestis' haptic contacts are entirely developed on, and confined to, an epidermic

---

[7]   See Gavrilenko 2011: 200: 'Alceste, son partenaire sexuel, ne semble pas être à ses côtés même s'il est effectivement présent'.

[8]   See on this point Bassi 2018: 46–7, who argues that the adjective ψυχρός is used for corpses (see i.e. Soph. *OC* 622), and further emphasises the 'out-of-placeness' and simultaneous centrality of Alcestis' corpse, which is stressed by the fact that she dies before the eyes of the audience, something atypical in Greek tragedy.

level, highlighting the limits of her characterisation.[9] The skin of the heroine, whose state is suspended between life and death, functions as an impermeable barrier: interestingly, while Alcestis is able to cry (176; 183–5), she does not bleed, nor is any other bodily fluid described in the account of her malady (203–12) – the heroine appears to be caught in a permanent state between life and death.

## 2. To Hades and Back: Admetus and Alcestis Between Life and Death

Whereas Euripides emphasises how Alcestis, though still living, already behaves and is treated as a dead woman, Admetus' ontological status is more complex to analyse. I argue that the image of Alcestis' simulacrum highlights another ontological paradox in the play, which will become clear in the recognition scene: the corpse that is actually missing is not Alcestis', but Admetus'.[10] Admetus *is* the one who should technically be dead, had Alcestis not agreed to die on his behalf, and this is repeatedly stressed throughout the play. The exchange between Death and Apollo taking place at the outset of the tragedy already reveals to the audience that Admetus is alive thanks to Apollo's tricks (12), which Thanatos considers an injustice (30: ἀδικεῖς).[11] This is also reiterated in lines 462–3, where the chorus specify that Alcestis has redeemed her husband from Hades, which would make Admetus a revenant, rather than a proper living being. It is the exchange between Admetus and his dying wife, and the image of her simulacrum, however, that trigger a new development in his character, whose ontological ambiguity is revealed from this point onwards with increasing clarity.

As noted by Mary Stieber, 'Admetus couches sentimental and sexual thoughts in formal religious and funerary language'.[12] More specifically, Stieber argues that the use of verbs such as ἐκτείνω (349), προσπίπτω (350) and περιπτύσσω (350) highlights the ambiguity of the scene, which is simultaneously erotic, as suggested by Admetus' desire to embrace the body of the statue in bed, but also funereal, as the artifact would have the

[9] Worman 2020: 43 notices that while her death scene is dominated by the constant reminder of the proximity of the Underworld, 'those living bodies around her seem barely proximate and do not, for the most part, touch her. The lack of touch also distinguishes this body *in extremis*'.
[10] Cf. Segal 1993: 45, who argues that the simulacrum of Alcestis is a *kolossos*, put in place of a missing corpse, Alcestis' in this case.
[11] On Apollo's relationship with Admetus and guest-friendship in the play see Schein 1988: 179–206.
[12] Stieber 2011: 73. See also Markantonatos 2013: 149 n. 42, who argues that although the image of Admetus sharing the marriage bed with a simulacrum of his dead wife 'holds the potential of the horrifyingly derisory, not to say the sexually deviant, it would be unwise to read too much into the comic aspect of the idea', and further notes (148) that the verb σέβομαι at line 279, suggests a connection with the divine.

role of a shrine, for Admetus to remember and venerate his dead wife.[13] What Stieber has not focused on, however, is the relevance of touch in the passage and its relation to the crucial role it plays in funerary scenes: haptic interactions between the deceased and their close relatives are significantly present both in ancient Greek art and literature.[14] As Arrington notes, touching the dead allowed the mourners 'to understand the presence of death with their bodies as well as their minds'.[15] I argue that this also applies to the case of Admetus, as lines 348–54 bring to the forefront his own ontological paradox, of which he seems to become progressively more aware.[16] *Alcestis* 350 (ᾧ προσπεσοῦμαι καὶ περιπτύσσων χέρας, 'I shall fall into its arms … as I embrace it') closely recalls lines in the *Hecuba* where the ghost of Polydorus wishes to be allotted a proper burial, after receiving the last embrace of his mother:

τοὺς γὰρ κάτω σθένοντας ἐξῃτησάμην
τύμβου κυρῆσαι κἀς χέρας μητρὸς πεσεῖν. (49-50)

I have won permission from the powers below
to pass into my mother's hands and receive burial.[17]

---

[13] Stieber 1998: 77. See also Harsh 1944: 169, who argues that the statue represents Admetus' tangible intention to establish a cult to honour the memory of his late wife. Segal 1993: 39 argues that Alcestis' statue is 'a point of crossing between artistry and ritual commemoration, between the aesthetic and the religious'.

[14] Classical Greek funerary art provides many examples of haptic interactions between the living and the deceased, both in inscriptions (e.g. *CEG* 1, n. 171; 2, n. 586), and vases (e.g. an Attic red-figure *loutrophoros*, now in the National Archaeological Museum, Athens, 1452). See Arrington 2018: 15–16. With regard to literature, perhaps the best known and most *touching* example is provided by Eur. *Med.* 1403 when Jason begs his wife to allow him to bid the last farewell to their dead children at the end of the play, he expresses his wish to touch their skin for the last time – a wish that Medea does not grant him. Jason replies by calling the gods to witness that Medea, after killing their children, also forbids him to touch them and bury them (1410–12). In Eur. *Supp.* 943, Adrastus suggests that the mothers of the slain chieftains must touch them before the burial. Another interesting example is found in Soph. *Aj.* 1410–11, where Teucer invites Ajax's son Eurysaces to touch the corpse of his father and help him to carry the body. See also Eur. *Phoen.* 1699–700, in which the touch of blind Oedipus functions simultaneously as recognition of and farewell to the dead bodies of his children. The motif of touching the deceased was also present in Archaic Greece: see e.g. Hom. *Il.* 23.136–7, 24.710–12. For visual evidence see e.g. Metropolitan Museum of Art, New York, inv. 14.130.15, Beazley Archive Database, 9018110.

[15] Arrington 2018: 16.

[16] See Beye 1959: 115: 'He [*sc.* Admetus] closes upon the subject of his own death, a subject with which he becomes increasingly more involved'. As argued by Segal (1993: 39): 'Admetus' realisation of Alcestis' sacrifice does not make his existence livable: his life is in fact a nonlife'. See on this point Gavrilenko 2011: 196, who argues that after seeing his wife dying Admetus is strongly and irretrievably attracted to death: 'le cas d'Admète peut relever de la "maladie du deuil" qui se manifeste par un fort èlan vers un être cher décédé, vers son "cadaver exquis."'

[17] Translation from Kovacs 2002.

The expressions used by both Admetus and Polydorus are strikingly similar: the verb πίπτω is present in both passages to express the action of falling into the arms (χέρας) of the women. What is interesting to notice, however, is that whereas Polydorus is dead, Admetus is still alive, and Alcestis, in whose arms he wishes to fall, is the dying character in the play.[18] As the language shows, Admetus is already thinking of himself as deceased, and employs words and expressions which are suggestive of his liminal status in between the realm of the dead and that of the living. For from this point onwards, Admetus' attitude drastically changes, and reveals a new preoccupation concerning death – not his wife's, this time, but his own. As discussed above, Admetus' wish is not only that of having a simulacrum of his wife, but also to lie together with her in death:

εἰ δ᾿ Ὀρφέως μοι γλῶσσα καὶ μέλος παρῆν,
ὥστ᾿ ἢ κόρην Δήμητρος ἢ κείνης πόσιν
ὕμνοισι κηλήσαντά σ᾿ ἐξ Ἅιδου λαβεῖν,
κατῆλθον ἄν, καί μ᾿ οὔθ᾿ ὁ Πλούτωνος κύων
οὔθ᾿ οὑπὶ κώπῃ ψυχοπομπὸς ἂν Χάρων
ἔσχ᾿ ἄν, πρὶν ἐς φῶς σὸν καταστῆσαι βίον.
ἀλλ᾿ οὖν ἐκεῖσε προσδόκα μ᾿, ὅταν θάνω,
καὶ δῶμ᾿ ἑτοίμαζ᾿, ὡς συνοικήσουσά μοι.
ἐν ταῖσιν αὐταῖς γάρ μ᾿ ἐπισκήψω κέδροις
σοὶ τούσδε θεῖναι πλευρά τ᾿ ἐκτεῖναι πέλας
πλευροῖσι τοῖς σοῖς· μηδὲ γὰρ θανών ποτε
σοῦ χωρὶς εἴην τῆς μόνης πιστῆς ἐμοί. (357–68)

If I had the voice and music of Orpheus so that I could charm Demeter's daughter or her husband with song and fetch you from Hades, I would have gone down to the Underworld, and neither Pluto's hound nor Charon the ferryman of souls standing at the oar would have kept me from bringing you back to the light alive. But now wait for me to arrive there when I die and prepare a home where you may dwell with me. For I shall command my children here to bury me in the same coffin with you and to lay out my body next to yours. Never, even in death, may I be parted from you, the woman who alone has been faithful to me!

[18] See on this point also the recognition scene in Eur. *Ion* 1443–4, where Ion ironically claims that by being in the arms of his mother, who deemed him to be dead, he seems to be simultaneously dead and not dead (ἀλλ᾿ ὦ φίλη μοι μῆτερ, ἐν χεροῖν σέθεν | ὁ κατθανών τε κοὐ θανὼν φαντάζομαι).

The sight of his wife wasting away before his eyes, triggers in Admetus the desire to go to Hades and rescue her – a wish with a clearly ironic undertone, as it comes from the very same man who condemned her to die in order to spare his own life.[19] Furthermore, as Admetus realises that his wish will not be attainable, he starts planning their future life in the Underworld, and even goes as far as to ask Alcestis to prepare a home for them, claiming that he will ask their children to bury him in the same coffin with her – a point which, as I will show below, will be crucial to the interpretation of the recognition scene. Admetus' abrupt preoccupation with death puzzles the audience, so that by the time of his first encounter with Heracles, they are left to wonder whether the solemnity and ambiguity of Admetus' words refer to his dead wife or, rather, to himself:

Ηρ. ἆ, μὴ πρόκλαι᾽ ἄκοιτιν, ἐς τότ᾽ ἀμβαλοῦ.
Αδ. τέθνηχ᾽ ὁ μέλλων καὶ θανὼν οὐκ ἔστ᾽ ἔτι.
Ηρ. χωρὶς τό τ᾽ εἶναι καὶ τὸ μὴ νομίζεται.
Αδ. σὺ τῇδε κρίνεις, Ἡράκλεις, κείνῃ δ᾽ ἐγώ. (526–9)

HERACLES. Oh, do not mourn your wife beforehand! Put it off till the day!
ADMETUS. Someone who is doomed to die is dead, has died and is no more.
HERACLES. Existence and non-existence are deemed to be separate things.
ADMETUS. You have your view on this, Heracles, and I have mine.

Just like Alcestis, Admetus is indeed doomed to die: this point, at which Euripides hints in the first part of the play, is made clearer in the exchange between Admetus and his father. King Pheres states that his son lives beyond his fated day (695: ζῇς παρελθὼν τὴν πεπρωμένην τύχην), thus implicitly suggesting that Admetus *should* be already dead. Pheres continues to provoke his son, by stating that one should just live one life instead of two (712), and asking him if he intends to remarry so that he could let his other wives die on his behalf (720), thus making it clear that Admetus himself is not only part, but the actual origin of the ontological paradox taking place on stage. Later in the play, Admetus' wish to die is expressed with increased vigour:

πῶς ἂν ὀλοίμην;
ἦ βαρυδαίμονα μήτηρ μ᾽ ἔτεκεν.
ζηλῶ φθιμένους, κείνων ἔραμαι,
κεῖν᾽ ἐπιθυμῶ δώματα ναίειν.

---

[19] For a full list of works discussing the ironic elements in *Alcestis* and its status as 'prosatyric drama' see Markantonatos 2013: 92 n. 10; see also Marshall 2000: 229–38. Cf. Lloyd-Jones 1990: 231.

οὔτε γὰρ αὐγὰς χαίρω προσορῶν
οὔτ᾽ ἐπὶ γαίας πόδα πεζεύων·
τοῖον ὅμηρόν μ᾽ ἀποσυλήσας
Ἅιδῃ Θάνατος παρέδωκεν.

...

ὦ μακρὰ πένθη λῦπαί τε φίλων
τῶν ὑπὸ γαίας.
τί μ᾽ ἐκώλυσας ῥῖψαι τύμβου
τάφρον ἐς κοίλην καὶ μετ᾽ ἐκείνης
τῆς μέγ᾽ ἀρίστης κεῖσθαι φθίμενον;
δύο δ᾽ ἀντὶ μιᾶς Ἅιδης ψυχὰς
τὰς πιστοτάτας σὺν ἂν ἔσχεν, ὁμοῦ
χθονίαν λίμνην διαβάντε. (864–71, 895–902)

I wish I could die! It was to an ill fate that my mother bore me. I envy the dead,
I long for their state, I yearn to dwell in those halls below. For I take no joy in
looking on the light or in walking about on the earth. Such is the hostage Death
took from me and handed over to Hades.

...

Oh, how great is the pain and grief for loved ones who lie beneath the earth!
Why did you keep me from throwing myself into the open grave and lying there
dead with her, the best of women? Hades would have had two most faithful souls
instead of one, crossing the Underworld's lake together.

In the short span of thirty-three lines Admetus' desire of death quickly escalates: 'I
wish I could die' (πῶς ἂν ὀλοίμην;) at line 864, followed by 'I envy the dead, I long for
their state, I yearn to dwell in those halls below' (ζηλῶ φθιμένους, κείνων ἔραμαι, | κεῖν᾽
ἐπιθυμῶ δώματα ναίειν) at lines 866–7, reaching a peak at line 897 when he asks the
chorus why they kept him from jumping in his wife's coffin (τί μ᾽ ἐκώλυσας ῥῖψαι τύμβου
| τάφρον ἐς κοίλην καὶ μετ᾽ ἐκείνης | τῆς μέγ᾽ ἀρίστης κεῖσθαι φθίμενον;). In what follows,
I argue that this climactically built ambiguity and tension find their final resolution in the
recognition scene between the two spouses.

## 3. Till Death Do Us Part, and Beyond

Euripides, it would appear, blurs the line between life and death not only regarding Alcestis, but also Admetus. Repeatedly wishing to die and yet desperately defending his right to live with his father, Admetus seems to become an increasingly liminal, borderline character, just like Alcestis had been. And yet, I would argue, Euripides takes this ambiguity a step further by employing references to well-known funerary motifs, which move away from the verbal sphere and towards the visual impact of contemporary funereal art.

The first reference to an artifact reproducing Alcestis' features is found in lines 348–54, where Admetus expresses his wish to have a simulacrum of his wife placed on their marital bed after her death. As discussed above, this device already instils in the audience the doubt that Alcestis' attitude might not be too different from that of the mentioned artifact, as the rigidity of her limbs and limited movements would suggest. This section becomes particularly relevant to the analysis of the recognition scene taking place at the end of the play.

Many interpretations have been put forward with regard to the identity of the woman brought to Admetus by Heracles.[20] What is striking about her is the lack of any cognitive, emotional or indeed vital signs, and how touch is, again, used to denote her passive attitude.[21] The prevailing reading of the scene is that the woman on stage is the dead Alcestis whom Heracles has brought back to life.[22] I disagree with this claim on account of several arguments: first, Heracles himself expresses his wish, and simultaneously his inability, to fetch Admetus' dead wife in lines 1072–4. Second, Admetus' rhetorical question about the prospect of placing the woman in his marriage bed (1055) immediately connects her with the artifact of Alcestis mentioned in lines 348–54. Stieber argued that the silent immobile woman whom Heracles presents on

---

[20] Segal 1993: 46 follows Cook 1971: 97 and argues that the woman brought on stage by Heracles is Alcestis, although 'her silence and Admetus' term *demas* (form, body, 1133; cf. 348) also make her, initially, a semblance of the statue'. Drew 1931: 295–319 argues that Heracles brings on stage the actual corpse of Alcestis, whereas Kott 1973: 88–9, 108 argues that the woman is not Alcestis but another woman, whom Admetus symbolically marries at the end of the play.

[21] Much has been written on Alcestis' silence and passive attitude in the end of the play. Some scholars have argued that her silent is consistent with her passive attitude in the play, and subordination to Admetus (e.g. Foley 2001: 317; cf. Burnett 1965: 255 n. 24), or might even be a reaction to Admetus' choice to let her die on his behalf (Drew 1931: 305, Paduano: 1969: 196). Other hypotheses range from Euripides' aversion to the use of a third speaking actor (Paley 1857: 301, Hayley 1898 ad loc., Dale 1961: 129, Paduano 1969: 196; cf. Verrall 1895: 69–70), to a parodic reference to Aeschylean silences (Taplin 1972: 57–97).

[22] Markantonatos 2013: 151–9 links the return of Alcestis from the Underworld to Attic Eleusinian–Orphic traditions; see also Sourvinou-Inwood 2003: 318. As noticed by Worman 2020: 232, although at line 1062 we find the only mention of Alcestis' name, 'this name is not attached to the woman standing [on stage]'.

stage as Alcestis is meant to be understood as a funerary statue of Admetus' deceased wife.[23] Despite considering both the possibility that the artifact might be either a statue-in-the-round or a funerary relief, she concludes that the former might be more plausible, and further hypothesises that, considering the setting of the play, 'an Archaic Attic *kore* would seem perfectly appropriate'.[24] Although I agree with Stieber's hypothesis that the woman on stage is a funerary statue of Alcestis, I argue that what Euripides has in mind is a very specific funerary motif, borrowed from Attic grave reliefs, around which he fashions the *anagnōrisis* between the two spouses. Touch is again crucial in the analysis of the motif.

Attic funerary monuments from the fifth century are replete with scenes involving the haptic sense, with particular regard to the 'handshake' motif, known as *dexiōsis*. This motif, which is mostly present on Athenian classical reliefs, does not seem to be confined to funerary art: the gesture also appeared in fifth-century vases in a matrimonial context.[25] Late Archaic and classical black- and red-figure vases also display scenes of *dexiōsis* involving well-known mythological characters, Heracles in particular. The hero is often portrayed clasping hands with the gods, as a confirmation of their endorsement of his divine nature, mostly with Athena.[26] One example in particular, a *lekythos* in Berlin, shows Heracles' attempt to rescue Peirithoos from the Underworld.[27] From the mid fifth century BC, however, the *dexiōsis* began to be applied more frequently to non-mythological characters, as for example in a well-known large krater in New York, where a woman and a young man greet each other in Hades by clasping hands.[28] Davies further argues that in the classical period the motif became particularly popular on Attic grave stelai, where the two main figures shaking hands are either portrayed one seated and one standing, or both standing. Interpreting these scenes has proven difficult, and many hypotheses have been put forward, according to the different contexts of these representations: whereas some scenes have been interpreted as greeting scenes, others seem to portray farewells.[29] What seems to be unquestionable, however, is that the act of

[23]  Stieber 1998: 77 argues that 'contrary to traditional Greek practice, which required ἐκφορά ("carrying out") and burial on the third day, Admetus has Alcestis buried within the day', simultaneously admitting that the 'apparently incongruous chronology' which significantly condenses Greek traditional funerary rituals can be explained by 'poetic license' and 'dramaturgical logic'. See also Segal 1993: 39, who argues that 'Heracles becomes the bearer of art's victory over death'.

[24]  Stieber 1998: 78.

[25]  See e.g. British Museum, inv. GR 1923.1–18.1; Boston, Museum of Fine Arts, inv. 33.56

[26]  Some examples include: Boston Museum of Fine Arts, inv. 97.205; Munich, Antiken Sammlung, inv. 1556; Museo Nazionale di Antichità, inv. C3; British Museum, inv. B226.

[27]  Berlin, Antikenmuseen, inv. 30035.

[28]  New York, Metropolitan Museum, inv. 08.258.21.

[29]  Davies 1985: 628.

touching and clasping hands creates 'powerful, effective, and comforting memorials', as can be inferred from one of the best known examples, the so called relief of Philoxenos and Philoumene, from ca 430–390 BC.[30] Here two standing figures, a man and a woman, are touching and clasping hands.[31] The intensity of the encounter is palpable, and also highlighted by the fact that both appear to look into each other's eyes, while engaging in the *dexiōsis*. The scene is arguably recurrent and I would argue that in many ways it appears to recall what the text of *Alcestis* invites us to imagine happening on stage at the end of the play. Not only are we looking at a still frame of Admetus and the veiled woman during the act of *dexiōsis*, but what is more the very act of clasping hands between Alcestis and Admetus is induced by Heracles – a character that, as discussed above, was traditionally associated with representations of *dexiōsis*. Further to that, the exchanges between Heracles and the manservant first, and Admetus later, seem to imply that funerary motif of the *dexiōsis* is constantly present during the *anagnōrisis* scene:

Θε. ὀρθὴν παρ' οἶμον ἢ 'πὶ Λάρισαν φέρει
τύμβον κατόψῃ ξεστὸν ἐκ προαστίου.
Ηρ. ὦ πολλὰ τλᾶσα καρδία καὶ χεὶρ ἐμή,
νῦν δεῖξον οἶον παῖδά σ' ἡ Τιρυνθία
ἐγείνατ' Ἠλεκτρύωνος Ἀλκμήνη Διί.
δεῖ γάρ με σῶσαι τὴν θανοῦσαν ἀρτίως
γυναῖκα κἀς τόνδ' αὖθις ἱδρῦσαι δόμον
Ἄλκηστιν Ἀδμήτῳ θ' ὑπουργῆσαι χάριν.
ἐλθὼν δ' ἄνακτα τὸν μελάμπεπλον νεκρῶν
Θάνατον φυλάξω, καί νιν εὑρήσειν δοκῶ
πίνοντα τύμβου πλησίον προσφαγμάτων.
κἄνπερ λοχαίας αὐτὸν ἐξ ἕδρας συθεὶς
μάρψω, κύκλον γε περιβαλὼν χεροῖν ἐμαῖν,
οὐκ ἔστιν ὅστις αὐτὸν ἐξαιρήσεται
μογοῦντα πλευρά, πρὶν γυναῖκ' ἐμοὶ μεθῇ.
ἢν δ' οὖν ἁμάρτω τῆσδ' ἄγρας καὶ μὴ μόλῃ
πρὸς αἱματηρὸν πελανόν, εἶμι τῶν κάτω
Κόρης Ἄνακτός τ' εἰς ἀνηλίους δόμους,
αἰτήσομαί τε καὶ πέποιθ' ἄξειν ἄνω
Ἄλκηστιν, ὥστε χεροῖν ἐνθεῖναι ξένου … (835–54)

---

[30] Los Angeles, Paul Getty Museum, 83.AA.378.
[31] Arrington, 2018: 12.

MANSERVANT. You will see from the outskirts of the city, next to the straight road that leads to Larisa, a sculpted tomb.

HERACLES. O heart and hand that have endured so much, now show what kind of son Tirynthian Alcmene, daughter of Electryon, bore to Zeus! I must save the woman who has just died and show my gratitude to Admetus by restoring Alcestis once more to this house. I shall go and look out for the black-robed lord of the dead, Death himself, and I think I shall find him drinking from the offerings near the tomb. And if once I rush from ambush and catch him in my side-crushing grip, no one shall take him from me until he releases the woman to me. But if I fail to catch this quarry and he does not come to the blood offering, I shall go down to the sunless house of Persephone and her lord in the world below and shall ask for Alcestis, and I think I shall bring her up and put her in the hands of my friend.

The ironic undertone of the passage is clear from Heracles' words, as he describes his intention of wrestling with Thanatos, who he suspects might be drinking the offerings near Alcestis' tomb. There are two details in this passage which I would like to focus on in particular: first, when Heracles asks the manservant where he could find Alcestis, the latter mentions her tomb. As already noted by Stieber, the proximity to the tomb indicates that Heracles' Alcestis is closely linked to the funerary sphere.[32] The expression used by the servant, τύμβον ξεστόν, is also relevant in the identification of the funerary artifact: the adjective ξεστόν means 'carved, sculpted' (LSJ s.v.), as is the case in Euripides' *Iphigeneia in Tauris* (111–12: ξεστὸν ἄγαλμα) and in Euripides' Helen, where it again refers to a tomb (986: τῷδ' ἐπὶ ξεστῷ τάφῳ).

The manservant therefore refers here specifically to at least a part of a carved tomb. It is at this point that Heracles claims that he will fetch Alcestis, by fighting Thanatos with his 'side-crushing grip': his ironic reply betrays the ambiguity of his task. If we take Thanatos here to refer, in a figurative sense, to Alcestis' tomb, Heracles is saying that he will be crushing its sides, indeed in a rather literal sense, so that he could remove the figure of Alcestis, thus setting her free (849).[33] In other words, the hero, who admittedly is not able to fetch dead Alcestis from the Underworld, opts for an alternative solution: crushing the 'sides' of her funerary monument to remove her statue instead. The crucial role of the tomb in Heracles' rescue of Alcestis is also reiterated at line 1142, where

[32]  Stieber, 1998: 75–6; Stieber also argues that lines 1002–4, where the chorus address the woman directly, is a funerary epitaph, which would prove that the statue has also been inscribed.

[33]  Cf. Segal 1993: 71: 'Heracles' victory over Death in an all-male, agonistic setting …. also validates the "contest" of dramatic performance itself, the theatrical activity that can represent an escape from death'.

the hero reveals to Admetus that his fight with Thanatos took place near the woman's tomb. It is Heracles himself, however, who discredits the final version he provides to Admetus, namely that he has rescued Alcestis from Thanatos, and induces disbelief in the audience: when the demigod first presents the woman on stage, he claims that he won her in a public contest (1026–33).

Even more suspiciously, when Heracles denies that he has stolen the woman, his *excusatio non petita* implicitly instils this very same doubt in the audience, which the hero seeks to dispel by adding that he seized her with much labour (1035–6): the words he uses, σὺν πόνῳ λαβών, express a physical effort which is apparently linked to the act of seizing the woman, but not necessarily related to a heroic deed. The same idea of physical effort is also expressed at lines (1025–7: πολλῷ δὲ μόχθῳ…. | …ἀθληταῖσιν ἄξιον πόνον). As the audience are aware of what Heracles' plan was, one would be tempted to connect his physical labour to the equally physical removal of the artifact, which he has supposedly dragged all the way from the cemetery to Admetus' palace (835–6).[34] The same ironic ambiguity dominates the recognition scene:

Αδ. κομίζετ᾽, εἰ χρὴ τήνδε δέξασθαι δόμοις.
Ηρ. οὐκ ἂν μεθείην τὴν γυναῖκα προσπόλοις.
Αδ. σὺ δ᾽ αὐτὸς αὐτὴν εἴσαγ᾽, εἰ δοκεῖ, δόμους.
Ηρ. ἐς σὰς μὲν οὖν ἔγωγε θήσομαι χέρας.
Αδ. οὐκ ἂν θίγοιμι· δῶμα δ᾽ εἰσελθεῖν πάρα.
Ηρ. τῇ σῇ πέποιθα χειρὶ δεξιᾷ μόνῃ.
Αδ. ἄναξ, βιάζῃ μ᾽ οὐ θέλοντα δρᾶν τάδε.
Ηρ. τόλμα προτεῖναι χεῖρα καὶ θιγεῖν ξένης.
Αδ. καὶ δὴ προτείνω, Γοργόν᾽ ὡς καρατομῶν.
<Ηρ. ἔχεις; Αδ. ἔχω, ναί. Ηρ. σῷζέ νυν, καὶ τὸν Διὸς
φήσεις ποτ᾽ εἶναι παῖδα γενναῖον ξένον.>
βλέψον πρὸς αὐτήν, εἴ τι σῇ δοκεῖ πρέπειν
γυναικί· λύπης δ᾽ εὐτυχῶν μεθίστασο.
Αδ. ὦ θεοί, τί λέξω; θαῦμ᾽ ἀνέλπιστον τόδε·
γυναῖκα λεύσσω τήνδ᾽ ἐμὴν ἐτητύμως,
ἢ κέρτομός μ᾽ ἐκ θεοῦ τις ἐκπλήσσει χαρά;
Ηρ. οὐκ ἔστιν, ἀλλὰ τήνδ᾽ ὁρᾷς δάμαρτα σήν.
Αδ. ὅρα δὲ μή τι φάσμα νερτέρων τόδ᾽ ἦ.

[34] From the instructions given to Heracles by the manservant, Markantonatos (2013: 145) infers that Alcestis' tomb might be in 'the northern cemetery of Pherae, an important Thessalian cult-centre'. Cf. Parker (2007 ad loc.), who argues that there is no certain connection between Alcestis' funerary monument and the cemetery of ancient Pherae, since ancient Greeks preferred to build tombs beside main roads.

Ηρ. οὐ ψυχαγωγὸν τόνδ᾽ ἐποιήσω ξένον.
Αδ. ἀλλ᾽ ἣν ἔθαπτον εἰσορῶ δάμαρτ᾽ ἐμήν; (1110–29)

ADMETUS. Take her in, since I must receive her into my house.
HERACLES. I will not release the woman into the hands of servants.
ADMETUS. Take her into the house yourself, if you like.
HERACLES. No, I shall put her into your hands.
ADMETUS. I will not touch her. She may go into the house.
HERACLES. I trust only your right hand.
ADMETUS. My lord, you compel me to do this against my will.
HERACLES. Have the courage to stretch out your hand and touch the stranger.
ADMETUS. There, I stretch it out, as if I were cutting off a Gorgon's head.
HERACLES. Do you have her?
ADMETUS. Yes, I have her.
HERACLES. Then keep her safe, and one day you will say that Zeus's son is a noble guest-friend. Look at her! See whether she bears any resemblance to your wife. Now that you are fortunate, cease your grieving!
ADMETUS. O gods, what shall I say? Here is a wonder past all hoping. Is this truly my wife I see here, or does some delusive joy sent by a god steal my wits?
HERACLES. Not so: the woman you see here is your wife.
ADMETUS. Perhaps it is some ghost from the Underworld.
HERACLES. No raiser of spirits is the man you made your guest-friend.
ADMETUS. But do I see my wife, whom I buried?

Admetus seems to be reluctant to acquiesce Heracles' request to put the woman into his hands. Heracles, however, is adamant: he will not let the servants touch the woman, only Admetus, thus stressing the importance of the spouses' haptic interaction. Even after their contact, Alcestis does not have any reaction: as discussed above, differently from other characters, tactile exchanges do not reveal any emotional depth or agency in her characterisation. First, just like Admetus openly admits that he is not Orpheus, and as such he does not have the power to rescue Alcestis from Hades (357), the same applies to Heracles, as he admits that he cannot raise dead spirits (1128), thus once more denying the possibility that the woman on stage might be dead Alcestis.[35] Second, the scene where Alcestis lies as a pitiful burden in Admetus' arms, in line 204, is what Heracles seeks to recreate on stage again, as he states that he will himself put Alcestis, or

[35] See on this point Dova 2012: 185: 'His [sc. Admetus'] use of the myth of Orpheus remains tangential, hypothetical and imaginary'.

rather her statue, a βάρος indeed, in the arms of her husband (1113). Finally, the act of touching his wife does not suggest any passionate exchange and is instead the realisation of the ψυχρὰν τέρψιν which Admetus had envisaged at line 353, while imagining his interaction with the simulacrum of Alcestis.

Haptic interactions taking place in the recognition scene (1110–15; 1117–18), of which Alcestis is again a mere passive receiver, establish a continuity between living Alcestis (200–4), her simulacrum envisaged by Admetus (348–54), and the artifact brought on stage by Heracles at the end of the play. Likewise, the exchange above seems to exclude the possibility that the woman on stage might be a living woman, as she does not seem to show any signs of movement or agency alike: Admetus asks Heracles to take her in (1110, 1113), whereas the demigod refuses to put her in the hands of the servants (1112, 1114), and it is Admetus who has to stretch his arm to touch her (1118). Finally, what Admetus wishes for himself in lines 363–4, namely to start a new life with his wife in the Underworld is, I argue, what we witness in the final part of the play.

For the *anagnōrisis* finally makes the ironic element in Euripides' characterisation of Admetus unequivocable, as the audience realise that the king's anxiety goes beyond the risk of offending the memory of his wife: Admetus is afraid of touching the speechless woman on stage not because he fears Alcestis' wrath, but because he recognises in her the funerary representation of his dead wife. In light of the above, it is easy to understand why Heracles does not want other people to touch Alcestis, except from Admetus, whose ambiguous ontological status finds its resolution in the *dexiōsis* taking place on stage: Admetus clasps the statue of dead Alcestis thus suggesting to the audience the motif that was so popular in the Attic funerary stelai representing a scene of greeting in the Underworld. What Admetus asked in line 363, namely that Alcestis might wait for him in the Underworld to greet him (ἀλλ᾽ οὖν ἐκεῖσε προσδόκα μ᾽, ὅταν θάνω), is now represented on stage.[36] Admetus' mention of the Gorgon suggests his anxiety of looking at the woman, while simultaneously betraying his fear of turning into stone himself.[37] Indeed, as discussed above, locking eyes was another recurrent element in funerary scenes of *dexiōsis* which, just like the act of clasping hands between the two spouses, is initiated by Heracles in the tragedy (1121: βλέψον πρὸς αὐτήν).[38] The motif puts emphasis on the intimate reunion between loved ones after death, and thus reminds Admetus of his precarious ontological status.

---

[36] Markantonatos 2013: 149 argues that Admetus' words are suggestive of a *hieros gamos* and bring together 'votaries and infernal powers, life and death'.

[37] On the comic effect of the mention of the Gorgon see Kott 1973: 101.

[38] See also Worman 2020: 232: 'Like so many other scenes that stage haptic experiencing as significant and propulsive, here too the eye–hand co-ordination makes for conclusive recognition'. On the importance of seeing in the play, see Craik in this volume.

The final scene in the play corroborates this reading: Heracles leaves the stage in a hurry, and when Admetus questions Alcestis' irresponsiveness, thus revealing an evidently comic effect, the hero explains that three days have to pass for the woman to be purified, or rather deconsecrated (1146: ἀφαγνίσηται). Heracles' answer is strikingly vague and disingenuous: as Thanatos claims at lines 74–6, those whose hair has been cut by his sword are the sacred property of the nether gods. Interestingly, Thanatos' claim follows Apollo's forecast of Heracles' arrival at lines 64–71 and confirms the vanity of the hero's intervention. Furthermore, it seems striking that Heracles spends more words seeking to convince Admetus to take the woman, or inventing implausible stories about her retrieval, than he does in the end to reveal the truth to his friend or share his supposed joy. Even his exit from the stage seems rushed: after realising that Heracles' story about the public contest was false (1026–33), the audience would feel inclined not to believe that his other impending labour is real either.[39]

As a result, the audience understand that what they see before their eyes is a remake of a well-known funerary motif and are able to interpret Heracles' urge to leave the stage as an admission that the hero has tricked Admetus (1152: νῦν δ' ἐπείγεσθαί με δεῖ). The reply of the latter, also his final words in the play, supports this interpretation: the king summons the servants and asks to organise a celebration for his new life with Alcestis which he calls βελτίω βίον τοῦ πρόσθεν, 'better than the old' (1157–8), even adding that he has been blessed with fortune (οὐ γὰρ εὐτυχῶν ἀρνήσομαι): an ironic reference to the representation of his new life, or rather afterlife, which he will soon share with his wife.[40]

Thus, whether on the one hand this final revelation must have caused shock in the audience, albeit coated by distinctive Euripidean irony, on the other, what the playwright had hinted at in the first part of the play seems to finally make sense to the spectators.[41] Admetus seeks to escape his destiny through the death of his wife; however, as specified by Thanatos at lines 30 and 41, the compensation orchestrated by Apollo is unjust. The exchange taking place at the beginning of the play between the god and Thanatos, which has the tone of a sophistic word battle, provides the key to the interpretation of the final scene:

Θα. καὶ νοσφιεῖς με τοῦδε δευτέρου νεκροῦ;
Απ. ἀλλ᾽ οὐδ᾽ ἐκεῖνον πρὸς βίαν σ᾽ ἀφειλόμην.

---

[39] See on this point Gavrilenko 2011: 202: 'Héraclè, toujours évasif dans ses réponses à Admète, le torture'.

[40] On the ambiguous tone permeating the whole play see Dellner 2000: 2: 'the play follows suit by exploiting the symbolic parallels of weddings and funerals in order to set a story of Alcestis as the ultimate commodities broker, choosing to die in Admetus' place, against the paradigmatic imagery and actions which try to return her to the status of a bride'. For a discussion of marriage and death in the Alcestis see Foley 2001: 310–27.

[41] Smith 1960: 129 argues that Thanatos and his treatment in the play are a clear example of Euripidean irony.

Θα. πῶς οὖν ὑπὲρ γῆς ἐστι κοὺ κάτω χθονός;
Απ. δάμαρτ᾽ ἀμείψας, ἣν σὺ νῦν ἥκεις μέτα.
Θα. κἀπάξομαί γε νερτέραν ὑπὸ χθόνα.
Απ. λαβὼν ἴθ᾽· οὐ γὰρ οἶδ᾽ ἂν εἰ πείσαιμί σε.
Θα. κτείνειν γ᾽ ὃν ἂν χρῇ; τοῦτο γὰρ τετάγμεθα.
Απ. οὔκ, ἀλλὰ τοῖς μέλλουσι θάνατον ἀμβαλεῖν.
Θα. ἔχω λόγον δὴ καὶ προθυμίαν σέθεν. (43–51)

DEATH. Will you then rob me of a second corpse?
APOLLO. But not even the first did I take from you by force.
DEATH. Then how is he still on earth and not beneath the ground?
APOLLO. By giving in exchange the wife you have now come to fetch.
DEATH. Yes, and I will take her down below.
APOLLO. Take her and go: I doubt if I can persuade you.
DEATH. To kill my fated victims? Yes, for those are my orders.
APOLLO. No, to postpone death for the doomed.
DEATH. I now understand your purpose and your desire.

As the passage above highlights, not even Apollo can prevent Thanatos from killing his designated victims nor postpone death for the doomed. Such ambiguous expressions can easily refer to either Alcestis or Admetus, or both. This latter option becomes increasingly more plausible in the following lines: as Thanatos specifies (63), Apollo will not get what he should not have. Furthermore, when the god foreshadows Heracles' intervention and rescue of Alcestis (64–71), Thanatos' reply is that Apollo's talk will earn him nothing: whoever is doomed to die will do so (72–6). Whereas *prima facie* these words seem to concern the specific case of Alcestis, the second part of the play, and its final scene in particular, shows that Thanatos' plan cannot be altered, and Apollo has indeed failed to appreciate what a σοφός he is (58): doomed Admetus must, and will, finally meet his end.

## 4. Conclusion

To conclude, in this chapter I have argued that Euripides deploys touch in the play to denote the emotional and cognitive sphere of the characters, or lack thereof, as in the case of Alcestis, whose characterisation makes her closer to a statue-like figure even in her human form, since her first appearance on stage. The prominent role of touch and its involvement in the intellectual and emotional spheres are emphasised in the recognition scene, where Euripides assigns to the haptic sense an additional function:

the 'final touch' between Admetus and Alcestis is evocative of the *dexiōsis*, a funerary motif populating Attic stelai in the fifth and fourth centuries. Euripides leaves hints to the audience throughout the play, to allow them to decipher the *anagnōrisis*: the passive, almost motionless characterisation of dying Alcestis, followed by Admetus' own wish to commission a statue of his already statue-like wife, the simulacrum of Alcestis brought on stage by Heracles in the end of the play and, finally, Admetus' own role in the ontological paradox. Although he is not dead, Admetus is living an existence which is a non-life, being simultaneously doomed and bound to suffering. The recognition with his wife finally liberates him: as the funerary statue of Alcestis greets him, their *dexiōsis* makes Admetus aware of a possibility for a new life, better than their previous one with Alcestis – in the Underworld, just as he had wished.

# PART IV

## Senses and Audiences

# Bodies That Shock: The Erinyes and Lyssa

*Naomi Weiss*

'Theatre is an art of bodies witnessed by bodies'.[1]

According to the *Life of Aeschylus*, apparently, at the first performance of the *Oresteia*, the entrance of the Erinyes was so terrifying that children fainted and women miscarried.[2] For the author of this *Life*, the Erinyes exemplify Aeschylus' capacity for effecting 'portentous shock' (ἔκπληξιν τερατώδη, 7) through visual effects. Later in the *Life* we hear again of such 'shock' (*ekplēxis*): with his use of various theatrical technologies, as well as with figures like ghosts and the Erinyes, Aeschylus 'shocked the spectators' gaze' (τὴν ὄψιν τῶν θεωμένων κατέπληξεν, 14). The repeated use of words with the root *plēgē* (ἔκπληξιν, κατέπληξεν), meaning 'blow' or 'strike', stresses the physical impact of this viewing experience.[3] Whatever the veracity of the *Life's* anecdotes, the Erinyes were remembered for inflicting a deeply visceral blow on their audiences.

Ancient Greek theorists of performance and spectatorship were deeply aware of the potential for a bodily response to an object of representation on the part of both performers and audiences. Gorgias, for example, claims that the audience of poetry can experience 'very fearful shuddering and pity full of tears and desire that loves to lament' (φρίκη περίφοβος καὶ ἔλεος πολύδακρυς καὶ πόθος φιλοπενθής, *Encomium of Helen* 9) in response to the fortunes of the characters represented.[4] Ion, the rhapsode in Plato's dialogue, describes how he himself sheds tears when he narrates something pitiable and feels his hair stand on end and heart leap when his subject is frightening, and how his spectators exhibit

---

[1]   Shepherd 2006: 73.
[2]   *Vit. Aesch.* 9, Pollux 4.110.
[3]   Cf. Ar. *Ran.* 962. On *ekplēxis* in relation to tragedy, specifically in terms of its captivating or mystical power see Lada-Richards 1993: 97–8.
[4]   On this account of audience engagement see esp. Halliwell 2011: 274–5, 280–1, Cairns 2015: 82–3.

the same reactions (Plato *Ion* 535b–e).[5] In *Poetics*, Aristotle also mentions 'shuddering' (φρίττειν, 1453b) as a response to tragedy.[6] In that treatise he famously talks of pity and fear as the primary emotions generated by this art form; in *Rhetoric*, he considers at more length the extent to which pity, as well as fear, can be 'a kind of pain' (λύπη τις, 1385b14) – that is, a bodily reaction to someone else's state of suffering.[7] In *Politics*, in a discussion specifically concerning music, especially 'theatrical music' (ἡ θεατρικὴ μουσική, 1342a18), he explores how 'everybody when listening to representations [*mimēseōn*] is thrown into a corresponding state of feeling [*sympatheis*]' (ἀκροώμενοι τῶν μιμήσεων γίγνονται πάντες συμπαθεῖς, 1340a12–14), including the feeling of pain.[8] Such *sympatheia* could be a corporeal response, not simply an emotional one.

Modern theatre scholarship also often highlights drama's somatic potential. This approach to theatre took off in the 1980s, with the publication of Bert States' seminal book, *Great reckonings in little rooms: on the phenomenology of theatre*.[9] Drawing from Maurice Merleau-Ponty's emphasis in *Phénoménologie de la perception* (1945) on embodied subjectivity (or *Leiblichkeit*, 'lived bodiliness'), States emphasises the actuality or 'affective corporeality' of the theatrical medium itself and the bodies within it over the signifying systems of textual semiotics, which tend to privilege text over material presence. Many theorists since States have focused on the bodied experience of theatre – its phenomenology – in terms of the bodily presence of both performers and audiences.[10] When Simon Shepherd, quoted in this chapter's epigraph, states that 'theatre is an art of bodies witnessed by bodies', he means that this artform does not simply present bodies onstage but engages the audience's own bodies in response. Scholars in film studies have for some time emphasised a similar sort of bodily reciprocity as an experience of film.[11] As Vivian Sobchack has argued, this experience is simultaneously literal and figural, as we make sense of filmic images through our own sensual bodies: 'we are

---

[5] On this passage see esp. Cairns 2015: 84–5. On the degree to which, according to Plato, audiences (as opposed to performers) of tragedy and Homer may assimilate themselves to a character see esp. Halliwell 2002: 80–1.

[6] On *phrikē* as a response to visual or verbal representation in ancient Greek thought see Cairns 2015.

[7] Cf. Arist. *Rhet.* 1382a20–6, 1386a25–29. On what Aristotle means here by 'a kind of pain' and the extent of equivalence between the state of the pitier (or fearer) and that of the pitied see esp. Nehamas 1992: 300–3, Nussbaum 1992: 273–6, Konstan 2001: 128–36, Halliwell 2002: 207–16. See also Arist. *De an.* 403a5–b19 on how these and other emotions are closely connected with the body.

[8] On this passage see esp. Kivy 1984: 33–5, Weiss forthcoming. Cf. Pl. *Resp.* 605c10–d5 on listening to a lament in epic or tragedy: 'surrendering ourselves, we follow it, feeling with it [*sympaschontes*] and responding earnestly' (ἐνδόντες ἡμᾶς αὐτοὺς ἑπόμεθα συμπάσχοντες καὶ σπουδάζοντες).

[9] States 1985.

[10] See e.g. Garner 1994, Shepherd 2006, Nevitt 2013. See also States 1992.

[11] See esp. Sobchack 1992, 2004, Marks 2000, 2002, Barker 2009.

caught up without a thought … in this vacillating and reversible sensual structure that *both* differentiates *and* connects the sense of my literal body to the sense of the figurative bodies and objects I see on the screen'.[12] Though the screen has its own particular forms of tactility, theatre, too, is able to produce a sort of intercorporeality – a connection, though not necessarily a one-to-one match, between what we see onstage and our sense of our own physical bodies.[13]

It is productive, I think, to bring a phenomenological approach to theatre's bodies – as well as film's – together with the recent turn toward affect and the senses in the study of classical Greek drama. Scholarship concerned with affect tends to highlight how emotion can act as a physical exchange or contagion between a play's bodies. In a recent discussion of tragedy's affective materiality, for example, Mario Telò and Melissa Mueller draw on Sara Ahmed's conceptualisation of fear as an emotion that 'works through and on the bodies of those who are transformed into its subjects, as well as its objects'.[14] They apply this sort of affective reading to the parodos of Sophocles' *Philoctetes*, demonstrating the circulation of fear in this scene as a material force that breaks down the boundaries between subject and object: 'the Chorus's fear of the bow and its abject possessor … has a reverberative effect – seeing the terrified sailors, Philoctetes becomes terrified himself'.[15] This sort of focus on affect is important in bringing to light some of the text's intercorporeal patterns, but it tends not to include much consideration of how they might involve an audience.[16]

In this chapter, I bring these two methodologies together by using two case studies: the Erinyes in Aeschylus' *Libation Bearers* and *Eumenides*, and Lyssa in Euripides' *Heracles*, divine agents of madness and some of the most terrifying characters to appear in physical form in extant tragedy. Through these case studies, I examine the contagion or reverberation of somatic affect both between dramatic bodies and between those

---

[12] Sobchack 2004: 77 (original emphasis).

[13] On film's 'tactility' see esp. Barker 2009. I take the term 'intercorporeality' from Larocco (2016)'s critique of Elaine Scarry's *The body in pain* (1985). Larocco argues that, while pain may not be representable in any simple one-to-one way, it can still involve communication between bodies: 'Pain's withering cries may not create empathetic transfer, the re-representation of the self's suffering in the other, but they do, almost invariably, disturb, altering the intercorporeal realm' (349).

[14] Ahmed 2004: 62, partially quoted by Telò and Mueller 2018b: 7. Worman 2020 also draws on Ahmed's work to explore how interbodily contact in Greek tragedy generates affects such as disgust, fear and erotic desire.

[15] Telò and Mueller 2018: 7. See also Telò's lengthier discussion in the same volume of the circulation and contagion of affect in *Philoctetes*, drawing in particular from Deleuze and Guattari 1987 (Telò 2018).

[16] An affect-oriented study of tragedy need not, however, exclude the audience: 'Thinking of tragic emotion in terms of affect encourages us to heed the multiple levels of between-ness created by the extant texts of the three tragedians – to imagine how the fraught intensities passed between characters onstage relate to those passed on to an audience, whether spectators/listeners or readers (including critics)' (Telò forthcoming).

bodies and their audiences within the theatre. In this respect, the chapter is aligned
with affect-oriented approaches to Greek tragedy. However, my focus on these dramas'
intercorporeality also looks towards phenomenological studies of theatre like States'
and Shepherd's, by foregrounding the experiential role of the audience, especially
in relation the physicality of onstage bodies.[17] I am interested both in these bodily
relationships themselves and in the role they play within the dramas' representational
processes: specifically, how the difficulties and dangers of viewing such shocking bodies
are bound up with their viscerality, and how it is through such somatic impact that
apparently unviewable bodies are materialised. I suggest that Aeschylus and Euripides
explore the extremes of theatre's representational potential, not just through the sorts
of visual effects and technologies on which the *Life of Aeschylus* focuses but also through
the intercorporeal dynamics at work within each play and extending to the audience's
own physical involvement.

## The Erinyes

Before the Erinyes come onstage, the audience of the *Oresteia* first experiences them
through the language and bodily affect of two internal spectators, Orestes at the end of
*Libation Bearers* and the Pythia priestess at the start of *Eumenides*. Their manifestation via
these two characters generates suspense for their actual entrance and, moreover, shapes
the audience's comprehension of their form and power. In this respect, the Erinyes are
the most dramatic example of a play throughout the *Oresteia* trilogy with the shift from
immaterial to material, invisible to visible, with objects and bodies extensively prepared
for in language before finally appearing in physical form.[18] Paradoxically, however, the
responses of Orestes and, in particular, the Pythia also prevent any clear visualisation,
thus disorienting the audience's own viewing experience as much as constructing it.

The Erinyes' presence in *Libation Bearers* is disconcertingly ambiguous, invisible to
the chorus but both visible and physically threatening to Orestes himself. When he first
becomes aware of them, he remarks that 'fear is by my heart, ready to sing and dance to
wrath's accompaniment' (πρὸς δὲ καρδίᾳ φόβος | ᾄδειν ἕτοιμος ἠδ' ὑπορχεῖσθαι κότῳ,
1024–5). Hinting at the singing and dancing of the chorus of Erinyes that will surround

---

[17] On the audience's sensory, bodily engagement in tragedy see esp. Worman 2017, 2018, 2020, Weiss
2018a: 236–44, Weiss 2023a esp. 122–61, Angelopoulou 2020, 2021, Olsen 2020. My approach here also
complements cognitive approaches to ancient Greek theatre and its audiences: see esp. Meineck 2017: 120–
46, Angelopoulou 2021; also Meineck's chapter in this volume. See also Lada-Richards 1993 on forms of
'empathic understanding'.

[18] On such play see Ferrari 1997, Frontisi-Ducroux 2007, Elmer 2017: 59, Bakola 2018, Weiss 2018b: 176–84,
Noel 2019.

him physically in the following play, he feels them as the embodiment of fear and wrath, an external force attacking him internally.[19] Some twenty lines later, Orestes' non-verbal cry of ἄ ἄ (1048) marks the change in his mental and bodily state as he appears not just to sense the Erinyes' imminent attack but to see them vividly before him. Though these creatures are not yet physically onstage, Orestes insists so forcefully on their existence that they hover between visible and invisible, present and absent.[20] He repeatedly uses the deictic αἵδε ('these [women] here', 1048, 1054, 1057, 1061) to refer to the Erinyes, as if they are there for all to see. Yet he also acknowledges that 'you don't see these women here, but I do' (ὑμεῖς μὲν οὐχ ὁρᾶτε τάσδ᾽, ἐγὼ δ᾽ ὁρῶ, 1061).[21] This address is to the audience as much as it is to the chorus. At the same time, however, the audience does to some degree already see the Erinyes, since the chorus of libation bearers, the only bodies present to whom the feminine plural pronoun αἵδε could refer, is about to be transformed into that other chorus in the following play.

Orestes' description of the Erinyes further underscores not only the ambiguity of their visual presence but also their somatic impact. He begins by likening them to Gorgons (Γοργόνων δίκην, 1048), the female monsters who turn anyone who looks at them into stone. In the following lines he talks of their dark clothes and the snakes in their hair (1049–50); later he mentions the 'loathsome' (δυσφιλές, 1058) fluid dripping from their eyes. As Françoise Frontisi-Ducroux has shown, the Erinyes in this trilogy are an especially notable example of the paradox of representing Gorgonic figures at whom none should look.[22] While the audience can visualise them here through Orestes' vivid language and, as we noted, may prematurely sense them in the bodies of the chorus, it is also protected from the Erinyes' gaze, by not witnessing them as their onstage victim does. It is in Orestes' body that their powerful Gorgonic presence is revealed. When the chorus asks Orestes, 'what imaginings are spinning you around?' (τίνες σε δόξαι … στροβοῦσιν, 1051–2), it keeps open the question of what, if anything, Orestes sees – are they mere imaginings (δόξαι)? But it also highlights the Erinyes' kinetic impact by characterising his movement as like that of a top (στρόμβος), an object entirely at the mercy of the agent who spins it. The physicality of their attack continues to be

---

[19] Cf. Frontisi-Ducroux 2007: 168.

[20] Cf. Ps.-Longinus' comment on Orestes' vision of the Erinyes in Euripides' *Iphigenia in Tauris* and *Orestes* and its transference to the audience: 'Here the poet himself saw the Erinyes, and he almost forced the audience too to see what he had imagined' (ὁ ποιητὴς αὐτὸς εἶδεν Ἐρινύας· ὁ δ᾽ ἐφαντάσθη, μικροῦ δεῖν θεάσασθαι καὶ τοὺς ἀκούοντας ἠνάγκασεν, *De subl*. 15.2).

[21] Cf. Frontisi-Ducroux 2007: 170 on how Orestes here sets 'two kinds of vision against each other, the hero's and that of the others, chorus and audience', even as the chorus is already oscillating between its present and future roles.

[22] Frontisi-Ducroux 1995: 132, 2007.

foregrounded as the chorus talks of a 'disturbance' (ταραγμός) that 'falls upon' (πίτνει) Orestes' mind (1056). Indeed, this is so powerful that it carries him offstage and brings the play to a close: as he says in his final line, 'I'm being driven off and can't stay any longer' (ἐλαύνομαι δὲ κοὐκέτ' ἂν μείναιμ' ἐγώ, 1062).

In *Eumenides*, Aeschylus continues to draw the audience's attention to the bodily state of the Erinyes' viewers and ties this to the danger involved in seeing them. This tragedy opens with the Pythia confidently delivering a prayer to the gods of Delphi and then entering Apollo's temple (represented by the *skēnē*). For a moment, extraordinarily for Greek drama, the stage is empty, but then she comes out again, utterly changed in her demeanor, posture, and concerns:

ἦ δεινὰ λέξαι, δεινὰ δ' ὀφθαλμοῖς δρακεῖν,
πάλιν μ' ἔπεμψεν ἐκ δόμων τῶν Λοξίου,
ὡς μήτε σωκεῖν μήτε μ' ἀκταίνειν στάσιν·
τρέχω δὲ χερσίν, οὐ ποδωκείᾳ σκελῶν·
δείσασα γὰρ γραῦς οὐδέν, ἀντίπαις μὲν οὖν. (34–8)

Truly terrible to say and terrible to see with one's eyes
[such things] have sent me back out of the house of Loxias,
that I have no strength nor can I keep myself upright;
but I run on my hands, not with my legs' swift-footedness.
For an old woman terrified is nothing – or, rather, she's like a child.

The Pythia's opening line upon her re-entry stresses both the difficulty of verbally representing these creatures and also the difficulty of looking at them: they are both 'terrible to say' and 'terrible to see with one's eyes'. It also suggests an equivalence between saying and seeing – between not just the two activities on her part, but between the audience hearing her say these words and seeing their materialisation in her own deformed movement.[23] For the Pythia is so affected by this sight that she herself, like Orestes, is physically transformed: now unable to stand, she crawls on her hands like a child – or like a beast, as if responding in kind to the bestial creatures that she has just seen.[24]

As she goes on to describe the scene within the temple, the Pythia emphasises her own viewing experience. Repeatedly using verbs of sight (ὁρῶ, 40; ἄπτεροί γε μὴν ἰδεῖν |

---

[23] Cf. Nooter 2017: 255: 'the priestess performs the transformative effect of this monstrousness by displaying and describing her own transformed affect'. Frontisi-Ducroux 2007: 171 notes that the 'passage from speaking to seeing' that the Pythia describes here 'adopts the spectator's standpoint and not her own, for she, conversely, has seen before she speaks'.

[24] On the characterisation of the Pythia as an animal here see Heath 1999: 33.

αὗται, 51–2), she invites the audience to visualise the Erinyes with her, just as Orestes did at the end of *Libation Bearers*. She also repeats three elements of that initial description: they wear dark clothes (52, cf. *Libation Bearers* 1049); they immediately make her think of Gorgons (48, cf. *Libation Bearers* 1048); they 'drip a loathsome drop from their eyes' (ἐκ δ' ὀμμάτων λείβουσι δυσφιλῆ λίβα, 54, cf. *Libation Bearers* 1058). As in Orestes' account, these latter two details stress the horror of meeting these creatures' oozy, bloody gaze. The viewer's repulsion is a bodily one: the Erinyes are βδελύκτροποι (52), a hapax word meaning 'nauseating' or 'vomit-inducing'.[25] The Pythia adds an acoustic element to this repulsiveness: not only are they terrifying to look at, but their bellowing snores are 'unapproachable' (οὐ πλατοῖσι, 53).[26] She thus urges upon the audience a visceral response of its own in anticipation of this chorus, especially as it begins to hear for itself the Erinyes' snores and groans (μυγμός, ὠγμός 117, 120, 123, 126, 129), probably before the chorus' bodies become fully visible.[27]

Even as she shapes the audience's reaction to these creatures, however, the Pythia prevents it from having any clear understanding of what they might look like. Frontisi-Ducroux has convincingly shown that, prior to the production of the *Oresteia* in 457 BC, the Erinyes had never been represented in theatre or visual art: these bodies were unprecedented.[28] The Pythia compares them to Gorgons and then to Harpies, whom she has seen in a painting (γεγραμμένας 50), and so prompts the audience to see the Erinyes in terms of representations of monstrous females in other media. Some might think of other comparable figures in Attic theatre, such as Lyssa in Aeschylus' *Wool Carders* (*Xantriai*), a play to which I shall briefly return below.[29] But the Pythia promptly shatters any such visualisation by declaring that she has never before seen such a race of wingless creatures in black (57) and so prevents the audience from making any assumptions based on its own cultural repertoire. Such visual uncertainty adds, of course, to the suspense leading up to their full appearance in the *orchēstra*. It also sets up the chorus' potential, when it does become physically visible, to shock the audience

---

[25]  Cf. Nooter 2017: 253 on the Erinyes' repugnancy here.

[26]  Cf. Nooter 2017: 245–88 on the emphasis in *Eumenides* on the Erinyes' bestial sounds as well as bodily fluids.

[27]  I believe that the full chorus is not meant to be physically present in the *orchēstra* until 94ff. at the earliest and most likely not until 140 (cf. Taplin 1977: 365–74). The text, however, has suggested different staging options to different scholars. A somewhat more popular view is that the Erinyes appear onstage from behind the *skēnē*, probably via an *ekkyklēma*, at line 64: see e.g. Sommerstein 1989: 33, 93, Ley 2007: 38–41. Another possibility, posited by Rehm 1988: 296–7, is that the chorus is already in the *orchēstra*, in an 'inside out' scene, at the start of the play, in which case the Pythia would then verbally frame the audience's visual understanding of what they already see – though the Erinyes would presumably only get to their feet and become fully visible upon beginning to sing at 140ff.

[28]  Frontisi-Ducroux 2007: 166.

[29]  We do not know when *Wool Carders* was produced in relation to the *Oresteia*.

quite viscerally – and, as we saw, the story in the *Life of Aeschylus* suggests that it became renowned for doing so. The viewing of these creatures is overdetermined as a fraught and dangerous act; like the Gorgons, they are 'terrible to see'.[30]

Thus, whatever the nature of the chorus' onstage appearance, it is framed by the Erinyes' effect on the bodies of others, as well as the difficulty and risk of viewing them in the first place. Certainly, the chorus could also have a marked physical appearance, such as dark clothing, unusual masks, or distinctive movements. A line in Aristophanes' *Wealth* indicates as much: when Poverty enters, Blepsidemus wonders if 'perhaps she's an Erinys out of tragedy: she's certainly got a manic and tragic look' (ἴσως Ἐρινύς ἐστιν ἐκ τραγῳδίας· | βλέπει γέ τοι μανικόν τι καὶ τραγῳδικόν, 423–4), suggesting that her mask resembles those of the Erinyes as they appear in tragedy.[31] But an audience's experience of these creatures is fundamentally tied to their somatic assault, which it finally witnesses onstage when the Erinyes perform the Binding Song at 307–96. As Yopie Prins and Albert Henrichs have shown, this is a remarkably performative song.[32] Beginning with the direction that they join together in dance since they have decided 'to make [their] horrifying music visible' (μοῦσαν στυγερὰν | ἀποφαίνεσθαι, 308–9), they announce the 'visual revelation of their verbal being'.[33] They draw attention to their full, bodily presence as they describe the 'hostile dancing of [their] feet' (ὀρχησμοῖς τ' ἐπιφθόνοις ποδός, 371) and the 'great leaping' (μάλα ... ἁλομένα, 372) that makes their victims fall (375–7), all while actually dancing in the *orchēstra*. In the second mesode, runs of paeons bring down the 'strike' (ἀκμάν, 374) of their feet, as much physical as metrical, in the last syllable of each line.[34] Thus they become most powerfully manifest in enacting such violence on Orestes. This performance, however, is also a visual, acoustic, and even visceral bombardment on the audience, which, now finally beholding these dangerous, Gorgonic beings onstage, itself becomes vulnerable to their attack.

We can therefore understand the Erinyes in Aeschylus' trilogy in terms of a radiation of bodily affect, spreading from Orestes at the end of *Libation Bearers* to the

[30] Cf. Frontisi-Ducroux 2007, who quotes the *Suda* on the Erinyes as 'faceless and painful to look at' (ἀπροσώπων καὶ δυσειδῶν): 'This definition, admittedly late, posits an equivalence between a revolting sight and ἀπροσωπία, the absence of face. The point is that the Erinyes are among those deadly powers whose relation to death places them in the field of the barely envisageable, or rather the invisible – such as Hades ... or such as the Gorgon, on whose face and eyes none can bear to gaze' (166).

[31] Halliwell 1993: 204–5. The Erinyes are included on the list of 'special' masks in Pollux 4.141, as is Lyssa (see below). At *Eum.* 990 Athena refers to 'these fearsome faces' (τῶν φοβερῶν τῶνδε προσώπων); Frontisi-Ducroux 2007: 176 sees here a reference to the stage masks (*prosōpa*), 'the mask that for the first time gives a visible face to these creatures never seen before'. On the likely rarity of non-generic masks in classical Greek theatre see also Marshall 1999.

[32] Prins 1991, Henrichs 1994–5: 60–5.

[33] Prins 1991: 183.

[34] Prins 1991: 189. See also Weiss 2023b: 247.

Pythia at the start of *Eumenides*, and then becoming manifest in the physical stampede performed against Orestes, while also extending out towards the audience itself. The first half of *Eumenides*, before the Erinyes are mollified by Athena, holds out the danger that they will transform the audience's own bodies, as they have transformed those of Orestes and the Pythia. It is in such embodied responses that these creatures, never before seen onstage, are materialised.

## Lyssa

The appearance of Lyssa in Euripides' *Heracles*, produced some 40 years later, initially seems very different from that of the Erinyes in the *Oresteia*. By the time Euripides produced this tragedy, probably around 416 BC, Lyssa was not an entirely new figure in the theatre nor in visual media.[35] As we have already seen, she had appeared in Aeschylus' *Wool Carders*; in a surviving fragment, she appears to be urging on the bacchants to tear Pentheus to pieces (fragment 169 Radt).[36] While there is no evidence that she actually came onstage in his *Archeresses* (*Toxotides*), she is included in a scene on an Attic red-figure bell krater from the mid fifth century that may be linked to that play.[37] She is also conceptualised very similarly to the Erinyes, who are likewise agents of madness and daughters of Night.[38] Like them, she is often associated with both snakes and dogs; in the vase painting just mentioned, she appears with a dog protruding from her head as she sets Actaeon's hounds against him.[39] Thus an ancient audience's viewing of her in *Heracles* could have been shaped by various representations across different media; at the time of its first production, she was not as apparently unrepresentable as the Erinyes were prior to the *Oresteia*.

Even if she may not have been a novelty, however, Lyssa's entrance in *Heracles* is a complete surprise.[40] Typically, divine epiphanies in Euripidean tragedy occur in the

---

[35] This dating is primarily based on metrical grounds: see Cropp and Fick 1985: 5.
[36] On dramatic precedents for Lyssa in Euripides' tragedy see esp. Duchemin 1967.
[37] Museum of Fine Arts, Boston 00.346, *BAPD* 213562. On the image's complicated relationship to tragedy see esp. Neer 1995: 141–6.
[38] Daughters of Night: Aesch. *Eum.* 321; Eur. *HF* 822, 834.
[39] On snakes in relation to Lyssa and particularly the Erinyes in both tragedy and art see esp. Padel 1992: 163–79; at *HF* 882–3 the chorus pictures her as surrounded by 'the hundred-headed | hissings of snakes' (ἑκατογκεφάλοις | ὄφεων ἰαχήμασι). On the shared canine associations of Lyssa and the Erinyes see esp. Franco 2014: 94–9. At Eur. Bacch. 977, the chorus calls on the 'hounds of Lyssa' (θοαὶ Λύσσας κύνες, 977) to goad the Theban women to madness. The hunting imagery in *Heracles* can also be understood in such terms (esp. 860, 898).
[40] Iris, however, does seem to be a novelty here, as she does not appear in any other surviving Greek tragedy. On surprise as a response to Greek tragedy see Meineck in this volume.

prologue and/or exodos; here, Lyssa and Iris appear, unusually, in the middle of the play.[41] There is none of the extensive preparation or speculation that we find prior to the Erinyes' onstage appearance in *Eumenides*. On the contrary, Lyssa and Iris enter with no warning, jarringly offsetting the prematurely joyful ode that the chorus has just sung. The chorus' own surprise, as it suddenly cries out in alarm (815), may mirror that of the audience. But there is no uncertainty as to the goddesses' identity, since Iris immediately tells the old men to 'have courage as you look upon this daughter of Night, | Lyssa ... and me, the gods' servant, Iris' (θαρσεῖτε Νυκτὸς τήνδ' ὁρῶντες ἔκγονον | Λύσσαν, 822–3). Lyssa is foregrounded here as the primary object of the old men's fear; the focus remains on her as Iris quickly announces their purpose (823–32) and gives detailed instructions to Lyssa on how to make Heracles mad (833–42). Initially, when Lyssa herself speaks, she tries to resist Iris (843–58), but soon she embodies her familiar function, describing the madness that she will inflict upon Heracles (861–74). The suddenness of their entrance, as well as their departure at the end of Lyssa's speech, means that no remark is made regarding her visual appearance before or during her presence onstage. It is therefore not so much Lyssa's actual form that is designed to shock the audience, but the abruptness with which she, along with Iris, appears, immediately altering the play's course.[42]

Beyond this initial shock, however, the audience's response to Lyssa is shaped by the impact she has on the bodies around her – and in this respect her appearance in this play does resemble that of the Erinyes in the *Oresteia*. Indeed, she is almost entirely presented in terms of others' affect and movement, beginning with the chorus' non-verbal cries of alarm at 815. The chorus then asks, 'have we come to the same onslaught of fear, | old men, because of such a vision that I see above the house?' (ἆρ' ἐς τὸν αὐτὸν πίτυλον ἥκομεν φόβου, | γέροντες, οἷον φάσμ' ὑπὲρ δόμων ὁρῶ, 816–17). According to the play's modern commentators, the word πίτυλος is to be understood as a 'rhythmic pulse', so that the chorus' question in line 816 is 'best explained as a vocal stage direction, prescribing proper choreography: "all now execute the same rhythmic movement indicating fear"'.[43] But πίτυλος also, primarily, means a torrent or attack, which falls upon the old Argives and prompts their attempt to flee (818–19). Like Orestes in *Libation Bearers* as he senses the Erinyes, the chorus thus grounds its viewing of the goddesses both in terms of fear as a

---

[41]  See Bond 1981: 279, Papadopoulou 2005: 71. Dionysus' epiphany at Eur. *Bacch.* 604 is an exception to this general rule, although he is already a character within the play. Gods appear midway through the drama in *Rhesus* (Athena at 595), Aeschylus' *Psychostasia* (Zeus), Sophocles' *Aias Lokros* (Athena, fr. 10c Radt) and possibly *Niobe* (Apollo and Artemis (fr. 441a Radt). Iris and Lyssa are most likely to appear on a *theologeion* or possibly a *mēchanē*: on this staging see Bond 1981: 299–300, Lee 1982: 44–6, Barlow 1996: 159.

[42]  Cf. Holmes 2010: 243: 'The goddesses' arrival is … rather like the symptom itself: sudden, shocking, disruptive'.

[43]  Barlow 1996: 160, Bond 1981: 280. Cf. πίτυλος as a torrent or onslaught of madness at Eur. *HF* 1187, *IT* 307 and as one of tears at *Hipp.* 1464.

physical onslaught and in its own bodily response. Its question is also directed outward to the audience, inviting it to see, feel and even move in the same way: that is, to look up at the same φάσμα (vision, apparition) above the *skēnē* and to react with physical terror.

Whatever her actual appearance, then, and however it may be constructed for an audience through encounters with other representations of her in theatre or the visual arts, Lyssa is primarily understood and experienced in this play through the somatic havoc she wreaks on others – the chorus as her internal audience, the spectators in the theatre and, of course, Heracles himself. As the scene builds up to the moment when he murders his family, his body becomes the focus of Lyssa's terrifying, maddening power. First, Iris instructs her to make Heracles crazy:

> μανίας τ᾽ ἐπ᾽ ἀνδρὶ τῷδε καὶ παιδοκτόνους
> φρενῶν ταραγμοὺς καὶ ποδῶν σκιρτήματα
> ἔλαυνε κίνει, φόνιον ἐξίει κάλων. (835–7)

> Against this man madness and child-killing
> confusion of senses and leaping of feet
> drive, set moving, let forth a deadly sail.

Like Orestes at the end of *Libation Bearers*, Heracles will display Lyssa's terrifying power through a confusion (ταραγμούς, 837, cf. *Libation Bearers* 1056) that is as much physical as mental, causing him to dance wildly. Io in *Prometheus Bound* describes her own crazed movement in similar terms, involving 'maddened leaps' (ἐμμανεῖ σκιρτήματι, 675) as she is stung by the gadfly.[44] At the same time, the 'leaping of feet' is the object being set against Heracles, along with the madness that Lyssa personifies, so that she is envisaged to act like the Erinyes do in the *Eumenides*, working upon him with a violent, bodily force. The relentless urgency of her attack is emphasised here by the asyndeton of line 838 and the imperatives ἔλαυνε κίνει (837); grammatically, these verbs' direct objects are the symptoms of madness, but they also govern Heracles himself, to be immediately driven astray and set moving. Unlike Orestes and the Pythia, however, Heracles is not onstage, even though Iris refers to him with a deictic (τῷδε, 835) as if he were – as Orestes refers to the Erinyes in *Libation Bearers*. Whereas in the *Oresteia* the audience sees the Erinyes' victims long before the creatures themselves, here Lyssa is visible, while Heracles is the one visualised. But Lyssa herself becomes more emphatically present and potent through her imagined impact on his mind and body.

---

[44] See Olsen 2020: 52–72 on Io's 'urgent corporeality' (p. 62) in *Prometheus Bound*. Cf. Worman 2020: 35–7 on the play's emphasis on Io's body and 'mobile intensity'.

Once Lyssa agrees to follow Iris' instructions, she describes her effect on Heracles entirely in terms of his corporeal response. She emphasises the physicality of her attack using the imagery of a chariot race running right into his body: no elemental force – wave, earthquake, or lightning bolt – will be so violent (λάβρος, 861) as 'the course I shall run into Heracles' chest' (ἐγὼ στάδια δραμοῦμαι στέρνον εἰς Ἡρακλέους, 863).[45] Then she calls on her audience – Iris, the chorus, the spectators in the theatre – to behold Heracles' devastating transformation, which is simultaneously happening offstage:

ἦν ἰδού· καὶ δὴ τινάσσει κρᾶτα βαλβίδων ἄπο
καὶ διαστρόφους ἑλίσσει σῖγα γοργωποὺς κόρας,
ἀμπνοὰς δ' οὐ σωφρονίζει, ταῦρος ὣς ἐς ἐμβολήν,
δεινὰ μυκᾶται δέ. Κῆρας ἀνακαλῶ τὰς Ταρτάρου
τάχος ἐπιρροιβδεῖν ὁμαρτεῖν θ' ὡς κυνηγέτῃ κύνας.
τάχα σ' ἐγὼ μᾶλλον χορεύσω καὶ καταυλήσω φόβῳ.
στεῖχ' ἐς Οὔλυμπον πεδαίρουσ', Ἶρι, γενναῖον πόδα·
ἐς δόμους δ' ἡμεῖς ἄφαντοι δυσόμεσθ' Ἡρακλέους. (867–73)

Look! There! He's shaking his head at the starting-posts
and silently whirls around his twisted, grim-looking eyes,
and he isn't restrained in his breathing, he's like a bull about to charge,
and he bellows terribly. I shall call upon the goddesses of death from Tartarus
quickly to whirr their wings and follow like dogs a huntsman.
Quickly I'll make you sing and dance still more and pipe you down in fear.
Go to Olympus, Iris, lifting your noble foot;
but I, unseen, will make my way into the house of Heracles.

Beginning with the direction to 'Look!' (ἰδού, 867), Lyssa urges everyone to see Heracles as if he is onstage, as Iris did with the deictic in line 835.[46] She follows this with the non-connective particle καὶ δή, which, so Denniston tells us, 'signifies, vividly and dramatically, that something is actually taking place at the moment'; it typically '[marks] vivid perception by mind, ear, or eye'.[47] What Lyssa presents as if visible are the violent movements and non-verbal sounds to which Heracles is reduced, as he shakes his head and bellows like a bull.[48] While the chorus and audience are encouraged to look upon the

---

[45] Cf. Holmes 2010: 243 on how Lyssa's entry into the house converges with her entry into the body of Heracles himself.

[46] On Lyssa's 'performative speech' here see Holmes 2010: 244. See also Barlow 1996: 162.

[47] Denniston 1954: 250.

[48] Cf. Nooter 2017 on the bodiliness of non-verbal, bestial sound in Aeschylean tragedy.

hero in this state, he in turn is pictured as a body that looks back: his pupils (κόρας, 868) are γοργωπούς, 'fierce-looking' but also 'gorgon-eyed' (868); he whirls them around as if to find the target of his deadly gaze. Later the chorus refers to Lyssa herself as 'Gorgon of the Night' (Νυκτὸς Γοργών, 882) with snakes in her hair. In her speech here, and again in the messenger's speech (ἀγριωπὸν ὄμμα Γοργόνος, 990), this attribute is transferred to Heracles, as if Lyssa's powers and appearance become manifest in his body, which the audience must visualise even as, like the Gorgonic Erinyes, it is dangerous to see.[49] Subject and object, agent and target, thus become blurred – perhaps even more so if the actor playing Heracles were to play Lyssa, just as he would earlier play Lycus, in a doubling that also blurs such boundaries.[50]

Before ending her speech and telling Iris to return to Olympus, Lyssa shifts from referring to Heracles in the third person to using a second person pronoun instead: 'Quickly I'll make you sing and dance [*choreusō*] still more and pipe you down [*kataulēsō*] in fear' (τάχα σ' ἐγὼ μᾶλλον χορεύσω καὶ καταυλήσω φόβῳ, 871). The target of her apostrophe here is ambiguous and inclusive. It is Heracles, whom she will drive still further mad, and whom she addresses as if actually present. It is also the chorus, which begins to respond in kind a couple of lines later, as it sings and dances (*choreuein*) to the piping of the *aulos*. Singing of the madness that Lyssa is inflicting, the chorus enacts her threat by producing a highly agitated performance. The singing here, in striking contrast to the stasimon just 60 lines earlier, lacks strophic structure and follows mostly dochmiac rhythms, a metre with a 'curious, irregular, checking movement' and associated with extreme emotion.[51] It also includes many non-verbal cries (beginning with ὀτοτοτοῖ in line 875) and is interspersed with the offstage shouts of Amphitryon, Heracles' father. There are indications of correspondingly frantic choreography. From the start of its singing, the chorus dwells on Heracles' maddened movement, but this soon becomes indistinguishable from both its dancing and Lyssa's, all presented in terms of distorted Dionysian ritual:[52] he is 'set dancing to the piped [*enaulois*] frenzied madness [*lyssais*]' (μανιάσιν λύσσαις | χορευθέντ' ἐναύλοις, 878–9); 'the dance begins without drums, | not pleasing to Bromius' thyrsus' (κατάρχεται χόρευμα' ἄτερ τυπάνων |

---

[49] Heracles' own 'fierce-looking' and 'gorgon-eyed' (γορ- | γῶπες) aspect is already prefigured at *HF* 131–2, as a trait he has passed on to his children.

[50] On the significance of the same actor playing, according to the 'three actor rule', Heracles and Lycus, the tyrant who is on the point of killing the hero's family at the start of the play and whom Heracles then murders offstage, see esp. Ruck 1976, Damen 1989: 328–9, Rehm 2002b: 175. Ruck 1976 assumes that the actors playing Amphitryon (rather than Heracles) and Megara would play Iris and Lyssa.

[51] Dale 1968: 110.

[52] On the imagery of destructive Dionysian music and dance in this part of the play see Henrichs 1994–5: 61–2; Wilson 1999–2000: 434–9.

οὐ Βρομίου κεχαρισμένα θύρσῳ, 889–90); 'deadly, deadly is this tune being piped ...
Lyssa will do a Bacchic dance through the house' (δάιον τόδε | δάιον μέλος ἐπαυλεῖται
... δόμοισι | Λύσσα βακχεύσει, 894–5). Thus the chorus displays in not just acoustic but
also bodily form the fear (φόβος) with which it, like Heracles, is 'pipe[d] down' – fear
that already earlier, as we saw, it presented as a physical attack. The hero's turmoil, as
he dances to Lyssa's *aulos* (λύσσαις ... ἐναύλοις, 878),[53] merges with that of the chorus
and its onstage performance. Meanwhile Lyssa herself is no longer in view – she has
gone 'unseen' (ἄφαντοι, 874) into the house – but she remains present through the tune
of the *aulos* and the impact she, as well as the instrument, has on the chorus, as its own
frenetic sounds and movements materialise the madness simultaneously suffered by
Heracles within the house. Once again, then, Heracles and Lyssa come together. The
chorus merges the agent and victim of madness as it makes both manifest through its
own singing and dancing bodies.

Such reverberation of bodily affect includes others as well. When Lyssa tells Iris to
go back to Olympus, her instructions recall the chorus' self-direction upon first seeing
her: the old Argives told themselves to 'lift [*pedaire*] your sluggish limb[s], move out of
the way [*ekpodōn*, more literally "out of feet's way"]' (νωθὲς πέδαιρε κῶλον, ἐκποδὼν ἔλα,
819); Lyssa tells Iris to 'lift [*pedairous'*] your noble feet [*poda*]' (πεδαίρουσ' ... γενναῖον
πόδα, 872). On the one hand, the use of the πεδαίρω at these two moments – the only
two occurrences of this uncommon verb (an Aeolic or Doric form of μεταίρω) in the
entire play and both in connection with legs and feet – frames Lyssa's appearance
between the two contrasting movements of the chorus' futile, faltering attempt to get
away and Iris' return on 'noble feet' to Olympus. On the other hand, the direction to
Iris, coming just after Lyssa's claim to 'make you sing and dance still more', indicates that
even this goddess' body is affected by Lyssa's power, as she moves her feet as the dancing
chorus did and exits the stage.[54]

A similar response is urged upon the audience in the theatre. We noted how, as
soon as Lyssa and Iris appear, the chorus, as her internal spectators, encourages the
audience to experience 'the same onslaught of fear'. From that moment onward, there
is a rapid crescendo of somatic affect, first with the chorus' agitated response, then
with the vivid descriptions of Heracles' wild movements, and with Lyssa's threatening
pronouncement followed by the chorus' own shouts and frenzied movement in
response, which simultaneously represent the hero's own contorted, maddened body
and violent actions. As in the Erinyes' Binding Song, such verbal descriptions and

[53] μανιάσιν λύσσαις is Hermann's proposal for the metrically problematic μανίαισιν Λύσσας [*Lyssas*] found in MS L.
[54] στείχω in line 872 also implies movement; occasionally this verb can be used with a sense of choreography, as at Eur. *El.* 173.

physical enactments of Lyssa's terrifying assault also, in a sense, bombard the audience, acoustically, visually and kinetically. Experiencing not just the chorus' disturbing song and dance but the penetrating sound of the *aulos*, the same instrument with which she claims to 'pipe down' her victims, the spectators are pushed to feel similarly vulnerable to Lyssa's attack.

Such a response could be a bodily one, not just as a visceral reaction to a physical threat, but also as a result of an audience's own deep familiarity with choral song and dance. Sarah Olsen has shown how frequently ancient Greek accounts of choral performance suggest a kind of 'kinesthetic empathy' or 'contagion', terms used by dance scholars to refer to a somatic identification with a dancer's movements.[55] As she writes, 'kinesthetic empathy ... is predicated on memory. A spectator feels as if he is dancing or singing along with a performance in part because he is able to remember his own past experiences of similar modes of movement or vocalization'.[56] I have argued elsewhere that such kinesthetic empathy may have been an especially pronounced experience for many audience members in fifth-century Athens as a result of their own extensive experience of *choreia*, as both performers and spectators.[57] At least for *Heracles*' early audiences, we may surmise that the chorus' sounds, rhythms, and movements at 875–905 – disturbing yet still within the familiar bounds of tragic *choreia* – would have the potential to generate particularly powerful sensations of embodied identification.

The radiation of Lyssa's somatic impact culminates with the messenger's speech. Following the chorus' performance, this is a detailed account of Heracles' frenzied murder of his wife and children. The onset of his madness is described partly in terms of a change in his bodily appearance: his eyes become bloodshot and start rolling; foam drips from his beard (932–4). It is also marked by constant movement: believing that he is mounting a chariot, he strikes (κἄθεινε, 949) his imaginary horses; he 'paces back and forth through the house' (εἷρπ' ἄνω τε καὶ κάτω κατὰ στέγας, 953); he 'rushes upon' (ἐσπεσών, 954) the men's quarters; he 'goes through' (διελθών, 957) the house again; he 'wrestles against no one' (πρὸς οὐδέν' ἡμιλλᾶτο, 960); he 'whirls in a circle in a terrible spinning movement' (ἐξελίσσων ... κύκλῳ | τόρνευμα δεινόν, 977–8) before shooting one child with an arrow; he clubs the second child and knocks down the door to the bedchamber before shooting the third and Megara; he 'races off' (ἱππεύει, 1001) to find his father before finally collapsing in sleep after Athena's intervention.[58] As a result of

---

[55] Olsen 2017, 2021, with particular reference to Sklar 2008 and Foster 2008, 2010.

[56] Olsen 2020: 159.

[57] Weiss 2018a: 236–8.

[58] After his madness, too, the drama continues to focus on Heracles' body in its final scenes: Holmes 2010: 245–6. Cf. Bond 1981: 330–1 on *HF* 1036. Worman 2020: 86 highlights the focus on Heracles' hands in the messenger speech as part of a pattern of 'manual menace' through the tragedy.

the earlier presentations of Heracles' madness, the audience is primed to understand his kineticism here also in terms of a sort of frenzied dance. Throughout, he is engaging in a sort of imaginary play akin to the performance of drama; the servants initially ask if he is mad or 'playing' (παίζει, 952), using a verb that is often connected to dance.[59] Some of Heracles' actions have an especially strong choreographic resonance: his 'whirling in a circle', as earlier he 'whirled' his eyes (ἑλίσσει ... κόρας, 868), evokes the sort of language typically used to describe a dancing chorus, especially in Euripidean tragedy; the imagery of horse racing, which is so dominant here, often appears in relation to a chorus' own dancing bodies in archaic and classical Greek lyric.[60] Instead of the *aulos*, the acoustic accompaniment for these movements is Heracles' own distorted noise, as he addresses his father with 'frenzy-stricken laughter' (γέλωτι παραπεπληγμένῳ, 935), 'bellows terribly' (δεινὰ ... βρέμων, 962) and shouts in triumph (ἠλάλαξε, 981).[61]

Thus the messenger's account seems to transfer the dancing and frantic sounds performed just previously by the chorus onstage into the offstage body of Heracles. At the same time, his distorted, moving, bellowing body comes in stark contrast with the 'beautifully formed chorus of his children' (χορὸς ... καλλίμορφος ... τέκνων, 925) that, just before Heracles' transformation, stood 'keeping holy silence' (φθέγμα δ᾽ ὅσιον εἴχομεν, 927) along with the rest of the attendants at the sacrifices to Zeus.[62] There, the language of circular movement (ἐν κύκλῳ, 926; εἵλικτο, 927) applied to the ritual regularity of handing the sacred basket from one family member to another. The earlier change in the chorus' type of song and dance, marking Heracles' onset of madness and the plot's new direction, is paralleled within this narrative in the hero's own manic performance, which transforms and destroys his family's orderly chorality. In this respect, he is like the transgressive and disruptive solo dancer, who often signifies the violation of social order in Greek literature, especially in contrast to the communal chorus.[63]

For the audience, this depiction of Heracles' body can also effect a form of kinesthetic contagion, now through the medium of spoken narrative rather than choral song and dance. In a study of Euripides' *Andromache*, Olsen has revealed how the description of Neoptolemus' death in the play's messenger speech has a 'choreographic quality

---

[59]  Naerebout 1997: 280. See also Lonsdale 1993: 1, 29–43.

[60]  On the choreographic resonance of ἑλίσσω and other words denoting circular movement in tragedy (especially Euripides) see Naerebout 1997: 281, Csapo 1999–2000: 422–4, Weiss 2018a: 9 and passim. On the choral associations of horses and horse racing see esp. Steiner 2021: 184–219; also Weiss 2018a passim.

[61]  Heracles' cry of ἀλαλή, combined with his imaginary chariot-racing and wrestling, marks the perverted culmination of the epinician imagery that runs through the play, especially in the first three stasima: on this see esp. Parry 1965, Foley 1985: 147–204, Swift 2010: 121–55.

[62]  Henrichs 1996: 62 sees this moment as 'the climax of the pattern of perverted *khoreia*'.

[63]  Olsen 2020.

in narration'. Like the chorus' own song and dance, this can trigger an audience's own 'embodied cultural knowledge' – the sort of familiarity with choral performance that I mentioned above, as well as with the language and imagery of *choreia* more broadly.[64] In its many choreographic traces, already overdetermined as such by the presentations of the hero that precede it, the messenger speech in *Heracles* is characterised by a similarly 'intense mode of audience engagement'.[65]

As the drama reaches its terrifying climax, then, across different verbal forms (speech and choral lyric) and via different characters (Iris, Lyssa, the chorus, the messenger), the audience's own bodies are drawn into the contagion spreading outwards from Lyssa. This agent of madness is materialised not so much through her actual appearance onstage as through her impact – affective but also physical, kinetic impact – on others, both those who experience her within the drama and, at least potentially, those who watch in the apparent safety of the theatre.

## Conclusion: Shocking Bodies

This study of Aeschylus' *Libation Bearers* and *Eumenides* and Euripides' *Heracles* has revealed a particular mode of representation for both the Erinyes and Lyssa. Uncertainty and danger surround the Erinyes' form, with the Pythia undoing her own attempts to describe them. In contrast, Lyssa, along with Iris, appears suddenly and without any prior visual description. Fundamental to the visuality of both the Erinyes and Lyssa, however, is their somatic power. We see in the three tragedies analysed here how these terrifying female deities are materialised both offstage and onstage through the bodies of others – through their visceral impact on Orestes, the Pythia, the chorus and Heracles. The latter, who never actually appears onstage while in his maddened state, has a sort of symbiotic relationship with Lyssa and the chorus, becoming present in turn through them both.

This chapter has also shown how these plays push the potentiality of theatre as 'an art of bodies witnessed by bodies'. We have seen both Aeschylus and Euripides experimenting not just with various bodily effects on and manifestations in characters within the dramas themselves, but also with the audience's own bodily engagement. The terrifying reach of the Erinyes and Lyssa threatens to extend to the spectators in the theatre, as the somatic danger of these petrifying agents of madness radiates beyond the confines of the dramatic world being represented. Such a danger, as we saw, was

---

[64] Olsen 2020: 173. The term 'embodied cultural knowledge' comes from Sklar 2008. As part of such knowledge, Olsen also includes an audience's potential experience of space, specifically the landscape and architecture of Delphi, where Neoptolemus is killed. See also Angelopoulou on how 'the kinetic style of both discourse and performance can invite a certain kind of corporealisation in the spectator's body' (2021: 600).
[65] Olsen 2020: 174.

frequently acknowledged as a product of the performance of poetry in general and of drama in particular. Aeschylus and Euripides participate in such an experience and conceptualisation of theatre by urging on their spectators' particularly visceral responses to the figures they see or visualise. In this respect, to return to the phrase used in the *Life of Aeschylus*, they both 'shock the spectators' gaze', even regardless of theatrical technologies like costumes, masks and stage machinery. In these tragedies, the audience's own bodies play an important role in theatre's representational process.

# Making Sense of Surprisal: *Thaumastos* on the Ancient Stage – A Cognitive Approach

Peter Meineck

Athenian drama in the fifth century BC was a multisensory experience capable of provoking profound perceptual associations between the mimetic displays performed in the theatre and the lived experiences of the five to six thousand spectators gathered on the southeast slope of the Acropolis.[1] Yet, the sensory information available to the *theates* extended far beyond scenes staged in the *theatron, skēnē* and *orchestra*, being also contiguously gathered from the surrounding environment. This view included the panoramic vistas of the southern city and its shrines and monuments, the sweeping Attic countryside beyond, then the Aegean Sea and most prevalent in these spectators' optic array, the vast expanse of the sky. This sensory elision between city, countryside, sky and stage was further intensified by the festival atmosphere within which the plays were embedded and its association with traditional cult practices. These included processions, pre-play events and the almost continual acts of animal sacrifice in the sanctuary below. It is not hard to imagine the sounds of those animals, the smell of their blood and the aroma of grilled meat carried by the light breeze of a Mediterranean spring day. Athenian drama was undoubtedly a feast for the senses.

But what happens when the sensory mechanisms humans depend on to perceive the world around them are confounded and disrupted, resulting in a 'cognitive gap' – a surprise that causes a mental stoppage that momentarily cannot be resolved? In this chapter, I suggest that much of the sensory power of Greek drama lay in its ability to do just that – induce temporary dislocations of sensory attenuation that could, in turn, increase attentionality, cognitive absorption, empathy and even a sense of self-realisation. If this description sounds like a mental description of *catharsis* as Aristotle frames it in *Poetics*, this is intentional, as perhaps it was this aspect of Athenian drama that was the most 'Dionysian', probably inherited from the dissociative mind-altering rituals of mystery cult practice. With this in mind, I am taking a cognitive approach to

---

[1]   On the size and form of the theatre in the fifth century BC see Papastamati-Von Mook 2020.

the sensory experience of ancient drama. I will be focusing on the opening scene of Aeschylus' *Eumenides*, where the Pythia is memorably portrayed suffering a startling perceptual failure that embodies how surprisal acts in and on our minds and bodies. In this volume, Naomi Weiss brings a phenomenological perspective to Aeschylus' Furies and explores how intercorporeality affected the audience. Here, rather than placing 'the senses' in their usual taxonomies, exteroceptive (vision, hearing, touch), interoceptive (taste, smell, pain, bodily functions) or proprioceptive (balance, movement, the sense of force and weight), I will be situating the total sensory experience within the perceptual theories of cognitive active inference and predictive processing. These define how human sensory perception forms a generative model of the world, continually gathering sensory information and making predictions about what it experiences.

Predictive processing is a fundamental mechanism of distributed cognition – the concept that the mind is *of* and *in* its surrounding environment and dynamically participates with the world in a continual sense-making feedback loop known as active inference.[2] Effectively, we receive sensory perceptual inputs 'bottom-up', such as sights, sounds, smells, physical sensations, tastes, shivers, heart rate increases, flinches, or feelings of temperature on our skin, to name but a few. But we do not possess the mental neuronal bandwidth, nor do we create enough glucose, the basic nutritional building block that helps maintain our neural chemistry, to mentally process the enormous array of perceptual stimuli in the world we sense around us at any one time.

Try it: look out of or imagine looking out of a window and attempt to count and then describe what you perceive: the people, trees, buildings, cars, signs, colours, textures, movements, plant life, animals, insects, physical features, clouds in the sky, etc. – you cannot – it is not possible, and even if you could perceive *everything*, there is a finite temporal limit on how long that would take and by then most of those initial sensory signals would have changed. Additionally, we are only sensing things from one dimension. To use Merleau-Ponty's famous example,[3] how do you know that the front of the table lamp you view is the same as the back? You cannot know for sure unless you gather more information through *action*, the active part of the inference system that underpins our cognitive productive mechanisms. So, without getting up and walking around to the other side of the lamp to view or touch it, we instead rely on our cognitive prediction systems. We set the bottom-up sensory information provided at that moment (I see one facet of a lamp) against the top-down stored percept of what we know through prior experience (that the back of the lamp resembles the front), and we

---

[2]   On predictive processing see Clark 2015.
[3]   Merleau-Ponty 1962: 68.

simply make our best guess, or as philosopher Andy Clark eloquently puts it, 'our mental states are coloured by delicate estimations of our own uncertainty'.[4] Because of this ability of the mind to use sensory information to create *eidolons* of the world around us, the theoretical neuroscientist Karl Friston has called the brain *the phantastic organ* from the Greek term *phantasia* – to make manifest or to imagine.[5]

Aristotle offers a complex and fascinating description of *phantasia* in *On the Soul*, where he asks if what we imagine is true or false. He concludes that basic sense perception only allows us to be aware of a thing. Yet, the process of *phantasia*, which he describes as a fluid movement of calibrating what we perceive with what we already know, allows us to form value judgements about what the thing is and how it might affect us (427b29–429a3).[6] Aristotle uses as an example the way we perceive the sun: it looks like it only measures a few inches when we see it in the sky, but we predict, based on our prior knowledge, that it is far larger than the world. In effect, we constantly cognitively 'correct' our perceptual 'errors'. When Aristotle states, 'imagination must be a movement produced by sensation actively operating', he describes the cognitive process of active inference (429a2–3).

Predictive processing is embedded in the mind's broader system of distributed cognition, the concept that mental processes are distributed in a continual cognitive feedback loop throughout our bodies and out into environmental perceptual networks. Thus, thoughts are *embodied* with our entire bodily form, *enacted* across the matter that bounds the organic matter we are made of, *embedded* within the environments and cultures where we live and *extended* out into the world.[7] The predictive mind uses a Bayesian form of error correction by actively and continually comparing those 'bottom-up' sensory signals with 'top-down' stored information held in the memory. As you survey the domain outside your window, your mind is employing a probabilistic (hence 'Bayesian' or inference updating) method to compare what it is presented with what it knows: tree: *check*, grass: *check*, sky: *check*; all these things sensed out in the world comport with our stored perceptions of that world. Suddenly, I see a shiny saucer-like object in the sky: what! The fluid, effortless process of sense perception suddenly lights upon something surprising, awe-inspiring, or frightening. As Aristotle suggests, we activate our inference systems to try to gain more information about the thing that we do not immediately understand – I focus my attention, heighten my senses, move to gain a better view, and as I do so, my neurochemical and endocrinal systems start to prepare my body for flight, flight, or freeze.

---

[4]   Clark 2015: xvi.
[5]   Friston et al. 2014.
[6]   Moss 2012: 53–4.
[7]   On distributed cognition see Hutchins 1995.

Of course, emotions play their part here, too. This is the error-correcting part of prediction at work, where we expend that precious glucose and other finite resources we possess to create homeostasis, the narrow biological bands within which we survive. But as Friston has convincingly demonstrated with the 'free energy principle' derived from theoretical thermodynamics, we are natural products of the environments in which we live (a fish cannot live out of the water, and we cannot live in it).[8] Suppose such a fish finds itself in that unfortunate position. In that case, it will expend a maximum amount of free energy to return to a state of homeostasis and convulse vigorously on dry land, attempting to get back in the water. We do the same if we find ourselves underwater for more than a few minutes without any external breathing apparatus. Friston maintains that we constantly strive to avoid entropy – a state of change that can result in our bodily functions ceasing to work. We maximise our free energy in these change states, but cannot do it for long. One might assume then that we would seek to minimise the expenditure of free energy by, as Friston puts it, seeking out a dark room and remaining there. However, sensory deprivation has been related to Greek cult practices, including the Mysteries. Humans cannot survive without the risk of leaving that cognitive 'dark room'. Living involves risk, and whether foraging for food, obtaining water, building shelter, or seeking a partner, our perceptual systems need to be ready to deal with all kinds of existential threats.

As for that flying saucer? I correct the error and move on when I find out later that I have been looking at a stray weather balloon. However, the energy I spend fixing this sensory error costs time, effort, emotional toll and mental health. These cognitive prediction errors create surprisal, and in so doing they stimulate our sensory and emotional mechanisms, heightening our attentionality and focusing our cognitive resources on dealing with what has caused that surprise. When we encounter such surprisal, suddenly or more gradually, our cognitive systems are heightened as we process the shocking and the amazing. In *Poetics*, Aristotle said that what is amazing (*thaumastos*) is essential to tragedy – and the improbable or incredible is the most critical aspect of what is amazing. For Aristotle, being enthralled by surprisal was a cause of pleasure for the audience but also one of the primary elements involved in provoking *eleos*, phobos and other emotions and, of course, the creation of tragic *catharsis* (1460a11–19).

Before processing any further and getting to my example from Aeschylus' *Eumenides*, it is crucial to address the applicability of cognitive science to antiquity – how can scientific and theoretical findings based on contemporary humans from distinct cultures apply to ancient Greek minds? Most neuroscience and AI studies initially approached the brain from a computational perspective. Still, more recently, philosophy, phenomenology and cognitive theory have advanced successfully integrated models of cognition that blend

---

[8]   Friston et al. 2012.

these computational approaches with distributed cognition.[9] As such methods hold that cognition exists in 'the wild',[10] in that thought is distributed through culture and environment, the study of ancient cultures might be reframed as what the archaeologists Colin Renfrew and Lambros Malafouris describe as 'the remnants of ancient thoughts'.[11]

A recent example of an effective application of cognitive theory to antiquity was a multi-year project at the University of Edinburgh on the history of distributed cognition, which produced a valuable volume on classical antiquity. In it, Anderson, Cairns and Sprevak comment, 'the paradigm of distributed cognition provides a middle way between relativism and universalism by highlighting the vital roles played by both physical and cultural resources in cognition'.[12] If the biological human mind, which has not fundamentally changed in the past 80,000 years, has been moulded by and has, in turn, moulded its environment and the culture it produced, then distributed cognition provides a bio-cultural paradigm to deepen our understanding of ancient cultures. In the same volume, Douglas Cairns adds that '[to] a considerable extent, traditional ways of doing Classics, ancient history, and classical archaeology either lend themselves to recasting in terms of distributed cognition or in fact already employ, usually without realising it, approaches and assumptions that can be expressed in those terms'.[13] Distributed cognition is particularly applicable to the theatre as a place of an active mimetic mental state between actors and audience.

Turning to the theatre, at the beginning of *Eumenides*, the final play of Aeschylus' *Oresteia* trilogy, the scene has moved from the House of Atreus in Argos to the Temple of Apollo at Delphi. The first character introduced is the Pythia, and she relates the succession of the shrine from a line of matriarchal goddesses to the current tenure of the Olympian deity Apollo. She enters the temple to receive her prophecies by the *skēnē* door, and for a moment the spectators are left gazing at a performance space empty of actors and completely quiet. Shouts suddenly break this silence and screams from inside are heard as the Pythia clambers out of the doorway on all fours, unable to stand and in a state of extreme distress:

ἦ δεινὰ λέξαι, δεινὰ δ᾽ ὀφθαλμοῖς δρακεῖν,
πάλιν μ᾽ ἔπεμψεν ἐκ δόμων τῶν Λοξίου,
ὡς μήτε σωκεῖν μήτε μ᾽ ἀκταίνειν στάσιν·
τρέχω δὲ χερσίν, οὐ ποδωκείαι σκελῶν·
δείσασα γὰρ γραῦς οὐδέν, ἀντίπαις μὲν οὖν.

---

[9]  For example, Seth and Critchley 2013, Clark 2018, Hutchinson and Barrett 2019, Hohwy 2020, Smith 2021.
[10]  Borrowing this phrase from Hutchins 1995.
[11]  Malafouris and Renfrew 2010: 1.
[12]  Anderson, Cairns and Sprevak 2019: 14–15.
[13]  Cairns 2019b: 18.

ἐγὼ μὲν ἕρπω πρὸς πολυστεφῆ μυχόν,
ὁρῶ δ' ἐπ' ὀμφαλῶι μὲν ἄνδρα θεομυσῆ
ἕδραν ἔχοντα προστρόπαιον, αἵματι
στάζοντα χεῖρας, καὶ νεοσπαδὲς ξίφος
ἔχοντ', ἐλαίας θ' ὑψιγέννητον κλάδον
ἀργῆτι μαλλῶι σωφρόνως ἐστεμμένον.
[ ∪ – ∪ – ∪ τῆιδε γὰρ τρανῶς ἐρῶ]
πρόσθεν δὲ τἀνδρὸς τοῦδε θαυμαστὸς λόχος
εὕδει γυναικῶν ἐν θρόνοισιν ἥμενος.
οὔτοι γυναῖκας ἀλλὰ Γοργόνας λέγω,
οὐδ' αὖτε Γοργείοισιν εἰκάσω τύποις.
εἶδόν ποτ' ἤδη Φινέως γεγραμμένας
δεῖπνον φερούσας· ἄπτεροί γε μὴν ἰδεῖν
αὗται μέλαιναί τ', ἐς τὸ πᾶν βδελύκτροποι,
ῥέγκουσι δ' οὐ πλατοῖσι φυσιάμασιν,
ἐκ δ' ὀμμάτων λείβουσι δυσφιλῆ λίβα·
καὶ κόσμος οὔτε πρὸς θεῶν ἀγάλματα
φέρειν δίκαιος οὔτ' ἐς ἀνθρώπων στέγας.
τὸ φῦλον οὐκ ὄπωπα τῆσδ' ὁμιλίας
οὐδ' ἥτις αἶα τοῦτ' ἐπεύχεται γένος
τρέφουσ' ἀνατεὶ μὴ μεταστένειν πόνον.
τἀντεῦθεν ἤδη τῶνδε δεσπότηι δόμων
αὐτῶι μελέσθω Λοξίαι μεγασθενεῖ·
ἰατρόμαντις δ' ἐστὶ καὶ τερασκόπος
καὶ τοῖσιν ἄλλοις δωμάτων καθάρσιος. (34–63)[14]

Horrors! Horrors to tell! Horrors before my eyes,
They have repelled me from Apollo's house!
I am terrified, they have taken all my strength! I cannot stand,
I have to scuttle out on my hands and knees
A scared old woman in nothing, no more than a helpless child.
I was entering the chamber where the wool wreaths
Hang, and I saw a man by the center-stone,
Stained in the sight of the gods and crouching
In supplication. His hands and drawn sword
Are dripping with blood, and he is clutching

---

[14] Text as in Podlecki 1989.

A tall olive branch, rightly wreathed
With a full woollen shank of silvery fleece.
In front of this man was an astounding throng
Of women propped against the benches asleep.
No, not women, they were a hideous sight,
More like Gorgons, but worse, much worse.
I have seen paintings of the beasts that plagued
Phineus and stole his food, but the creatures in there
Have no wings, they are shadowy, dank, and disgusting.
Their foul stench and hideous breath forced me back,
And their eyes seep a repulsive, putrid pus.
They are wrapped in dismal rags not fit for human sight.
A place of holy idols should not suffer such an evil apparition.
I have never known a place that spawned such creatures,
Nor have I seen a land that could boast to have bred them
Without suffering some terrible blight – terrible pain!
Apollo must decide what to do with them,
He is the master of this house,
He is the healer, the prophet,
He has the power of purification.[15]

The Pythia's entropy state is sudden and alarming: her environment is disrupted by the presence of the Furies and, as a result, she cannot function as a conduit to the divine. Moreover, the sensory experience of encountering the Furies has rendered her biologically incapable of her usual state of homeostasis: she cannot walk; her speech is frantic and rushed; and her emotional response, in this case, disgust and fear, has repelled her from the shrine where she is supposed to officiate. Yet Aeschylus provides us with far more than a simple emotional response, and here we experience the Pythia struggling to make sense of what she has just perceived. Her cognitive active inference mechanisms seem to have failed, and the predictive 'error' caused by the sensory experience (sight, smell, bodily functions) of the Furies cannot be reconciled and compared against any top-down percept stored in her memory. First, she tries categorising the furies by comparing them to women (48–9), an aspect of predictive processing known as precision. This is described as 'a fundamental aspect of inference in the brain … encoding the expected uncertainty in any given context'.[16] Precision is a vital part of the operation of the so-

---

[15] Meineck 1998.
[16] Friston et al. 2014.

called generative model of active inference, whereby the mind dynamically interprets the sensory information available to 'generate' an acceptable deduction about what the thing being sensed is. When an inference cannot be made quickly, the mind seeks more information, looking for precision. In the case of the Pythia, this cognitive function immediately fails; the Furies are not like women at all. The Pythia's predictive mental process is now under intense pressure as she desperately seeks cognitive precision to understand what she has perceived in the temple. She tells us that she has a percept of a Gorgon, but this mental image also fails to correct the cognitive error. The Furies do not even resemble Harpies as they have no wings, there is nothing the Pythia can compare them to, no category where they belong, they are shadowy, repulsive (βδελύκτροποι, 57) creatures that should not be looked upon at all.

There is a robust neural correlation between cognitive precision, which binds predictions within sense perception, and bodily movement through the active calibration of proprioception (the sense of one's own body in space), nociception (the sense of pain) and equilibrioception (the sense of balance). These are actively adjusted as top-down predictions interpret the available bottom-up sensory information. An involuntary reflex such as a flinch when we perceive that an object may be about to hit us is an example of precision and movement working together effectively. Yet the Pythia's disjointed and frenetic movements and her loss of bodily control are manifestations of her predictive failure. Aeschylus provides us with a good deal of detail about how the Furies have acted on her sense-making systems: she is physically repelled by the sound (and stench) of their foul breath, sickened by the detestable fluid oozing from their eyes and disgusted at the sight of such creatures in a sacred space. The reaction of disgust is an embodied, emotional one and leads to other affective states like fear, anger and shock (all emotions are an integral part of our predictive systems).

The Pythia's embodied expressions form an interoceptive feedback loop between exterior stimulus, mental percepts and the body's autonomic systems (heart rate, blood pressure, breathing, skin temperature, oxygen flow, etc.). This predictive model of emotions threads the needle between the James/Lange embodiment theory ('I tremble; therefore, I feel afraid') and appraisal theory, which posits that emotions derive from cognitive judgement. Within predictive processing, both can be tenable, operating simultaneously as bodily felt emotional states further contribute to the generative model by providing interoceptive bottom-up signals to compare with top-down contextual situations.[17] This process also involves neurochemical and endocrine production, such as adrenaline which, in the case of fear, certainly an emotion being experienced by the Pythia, prepares the body for immediate action.

---

[17]   Pezzulo et al. 2015.

In addition to fear, the Pythia experiences shock, disgust, anxiety and even anger when she says that the Furies (and their dismal rags) are not fit to be seen in such a holy place. Her fleeing from the temple is a physical and cognitive rejection of the indescribable things she has just perceived. Just as she tells of the failure of her mind to process and categorise the Furies, knowing of no place anywhere in the world that could have bred them, so her bodily functions also fail as she scurries out on all fours, hardly in recognisable human form herself. This state could be viewed as a form of echopraxia, a debilitating syndrome that can affect people with different forms of mental illness or temporary cognitive disruptions such as extreme anxiety. A person suffering from echopraxia starts to mirror the movements of the person they observe as their mirror neuron system fails to attenuate the actions under observation. Of course, I am not suggesting that Aeschylus created this scene with this specific diagnosis in mind, that he may well have observed people under tremendous stress in wartime or provoked to echopraxic behaviour from mystery and healing cults that utilised ritual overimitation, dance and collective movement.[18] Notably, the Pythia calls for *catharsis* at the end of the scene (65).

It must have been deeply unsettling for many in Aeschylus' audience to witness the Pythia forced from the Temple of Apollo, having lost control of her body. It was even more upsetting to hear how a priestess associated with producing knowledge and foresight could not articulate what she had perceived inside. The sense of cognitive dissonance established by the Pythia sets the scene for what is to come, the famous entry of the Furies, which have been presented as *phantasia* in *Agamemnon* and *Libation Bearers*.[19] The quasi-mythical *Life of Aeschylus* famously tells us that at the sight of the furies in *Eumenides*, children fainted, and women suffered miscarriages. While this story is as far-fetched as the turtle-bombing Eagle that cracked Aeschylus' bald skull, it retains a memory of the kind of sensory overload associated with this staging. It was as if the entropy of the Pythia communicated an extreme form of emotional and sensory contagion amongst the spectators. After only hearing about the Furies in *Agamemnon* and then experiencing them vicariously through Orestes in *Libation Bearers,* the sight of

---

[18] For example, the Corybantic Frenzies, where extreme repetitive movements practices in a group aid in healing. See Borthwick 1992 and Ustinova 2017: 118–25. On ritual overimitation in antiquity see Mackey 2019.

[19] Cassandra (*Ag.* 1186–92), Orestes (*Cho.* 1048–9). Orestes' visions are described by the chorus as δόξαι (1051), a term that conveys both imagination and prediction or what 'seems to be'. Aeschylus' attention to cognitive disruption is demonstrated by Orestes who is aware that he is losing grip of his senses and likens his mental state to an out-of-control chariot hurtling him far off course and into the unknown (1021–5). Like the Pythia, Orestes also seeks relief by seeking *catharsis* (1059). The chorus also call for *catharsis* in *Cho.* (968), where disturbingly they are referring to the killing of Clytemnestra and Aegisthus.

them creeping out of the *skene* or rising from the *ekkylēma* might have been both truly astounding and quite shocking – *phantasia* brought to vivid mimetic life.[20]

The first sight of the Furies embodied in the *Oresteia* may also have had a predictive element that has been overlooked. It was not only their physical appearance, the way they moved and sounded, the music that accompanied them and their disruption of the Olympian hierarchy that was unnerving, but the very idea of seeing Furies, albeit mimetic ones, in action at all. Such creatures made manifest may have been considered something right on the edge of impiety connected with the Furies' cultic connections with Demeter and the mysteries I will describe below. This was dangerous theatre, and apart from the spurious reference to it in the *Life of Aeschylus*, we can only imagine what it made those in the audience feel, undoubtedly different degrees of *thaumastos* – the very term the Pythia uses to describe what she had experienced (48).

We hardly need cognitive science to inform us that the entrance of the Furies in *Eumenides* was surprising, but how might we understand how theatrical *thaumastos* – the action of being surprised or 'surprisal' – operated in moments such as the Pythia's entrance? A cognitive approach can help shed light on *how* such moments of surprisal worked on stage and in what way they may have been received by the audiences they were initially intended for. This use of cognitive theory, applied to drama, might be described as cognitive performance studies and can offer us a valuable tool to place beside literary, cultural, historical and material approaches. The film theorist Phillip Auslander described this as 'liveness', embedding a performance within its social, political and environmental context.[21] What elements of liveness can we discern in the Furies' entrance that might further illuminate its *dramatic* experienced effect?

In *Poetics* 1455a27–9, Aristotle advises the ancient playwright to place the action before their sight so they can perceive it as an audience might and not just an internalised percept of what that action might look like. *Peripetia* (reversals) and *anagnorisis* (sudden recognitions) are his famous examples of dramatic surprisals, and we can also place *hamartia* within predictive processing as a failure of a character's cognitive systems to correct a perceptual error. According to Aristotle, these change elements are essential to producing *catharsis*, particularly in tragedy. However, they should not be so shocking that they go beyond probability. His example is of a statue of Mitys at Argos that falls on the murderer of Mitys at a festival – a surprise for the murderer, to be sure. Still, for the audience, the surprising event fits into a probabilistic cosmos of reciprocity (*Poetics*

---

[20]   Much has justifiably been written about the amazing entrance of the Furies. For a survey of the scholarship and recent spatial perceptual view see Bakola 2018; others that deal with perceptual elements include Bacon 2001, Easterling 2008, Mitchell-Boyask 2013.

[21]   Auslander 2008: 52.

1452a2–11). Aristotle knew that a prediction error is sublimely arresting and enthralling. Still, if unresolved, it will lead to distraction and reflection of the fragile cognitive artifice that is that act of theatre.

Plato takes a different view, of course. In *Laws* 797d–799c, he has his Athenian rail against change (μεταβολή) as a significant disruptive influence on the state. It is 'something evil and extremely dangerous' (797d). The Athenian wants ancient, unchanging laws that are revered and respected and thinks that when children introduce novelties (νεωτερίζοντας) into their games, they will grow up and demand political change, upsetting the status quo. Plato then goes on to have his Athenian refer to the earlier discussion on musical form and rhythm and how certain 'excitable' modes can negatively affect the audience member (654e, 668a). He concludes by stating that they must do all they can to prevent the young from 'presenting alternative subjects' (ἄλλων μιμημάτων), either in dance drama (ὀρχήσεις) or music and song (μελῳδίας). The remedy cited in this passage is to look to the Egyptians and sanctify all performances so that it would be deemed impious to change them, and anyone attempting to do so would be tried and expelled from the state.

Plato has the Athenian in *Laws* describe the theatre as being the place where the people were trained to express their aesthetic opinions and this, in turn, made them politically emboldened. For Plato, this was a 'vicious theatrocracy' where 'the conviction of their expectations' made them 'unafraid' (701a–b). Later, he says, 'we must do everything possible to distract the young from attempting to present new subjects in their choruses or their music' (798e); if they do this, they will be different from the previous generation and 'then they will demand a different kind of life, and this will make them want new institutions and laws' (798c). What Plato is railing about here is not only an aesthetic turn but a cognitive one, with significant political and social ramifications.

Recent neural mapping of the brain's default mode network has shown that when we encounter moments of surprisal, this complex network, normally active at moments of cognitive interiority (daydreaming, sleeping, meditation, etc.), is at its most dynamic when perceptual wonders engage us. It is not coincidental, then, that in Plato's Analogy of the Cave, the prisoners are enthralled by the shadows created by the θαυματοποιοῖς or 'amazement-makers' (*Republic* 514b). The term can also mean 'conjurer' or 'magician', even an acrobat or anyone who performs something awe-inspiring – the compelling cognitive gap between sensory input and mental percept. Based on Plato's general disparagement of drama, he surely means for us to see the shadow puppeteers in the cave as poets, enthralling their captive audience with myths – imitations of what Plato considered reality. So, when we think of dramatic *thaumastos* in these terms, we can understand the powerfully compelling nature of tragedy and its relationship to *phantasia*.

The studies on the Default Mode Network help explain the kind of sustained cognitive absorption that, in tragedy, is stimulated by feelings of dissociation and displacement. I have written elsewhere about how the foreign strains of the highly emotive *aulos*, elaborate costumes, surprising narrative twists, uncanny attributes of the mask, and the dopamine-inducing open-air environment of the performance space itself all contributed to the spectator feeling like 'a stranger in a strange land', while seated in the heart of Athens.[22] Though we only have a textual 'blueprint' of Aeschylus' *Eumenides*, with all its associated transmission issues, we can still detect traces of how the Pythia scene and the subsequent entrance of the Furies may have been sensed and felt by the spectators. It is understood that not all audience members will ever respond in the same way, and we must always consider the conditions of the scopic regime of Athens in the mid fifth century. Yet audiences can and do often respond collectively, and emotional contagion, shared kinesthetic empathy and collective autonomic responses (such as breathing rates) have been well documented in many studies.[23] Surprisal is often the key to creating the cognitive absorption necessary to produce these broad shared audience experiences.

In *Eumenides*, Aeschylus used the Pythia scene to prime the audience's predictive systems for what was to come – the actual manifestation of the Furies on stage. He used this staging to create a cognitive gap in their minds, one that was less extreme than the Pythia said she had experienced but nevertheless enough to create the kind of long-lasting reputation for active surprisal of women miscarrying and children fainting. Of course, this anecdote tells us more about some areas where the Furies were said to operate (fecundity, the nurturing of the young, familial blood ties) than any actual event that may have occurred. Still, the one thing we can at least take away from it is that the entrance of the Furies was a superb act of tragic *thaumastos*.

We left the Pythia at a profound moment of predictive error correction stoppage. I have already noted how disconcerting it must have been to watch a priestess famed for imparting knowledge to now have no way of expressing what she has just perceived. Here, Aeschylus pulls off a brilliant theatrical sleight-of-hand by confounding the audience's predictive mechanisms. When the Pythia comes scurrying out of the shrine after experiencing the Furies, she acts like a tragic messenger. This character is supposed to articulate unseen events that have happened offstage. But she fails and, whereas the audience may have begun to imagine the Furies in their minds prompted by Cassandra in *Agamemnon* or Orestes in *Libation Bearers*, the Pythia acts to obliterate any percepts that their imaginations may have created based on existing artistic representations of

---

[22]  Meineck 2017.
[23]  Reason and Reynolds 2010.

Gorgons, or Harpies or other such creatures.[24] At this point, the audience is misdirected. If a great seer like the Pythia cannot interpret what she has perceived, how can the audience member?[25] It is more than likely that they had no reason to think they would see them on stage, as even in Homer they are known as ἠεροφοῖτις, the 'unseen' or 'those who walk in darkness' (*Iliad* 9.571 and 19.87).[26]

There can be no doubt that producing the Furies on stage was a surprisal *coup de théâtre*, and we can only speculate on how it may have been staged: suddenly and shockingly, or as a slower disquieting event. It was a combination of both, like a 'jump-cut' from a horror movie where an atmosphere of eerie silence and dissonance is suddenly broken by a frightening image usually accompanied by a piercing noise. If Orestes entered on the *ekkyklema* surrounded by three sleeping Furies, as has been proposed, then initially, only a few inanimate sleeping figures with their masks turned away from the audience may have been seen. Urged on by the ghost of Clytemnestra, they slowly began to move. At this point, the audience's predictive systems are becoming fully engaged as they lean in on the 'edge of their seats' to gather more sensory information – are they really going to see Furies embodied, and how is Aeschylus going to depict them? Then more of them start to spill out of the *skēnē* door, filling the *orchestra*, the texts here perhaps reflective of their seeping breath sounds with their marked sibilance and long vowel sounds:

ἰοὺ ἰοὺ πύπαξ. ἐπάθομεν, φίλαι,
ἤ πολλὰ δὴ παθοῦσα καὶ μάτην ἐγώ
ἐπάθομεν πάθος δυσαχές, ὢ πόποι. (143–5)

No! No! Sisters we have been wronged!
All my work – all our work for, for nothing! Nothing!
No! No! I can't bear the pain, it hurts! It hurts!

That Aeschylus thoroughly surprised his audience with the appearance of the Furies is the accepted view of this moment in *Eumenides*. At some point during their entrance, the audience must have realised that these creatures embodied before them would comprise the chorus of the third play in the trilogy and this, on its own, would have been an astounding element. The entrance of the Furies is even given as the reason for Aeschylus'

---

[24]   Simas 2020 thinks that the Pythia is using the language of vase painting and referencing reliefs on temple pediments. Alongside this I would place wall painting, folklore and the masked daemon rituals mentioned above.

[25]   Brown 1983 proposed that the Pythia's description helped the audience 'come to picture the Furies more and more clearly in their own minds'. I think the opposite was the case.

[26]   Bakola 2018 has made a strong case that the Furies are pivotal throughout the *Oresteia* and fluctuate between the seen and unseen.

hasty departure to Sicily by later commentators, including Pollux (*Onomasticon* 4.110). However, if we explore this scene from a cognitive perspective, we can take a small step back and ask if the audience had any percepts about presenting Furies on stage. I have already pointed out that the Pythia's list of predictive failures moves the audience members' minds away from images they may have seen in other media available at that time, but what about the idea of staging them at all? How revolutionary was it to bring such figures to life on stage? Was the reaction to Aeschylus' Furies only about the *mise-en-scène*, or was there something else going on that provoked the audience's predictive systems?

Burkert pointed out that what he described as 'grotesque masks of old women' were associated with the rites of female deities in several archaic Greek communities.[27] He cites the Gorgon-like terracotta masks from the sanctuary of Artemis Orthia, which were probably based on masks initially worn in the rituals held there, and the pot-shaped masks from Tiryns dated to the eighth century and found at a shrine to Hera. Also, Pausanias writes of a mask of Demeter Kidaria worn by a priest in the mysteries held in Arcadia, where he beat 'those from the underworld' with a stick (8.14.1–3). Related to the Furies were masks associated with the Praxidikai, female avenging spirits who punished oath breakers (Hsch. s.v. Π). If Burkert is correct, there may well have been a tradition of representing chthonic female *daemons* by masked performers in older cult practice, and the fact that these rituals seem connected with eschatological cults and forms of chthonic justice involving the punishment of transgressions is significant to the narrative of *Eumenides*. Perhaps, then, it was not just the perception of Aeschylus' presentation of the Furies on stage. What could have been so shocking was not how Aeschylus embodied the Furies, but that he dared to stage them.

Aristotle alludes to a tale where Aeschylus was prosecuted for revealing the mysteries in his plays.[28] His defence was how could he tell what he did not know? It is a likely story from a playwright who reportedly hailed from a well-to-do family of Eleusis. His surviving plays teem with Eleusinian references. Aristophanes depicts him praying to Demeter as his 'nurturer' in *Frogs* and asking to be 'worthy of her mysteries' (886–7). His visits to Sicily may have been connected to Hieron's role as a priest of Demeter, with the cult of the two goddesses being used to bolster Syracusan expansionism and identity.

Furthermore, the connections between the Furies and Demeter are well known and, as Curbera has pointed out, 'we know that in several places Demeter had the title of Erinys'.[29] Suppose we place this evidence within the cognitive realm of the Athenian audience. In that case, it may well have been likely that some form of these elements

---

[27] Burkert 1985: 104.

[28] *Eth. Nic.* 1111a8.

[29] Curbera 1997. See also Dietrich 1962, Boedecker 1983, Stallsmith 2008. Pausanias writes of a cult of Demeter Erinys in Thelpousa (8.25.3–7).

(the connection between Demeter, Persephone and the Furies and the cult tradition of staging masked female *daemons'* ritual performances) existed as memory-based percepts ready to be compared to what Aeschylus presented. Might we then infer from this that revealing the Furies onstage could have been perceived as crossing a ritual line connected to what could and could not be shown related to the mystery cult of Demeter and Persephone? If this was the case, then, as the Furies enter, Aeschylus' audience is taken well beyond the comfort zone of their eschatological 'dark rooms'. Their *thaumastos* could well have been the thought that by encountering the multi-sensory experience of Aeschylus' mimetic Furies they were also participating in an act that was right on the edge of impiety.

By the end of the play, the Furies are transformed and incorporated into the city of Athens. Now they are displayed in a procession of full view, and 'kind minds' are perceived in their 'fearsome faces' (προσώπων, 990–2; the same term is used for 'mask'). They join a commonwealth, 'a joint spirit shared by all', and provide 'a cure for common suffering' (985–6). Those who once caused insensibility are now welcomed with all the sensations of a public religious spectacle. What Aeschylus had done was to expertly use the cognitive mechanisms of surprisal to actuate the active inference sensory-perceptual systems of his audience and, in so doing, deepen their cognitive absorption and increase their feelings of empathy. If Athens could make sense of and reconcile these most disturbing creatures, there was hope that the *stasis* that threatened the city in 458 BC might also be avoided. By experiencing the Pythia losing her senses, by the end of the play, the Athenians might come to theirs.

# Bibliography

Agamben, G. (1993) *Infancy and history*, trans. L. Heron, New York.

Agamben, G. (1998) *Homo sacer: sovereign power and bare life*, trans. D. Heller-Roazen, Stanford.

Ahmed, S. (2004) *The cultural politics of emotion*, London.

Akrigg, B. and R. Tordoff, eds (2013) *Slaves and slavery in ancient Greek comic drama*, Cambridge.

Allen, D. (2009) 'Angry bees, wasps, and jurors: the symbolic politics of ὀργή in Athens', in S. M. Braund and G. W. Most, eds, *Ancient anger: perspectives from Homer to Galen* (Cambridge) 76–98.

Alt, K. (1952) 'Untersuchungen zum Chor bei Euripides', unpublished PhD thesis, University of Frankfurt.

Anderson, M., D. Cairns and M. Sprevak, eds (2019) *Distributed cognition in classical antiquity*, Edinburgh.

Andò, V. (2021) *Euripide, Iphigenia in Aulide: introduzione, testo critico, traduzione e commento*, Venice.

Angelopoulou, A. (2020) 'Problematizing *aisthēsis*: the disruption of shared affectivity in the *Ajax*', *TAPhA* 150: 39–64.

Angelopoulou, A. (2021) 'Gesture, metaphor and the body in *Trojan Women*', *AJP* 142: 597–627.

Angelopoulou, A. (2022) 'Making sense of Plato's taste', *CP* 117: 24–44.

Armstrong, P. (2005) 'Phenomenology', in M. Groden, M. Kreiswirth and I. Szeman, *The Johns Hopkins guide to literary theory and criticism*, 2nd edn (Baltimore) 562–6.

Arrington, N. (2018) 'Touch and remembrance in Greek funerary art', *ABull* 100.3: 7–27.

Auslander, P. (2008) *Liveness: performance in a mediatised culture*, London.

Austin, C. and S. Olson (2004) *Aristophanes: Thesmophoriazusae*, Oxford.

Backhouse, A. (1994) *The lexical field of taste: a semantic study of Japanese taste terms*, Cambridge.

Bacon, H. (2001) 'The Furies' homecoming', *CP* 96.1: 48–59.

Bakola, E. (2018) 'Seeing the invisible: interior spaces and uncanny Erinyes in Aeschylus' *Oresteia*', in A. Kampakoglou and A. Novokhatko, eds, *Gaze, vision, and visuality in ancient Greek literature* (Berlin/Boston, MA) 163–86.

Barker, A. (2004) 'Transforming the nightingale: aspects of Athenian musical discourse in the late fifth century', in Murray and Wilson 2004: 185–204.

Barker, J. (2009) *The tactile eye: touch and the cinematic experience*, Berkeley.

Barlow, S. (1971) *The imagery of Euripides*, London.

Barlow, S., ed. (1996) *Euripides: Heracles*, Warminster.

Barzini, L. (2021) *Mystery cults, theatre and Athenian politics: a reading of Euripides' Bacchae and Aristophanes' Frogs*, London/New York.

Bassi, K. (1998) *Acting like men: gender, drama, and nostalgia in ancient Greece*, Ann Arbor.

Bassi, K. (2016) *Traces of the past: classics between history and archaeology*, Ann Arbor.

Bassi, K. (2018) 'Morbid materialism: the matter of the corpse in Euripides' *Alcestis*', in Telò and Mueller 2018a: 35–48.

Battezzato, L. (2005) 'The new music of the *Trojan Women*', *Lexis* 23: 73–104.

Beckett, S. (1994) *Trilogy: Molloy, Malone Dies, The Unnamable*, London.

Beekes, R. (2010) *Etymological dictionary of Greek*, Leiden.

Bélis, A. 1(991) 'Aristophane, *Grenouilles* v. 1249–1364: Eschyle et Euripide μελοποιοί', *REG* 104: 31–51.

Bergoffen, D. (2001) 'Toward a politics of the vulnerable body', *Hypatia* 18: 116–34.

Bernadete, S. (1999) *Sacred transgression: a reading of Sophocles' Antigone*, South Bend.

Betts, E. (2017) *Senses of the empire: multisensory approaches to Roman culture*, London/New York.

Beye, C. (1959) '*Alcestis* and her critics', *GRBS* 2: 111–27.

Biles, Z. (2011) *Aristophanes and the poetics of competition*, Cambridge.

Biles, Z. (2014) 'Exchanging metaphors in Cratinus and Aristophanes', in S. Olson, ed., *Ancient comedy and reception: essays in honor of Jeffrey Henderson* (Berlin) 3–12.

Biles, Z. (2016) 'Thucydides' Cleon and the poetics of politics in Aristophanes' *Wasps*', *CP* 111: 117–38.

Biles, Z. and S. Douglas Olson (2015) *Aristophanes: Wasps*, Oxford.

Billings, J. (2018) '*Bacchae* as palinode', *IJCT* 25.1: 57–71.

Bloesch, H. (1943) Ἄγαλμα *als Kleinod, Weihgeschenk und Götterbild*, Bern.

Bochicchio, L., M. Mazzeo and G. Squillace (2019) *A lume di naso: olfatto, profumi, aromi tra mondo antico e contemporaneo*, Macerata.

Boedeker, D. (1983) 'Hecate: a transfunctional goddess in the *Theogony*?', *TAPA* 113: 79–93.

Bond, G., ed. (1981) *Euripides: Heracles*, Oxford.

Borthwick, E. (1992) 'Observations on the opening scene of Aristophanes' *Wasps*', *CQ* 42.1: 274–8.

Borthwick, E. (1994) 'New interpretations of Aristophanes *Frogs* 1249–1328', *Phoenix* 48.1: 21–41.

Bourdieu, P. (2017) 'Tastes of luxury, tastes of necessity', in Korsmeyer 2017b: 54–9.

Bowie, A. (1993) *Aristophanes: myth, ritual and comedy*, Cambridge.

Bowie, A. (1997) 'Thinking with drinking: wine and the symposium in Aristophanes', *JHS* 117: 1–21.

Braden, G. (2017) 'Classical Greek tragedy and Shakespeare', *Classical Receptions Journal* 9.1: 103–19.

Bradley, M. (2014) 'Art and the senses: the artistry of bodies, stages, and cities in the Greco-Roman world', in Toner 2014: 163–82.

Bradley, M., ed. (2015) *Smell and the ancient senses*, London/New York.

Bradley, M., V. Leonard and L. Totelin (2021) *Bodily fluids in antiquity*, London/New York.

Breitenbach, W. (1934) *Untersuchungen zur Sprache der euripideischen Lyrik*, Stuttgart.

Bremmer, J. (1993) 'Aristophanes on his own poetry', in J. Bremmer and E. Handley, eds, *Aristophane: entretiens sur l' antiquité* 38 (Geneva) 125–65.

Brinkema, E. (2014) *The forms of the affects*, Durham, NC.

Brock, R. (2000) 'Sickness in the body politic: medical imagery in the Greek polis', in V. Hope and E. Marshall, eds, *Death and disease in the ancient city* (London) 24–34.

Brown, A. (1983) 'The Erinyes in the *Oresteia*: real life, the supernatural, and the stage', *JHS* 103: 13–34.

Budelmann, F. (2019) 'Group minds in classical Athens?: chorus and demos as case studies of collective cognition', in Anderson, Cairns and Sprevak 2019: 190–208.

Budelmann, F. and P. LeVen (2014) 'Timotheus' poetics of blending: a cognitive approach to the language of the New Music', *CP* 109.3: 191–210.

Budelmann, F. and T. Phillips, eds (2018a) *Textual events: performance and the lyric in early Greece*, Oxford.

Budelmann, F. and T. Phillips, eds (2018b) 'Introduction: textual events: performance and the lyric in early Greece', in Budelmann and Phillips 2018a: 1–28.

Burke, V. (2008) 'From ethical substance to reflection: Hegel's *Antigone*', *Mosaic* 41.3: 47–61.

Burkert, W (1985) *Greek religion*, Cambridge, MA.

Burnett, A. (1965) 'The Virtues of Admetus', *CP* 60.4: 240–55.

Butler, J. (1988) 'Performative acts and gender constitution: an essay in phenomenology and feminist theory', *Theatre Journal* 40: 519–31.

Butler, J. (2000) *Antigone's claim: kinship between life and death*, New York.

Butler, J. (2004) *Precarious life: the powers of mourning and violence*, New York.

Butler, J. (2009) *Frames of war: when is life grievable?*, London.

Butler, J. (2015) *Notes toward a performative theory of assembly*. Cambridge, MA/London.

Butler, J. (2022) *The force of nonviolence*, New York.

Butler, S. (2015) *The ancient phonograph*, New York.

Butler, S. and S. Nooter, eds (2019) *Sound and the ancient senses*, London/New York.

Butler, S. and A. Purves, eds. (2013) *Synaesthesia and the ancient senses*, London/New York.

Buxton, R. (1980) 'Blindness and limits: Sophokles and the logic of myth', *JHS* 100: 22–37.

Buxton, R. (2013) *Myths and tragedies in their ancient Greek context*, Oxford.

Cairns, D. (1993) *Aidōs: the psychology and ethics of honour and shame in Greek literature*, Oxford.

Cairns, D. (2015) 'The horror and the pity: *phrikē* as a tragic emotion', *Psychoanalytic Inquiry* 35: 75–94.

Cairns, D. (2019a) 'The politics of Antigone's lament from Sophocles to Heaney', Διεθνές συμπόσιο αρχαίου ελληνικού δράματος 14: 35–44.

Cairns, D. (2019b) 'Distributed cognition and the Classics', in Anderson, Cairns and Sprevak 2019: 18–36.

Campbell, D. (1993) *Greek lyric V: the new school of poetry and anonymous songs and hymns*, Cambridge, MA/London.

Carson, A. (1999) 'Dirt and desire: the phenomenology of female pollution in antiquity', in J. Porter, ed., *Constructions of the classical body* (Ann Arbor) 77–100.

Carter, D., ed. (2011) *Why Athens? A reappraisal of tragic politics*, Oxford/New York.

Carter, L. (1986) *The quiet Athenian*, Oxford.

Cartledge, P. (2002) *The Greeks: a portrait of self and others*, 2nd edn, Oxford.

Case, Z. (2021a) 'What's Nietzsche to Euripides? The aesthetics of suffering in Nietzsche's *Birth of Tragedy* and Euripides' *Trojan Women*', *CCJ* 67: 25–50.

Case, Z. (2021b) 'Hyper-democracy: the politics of Aristophanes', unpublished PhD thesis, University of Cambridge.

Cavarero, A. (2005) *For more than one voice: toward a philosophy of vocal expression*, trans. P. A. Kottman, Stanford.

Cavarero, A. (2007) *Horrorism: naming contemporary violence*, trans W. McCuaig, New York.

Cavell, S. (2003) *Disowning knowledge in seven plays of Shakespeare*, Cambridge.

Cazzato, V. and A. Lardinois, eds (2016) *The look of lyric: Greek song and the visual*, Leiden/Boston, MA.

Childs, W. (2018) *Greek art and aesthetics in the fourth century B. C.*, Princeton/Oxford.

Citron, F. and A. Goldberg (2014) 'Metaphorical sentences are more emotionally engaging than their literal counterparts', *Journal of Cognitive Neuroscience* 26: 2585–95.

Clark, A. (2015) *Surfing uncertainty: prediction, action, and the embodied mind*, Oxford.

Clark, A. (2018) 'A nice surprise? Predictive processing and the active pursuit of novelty', *Phenomenology and the Cognitive Sciences* 17: 521–34.

Classen, C., D. Howes and A. Synnott (1994) *Aroma: the cultural history of smell*, London.

Clay, J. S. (2002) 'Rowing for Athens', in J. Miller, C. Damon and K. Myers, eds, *Vertis in usum: studies in honor of Edward Courtney* (Munich) 271–6.

Clements, A. (2013) 'Looking mustard: Greek popular epistemology and the meaning of δριμύς', in Butler and Purves 2013: 46–59.

Clough, P. and J. Halley, eds (2007) *The affective turn: theorising the social*, Durham, NC.

Collard, C. and J. Morwood, (2017) *Euripides: Iphigenia in Aulis*, 2 vols, Liverpool.

Compton-Engle, G. (2015) *Costume in the comedies of Aristophanes*, Cambridge.

Cook, A. (1971) *Enactment: Greek tragedy*, Athens, OH.

Cousland, J. and J. Hume (2009) *The play of texts and fragments: essays in honour of Martin Cropp*, Leiden/Boston, MA.

Cowan, R. (2014) 'The smell of Sophokles' *Salmoneus*: technology, scatology, metatheatre', *Ramus* 43: 1–12.

Crane, G. (1989) 'Creon and the "Ode to Man" in Sophocles' *Antigone*', *HSP* 92: 103–16.

Croiset, M. (1891) *Histoire de la littérature grecque*, Paris.

Cropp, M. (1988) *Euripides: Electra*, Warminster.

Cropp, M. (1997) 'Antigone's final speech (Sophocles, *Antigone* 891–928)', *G&R* 44.2: 137–60.

Cropp, M. and G. Fick (1985) *Resolutions and chronology in Euripides: the fragmentary tragedies*. London.

Csapo, E. (1999–2000) 'Later Euripidean music', *ICS* 24–25: 399–426.

Csapo, E. (2003) 'The dolphins of Dionysus', in E. Csapo and M. Miller, eds, *Poetry, theory, praxis: the social life of myth, word and image in ancient Greece: essays in honour of William J. Slater* (Oxford) 69–98.

Csapo, E. (2004) 'The politics of the new music', in Murray and Wilson 2004: 207–48.

Csapo, E. (2008) 'Star choruses: Eleusis, Orphism, and new musical imagery and dance', in Revermann and Wilson 2008: 262–90.

Csapo, E. (2009) 'New Music's gallery of images: the "dithyrambic" first stasimon of Euripides' *Electra*', in Cousland and Hume 2009: 95–109.

Csapo, E. (2011) 'The economics, poetics, politics, metaphysics, and ethics of the "New Music"', in D. Yatromanolakis, ed., *Music and cultural poetics in Greek and Chinese societies, volume I: Greek Antiquity* (London/Cambridge, MA) 65–131.

Csapo, E. (2014) 'Performing comedy in the fifth through early third centuries', in Fontaine and Scafuro 2014: 50–68.

Csapo, E. and P. Wilson (2009) 'Timotheus the New Musician', in F. Budelmann, ed., *The Cambridge companion to Greek lyric*, (Cambridge/New York) 277–94.

Cullyer, H. (2005) 'A wind that blows from Thrace: Dionysus in the fifth stasimon of Sophocles' *Antigone*', *CW* 99.1: 3–20.

Curbera, J. (1997) 'Chthonians in Sicily', *GRBS* 38.4: 397–408.

D'Angour, A. (2006) 'The New Music: so what's new?', in Goldhill and Osborne 2006: 264–83.

D'Angour, A. (2011) *The Greeks and the new: novelty in ancient Greek imagination and experience*, Cambridge/New York.

Dale, A. (1961) *Euripides, Alcestis*, Oxford.

Dale, A. (1968) *The lyric meters of Greek drama*, 2nd edn, Cambridge.

Damen, M. (1989) 'Actor and character in Greek tragedy', *Theatre Journal* 41: 316–40.

Davidson, J. (1997) *Courtesans and fishcakes: the consuming passions of Classical Athens*, New York.

Davies, G. (1985) 'The significance of the handshake motif in classical funerary art', *AJA* 89.4: 627–40.

de la Fuente, S. (2002) 'El sufijo Griego -ώδης: origen, valore y fortuna literaria', *Myrtia* 17: 7–43.

de Romilly, J. (1958) La crainte et l'angoisse dans le théâtre d'Eschyle, Paris.

de Simone, M. (2008): 'The "lesbian" muse in tragedy: Euripides μελοποιός in Aristoph. *Ra.* 1301–28', *CQ* 58.2: 479–90.

De'Ath, L. (2016) 'Text considerations in the stage works of Carl Orff, *Journal of Singing* 73.1: 55–70.

Deleuze, G. (1968) *Différence et répétition*, Paris.

Deleuze, G. (1993) *The fold: Leibniz and the Baroque*, trans. T. Conley, New York.

Deleuze, G. (1994) *Différence and répétition*, trans. P. Patton, New York.

Deleuze, G. and F. Guattari (1987) *A thousand plateaus: capitalism and schizophrenia*, trans. B. Massumi, Minneapolis.

Dellner, J. J. (2000) 'Alcestis' double life', *CJ* 96.1: 1–25.

Delulle, H. (1911) 'Les répétitions d'images chez Euripide: contributions à l'étude de l'imagination d'Euripide', unpublished PhD thesis, University of Leuven.

Denniston, J. (1954) *The Greek particles*, 2nd edn, Oxford.

Denniston, J. and D. Page (1957) *Aeschylus: Agamemnon*, Oxford.

Destrée, P. (2015) 'Pleasure', in Destrée and Murray 2015a: 472–85.

Destrée, P. and P. Murray, eds (2015a) *A companion to ancient aesthetics*, Malden/Oxford.

Destrée, P. and P. Murray (2015b) 'Introduction', in Destrée and Murray 2015a: 1–13.

Detienne, M. (1994) *The gardens of Adonis: spices in Greek mythology*, trans. J. Lloyd and J.-P. Vernant, Princeton.

Dewar-Watson, S. (2009) 'The *Alcestis* and the statue scene in *The Winter's Tale*', *Shakespeare Quarterly* 60.1: 73–80.

Di Benedetto, S. (2010) *The provocation of the senses in contemporary theatre*, London.

Dietrich, B. (1962) 'Demeter, Erinys, Artemis', *Hermes* 90: 129–48.

Diggle, J. (1984) *Euripides fabulae tomus I: insunt Cyclops, Alcestis, Medea, Heraclidae, Hippolytus, Andromache*, Hecuba, Oxford.

Diggle, J. (1994) *Euripidis Fabulae Tomus III. Insunt Helena, Phoenissae, Orestes, Bacchae, Iphigenia Aulidensis, Rhesus*, Oxford.

Dillon, J. (2010) 'Shakespeare's tragicomedies', in M. de Grazia and S. Wells, eds, *The New Cambridge Companion to Shakespeare* (Cambridge) 169–84.

Diprose, R. (2002) *Corporeal generosity: on giving with Nietzsche, Merleau–Ponty, and Levinas*, Albany.

Dobrov, G. (2010) 'Comedy and her critics', in G. Dobrov, ed., *Brill's companion to the study of Greek comedy* (Leiden/Boston, MA) 1–33.

Dodds, E. (1960) *The Bacchae*, 2nd edn, Oxford.

Dova, S. (2012) *Greek Heroes in and out of Hades*, Lanham, MD.

Dover, K. (1972) *Aristophanic comedy*, Berkeley.

Dover, K. (1989) *Aristophanes: Clouds*, Oxford.

Dover, K. (1993) *Aristophanes: Frogs*, Oxford.

Drew, D. (1931) 'Euripides' *Alcestis*', *AJP* 52.4: 295–319.

Driver, T. (1960) 'Release and reconciliation: the *Alcestis* and *The Winter's Tale*' in *The sense of history in Greek and Shakespearean drama* (New York) 168–98.

Drobnick, J., ed. (2006) *The smell culture reader*, Oxford.

DuBois, P. (1991) *Torture and truth*, New York/London.

Duchemin, J. (1967 'Le personnage de Lyssa dans *Héraclès* d' Euripide', *REG* 80: 130–9.

Dunbar, N. (1995) *Aristophanes: Birds*, Oxford.

Dyson, M. (1988) 'Alcestis' children and the character of Admetus', *JHS* 108: 13–23.

Easterling, P. (2008) 'Theatrical Furies: thoughts on *Eumenides*', in Revermann and Wilson 2008: 219–36.

Edmonds, R. (2004) *Myths of the underworld journey: Plato, Aristophanes, and the Orphic gold tablets*, Cambridge.

Edwards, A. (1991) 'Aristophanes' comic poetics: τρύξ, scatology, σκῶμμα', *TAPA* 121: 157–79.

Elderkin, G. W. (1990) 'Aphrodite and Athena in the *Lysistrata* of Aristophanes', *CP* 35: 387–96.

Ellis, M. (2022) 'Beauty of form and concept: the aesthetics of late Euripidean tragedy', unpublished PhD thesis, University of Cambridge.

Elmer, D. (2017) 'Aeschylus' tragic projections', in K. Coleman, ed., *Albert's anthology* (Cambridge, MA) 57–9.

Elsner, J. (2006) 'Reflections on the "Greek Revolution" in art: from changes in viewing to the transformation of subjectivity', in Goldhill and Osborne 2006: 68–95.

England, E. (1891) *The Iphigenia at Aulis of Euripides*, London.

Enterline, L. (1997) '"You speak a language that I understand not': the rhetoric of animation in *The Winter's Tale*', *Shakespeare Quarterly* 48.1: 17–44.

Eskine, K., N. Kacinik and J. Prinz (2011) 'A bad taste in the mouth: gustatory disgust influences moral judgment', *Psychological Science* 22: 295–9.

Farenga, V. (2014) 'Open and speak your mind', in V. Wohl, ed., *Probabilities, hypotheticals, and counterfactuals in ancient Greek thought* (Cambridge) 84–100.

Fauçonnier, G. and M. Turner (1998): 'Conceptual integration networks', *Cognitive Science* 22: 133–87.

Fauçonnier, G. and M. Turner (2002) *The way we think: conceptual blending and the mind's hidden complexities*, New York.

Ferrari, G. (1997) 'Figures in the text: metaphors and riddles in the *Agamemnon*', *CP* 92: 1–45.

Finley, M. (1980) *Ancient slavery and modern ideology*, Cambridge.

Fletcher, J. (2008) 'Citing the law in Sophocles' *Antigone*', *Mosaic* 41.3: 79–96.

Foley, H. (1985) *Ritual irony: poetry and sacrifice in Euripides*, Ithaca, NY.

Foley, H. (1992) '*Anodos* dramas: Euripides' *Alcestis* and *Helen*', in R. Hexter and D. Selden, eds, *Innovations of Antiquity* (London) 301–32.

Foley, H. (2000) 'The comic body in Greek art and drama', in B. Cohen, ed., *Not the classical ideal: Athens and the construction of the other in Greek art* (Leiden/Boston, MA) 275–311.

Foley, H. (2001) *Female acts in Greek tragedy*, Princeton.

Foley, H. (2018) 'The _oices of *Antigone*', in Stuttard 2018: 162–76.

Fontaine, M. and A. Scafuro, eds (2014) *The Oxford handbook of Greek and Roman comedy*, Oxford.

Ford, A. (2002) *The origins of criticism: literary culture and poetic theory in classical Greece*, Princeton.

Ford, A. (2013) 'The poetics of dithyramb', in Kowalzig and Wilson 2013: 313–31.

Foster, S. (2008) 'Movement's contagion: the kinesthetic impact of performance', in T. Davis, ed., *The Cambridge companion to performance studies* (Cambridge) 46–59.

Foster, S. (2010) *Choreographing empathy: kinesthesia in performance*, New York.

Fraenkel, E. (1950) *Aeschylus: Agamemnon*, 3 vols, Oxford.

Franco, C. (2014) *Shameless: the canine and the feminine in ancient Greece*, Berkeley.

Franklin, J. (2013) '"Songbenders of circular choruses": dithyramb and the "demise of music"', in Kowalzig and Wilson 2013: 213–26.

Friston, K. et al. (2012) 'Free-energy minimisation and the dark-room problem', *Frontiers in Psychology* 130: 293–301.

Friston, K. et al. (2014) 'Computational psychiatry: the brain as a phantastic organ', *The Lancet Psychiatry* 1: 148–58.

Frontisi-Ducroux, F. (1995) *Du masque au visage: aspects de l'identité en Grèce ancienne*, Paris.

Frontisi-Ducroux, F. (2007) 'The invention of the Erinyes', in C. Kraus, S. Goldhill, H. Foley and J. Elsner, eds, *Visualizing the tragic: drama, myth, and ritual in Greek art and literature* (Oxford) 165–76.

Gagarin, M. (1996) 'The torture of slaves in Athenian law', *CP* 91: 1–18.

Garland-Thomson, R. (2002) 'Integrating disability, transforming feminist theory', *NWSA Journal* 14: 1–32.

Garner, S., Jr. (1994) *Bodied spaces: phenomenology and performance in contemporary drama*, Ithaca, NY.

Garvie, A. (1994) *Homer: Odyssey books VI–VIII*, Cambridge.

Gavrilenko, V. (2011) '*Toucher, ne par toucher, telle est la question*: réflexions autour du Corps d'Alceste chez Euripide', *Mètis* 9: 193–207.

Gerber, D. (1978) 'The female breast in Greek erotic literature', *Arethusa* 11: 203–12.

Giannakis, G. (2001) 'Light is life, dark is death: an ancient Greek and Indo-European metaphor', Δωδώνη: Φιλολογία 30: 127–53.

Gigante, D. (2005) *Taste: a literary history*, New Haven.

Goldhill, S. (1986) *Reading Greek tragedy*, Cambridge.

Goldhill, S. (1987) 'The Great Dionysia and civic ideology', *JHS* 107: 58–76.

Goldhill, S. (1991) *The poet's voice: essays on poetics and Greek literature*, Cambridge/New York.

Goldhill, S. (2012) *Sophocles and the language of tragedy*, Oxford.

Goldhill, S. and R. Osborne, eds (1999) *Performance culture and Athenian democracy*, Cambridge.

Goldhill, S. and R. Osborne, eds (2006) *Rethinking revolutions through ancient Greece*, Cambridge/New York

Gossett, S., ed. (2014) *Pericles*, London.

Gowers, E. (1993) *The loaded table: representations of food in Roman literature*, Oxford.

Grand-Clément, A. and C. Ribeyrol (2022) *The smells and senses of antiquity in the modern imagination*, London/New York.

Gray, B. (2015) *Stasis and stability: exile, the polis, and political thought, c. 404–146 BC*, Oxford.

Green, J. R. (1991) 'On seeing and depicting the theatre in classical Athens', *GRBS* 32: 15–50.

Gregg, M. and G. Seigworth, eds (2010) *The affect theory reader*, Durham, NC.

Grene, D. and R. Lattimore, eds (1955) *The complete Greek tragedies*, vol. 3, Chicago.

Grethlein, J. (2017) *Aesthetic experiences and Classical Antiquity: the significance of form in narratives and pictures*, Cambridge.

Griffith, M. (1999) *Sophocles: Antigone*, Cambridge.

Griffith, M. (2010) 'Psychoanalyzing Antigone', in S. E. Wilmer and A. Žukauskaitė, eds, *Interrogating Antigone in postmodern philosophy and criticism* (Oxford) 110–34.

Griffith, M. (2013) *Aristophanes: Frogs*, Oxford.

Gunders, J. (2002) 'Signal or noise? Information theory and the novel', *Double Dialogues* 3.

Gurd, S. (2005) *Iphigenias at Aulis: textual multiplicity, radical philology*, Ithaca, NY.

Gurd, S. (2013) 'Resonance: Aeschylus' *Persae* and the poetics of sound', *Ramus* 42: 122–37.

Gurd, S. (2016) *Dissonance: auditory aesthetics in ancient Greece*, New York.

Gurd, S. (2019) 'Auditory philology', in Butler and Nooter 2019: 184–97.

Hall, E. (2006) *The theatrical cast of Athens: interactions between ancient Greek drama and society*, Oxford/New York.

Hall, E., D. Braund and R. Wyles, eds (2019) *Ancient theatre and performance culture around the Black Sea*, Cambridge.

Hall, E. and S. Harrop (2010) *Theorising performance: Greek drama, cultural history and critical practice*, London.

Hall, E., F. Macintosh and O. Taplin, eds (2005) *Agamemnon in performance*, Oxford/New York.

Hall, E., F. Macintosh, P. Michelakis and O. Taplin, eds (2000) *Medea in performance 1500–2000*, Oxford.

Hall, E. and A. Wrigley, eds (2007) *Aristophanes in performance*, London.

Halliwell, S. (1986) *Aristotle's Poetics*, London.

Halliwell, S. (1993) 'The function and aesthetics of the Greek tragic mask', in N. Slater and B. Zimmermann, eds, *Intertextualität in der griechisch-römischen Komödie* (Stuttgart) 195–211.

Halliwell, S. (1998) *Aristotle's Poetics*, Chicago.

Halliwell, S. (2002) *The aesthetics of mimesis: ancient texts and modern problems*, Princeton.

Halliwell, S. (2011) *Between ecstasy and truth: interpretations of Greek poetics from Homer to Longinus*, Oxford.

Halliwell, S. (2012) '*Amousia*: living without the Muses', in Sluiter and Rosen 2012: 15–45.

Halliwell, S. (2022) *Pseudo-Longinus: On the Sublime*, Oxford/New York.

Halliwell, S., W. Fyfe, D. Russel and D. Innes (1999) *Aristotle: Poetics. Longinus: On the Sublime. Demetrius: On Style*, Cambridge, MA/London.

Halperin, D. (1990) *One hundred years of homosexuality*, New York.

Hamilakis, Y. (2013) *Archaeology and the senses: human experience, memory and affect*, Cambridge.

Hardt, M. (2007) 'Forward: what affects are good for', in Clough and Halley 2007: ix–xiii.

Harris, E. (2004) 'Notes on a lead letter from the Athenian agora', *Hesperia* 102: 157–70.

Harris, J. (2007) 'The smell of Macbeth', *Shakespeare Quarterly* 58: 465–86.

Harsh, P. (1944) *A handbook of classical drama*, Stanford.

Hartman, H.W. (1938) *A petite pallace of Pettie his pleasure*. London/New York.

Hawes, G. (2014) *Rationalising myth in antiquity*, Oxford.

Hawthorne, K. (2009) 'The chorus as rhetorical audience: a Sophoklean agōn pattern', *AJP* 130.1: 25–46.

Hayley (1898) *The Alcestis of Euripides*, Boston, MA.

Heath, J. (1999) 'Disentangling the beast: humans and other animals in Aeschylus' *Oresteia*', *JHS* 119: 17–47.

Heiden, B. (1991) 'Tragedy and comedy in the *Frogs* of Aristophanes', *Ramus* 20: 95–111.

Helg, W. (1950) 'Das Chorlied der griechischen Tragödie in seinem Verhältnis zur Handlung', unpublished PhD thesis, University of Zurich.

Henderson, J. (1987a) 'Older women in Attic old comedy', *TAPA* 117: 105–29.

Henderson, J. (1987b) *Aristophanes, Lysistrata*, Oxford.

Henderson, J. (1990) 'The *dēmos* and the comic competition', in Winkler and Zeitlin 1990: 271–313.

Henderson, J. (1991) *The maculate muse: obscene language in Attic comedy*, Oxford.

Henderson, J. (1998a) *Aristophanes: Acharnians, Knights*, Cambridge, MA/London.

Henderson, J. (1998b) *Aristophanes: Clouds, Wasps, Peace*, Cambridge, MA/London

Henderson, J. (2000) *Aristophanes: Birds, Lysistrata, Women at the Thesmophoria*, Cambridge, MA/London.

Henderson, J. (2002) *Aristophanes: Frogs, Assemblywomen, Wealth*, Cambridge, MA/ London.

Henrichs, A. (1969) 'Die Maenaden von Milet', *ZPE* 4: 223–41.

Henrichs, A. (1994–5) '"Why should I dance?": choral self-referentiality in Greek tragedy', *Arion* 3: 56–111.

Highmore, B. (2010) 'Bitter after taste: affect, food, and social aesthetics', in Gregg and Seigworth 2010: 118–37.

Hiscock, M. (2018) 'Sophoclean suicide', *ClAnt* 37.1: 1–30.

Hitch, S. (2018) 'Tastes of Greek poetry', in Rudolph 2018a: 22–44.

Hohwy, J. (2020) 'New directions in predictive processing', *Mind & Language* 35: 209–23.

Holmes, B. (2010) *The symptom and the subject: the emergence of the physical body in ancient Greece*, Princeton.

Honig, B. (2013) *Antigone, interrupted*, Cambridge.

Hose, M. (1990–1) *Studien zum Chor bei Euripides*, Stuttgart.

Howes, D., ed. (2005) *Empire of the senses: the sensual culture reader*, Oxford.

Howes, D., ed. (2018) *Senses and sensation: critical and primary sources*, 4 vols, London/New York.

Hubbard, T. (1991) *The mask of comedy: Aristophanes and the intertextual parabasis*, Ithaca, NY.

Hughes, A. (2006) 'The costumes of old and middle comedy', *BICS* 49: 39–68.

Hughes, T., ed (1999) *Alcestis*, London.

Hume, D. (2017) 'Of the standard of taste', in Korsmeyer 2017b: 197–204.

Hunter, R. (2009) *Critical moments in classical literature: studies in the ancient view of literature and its uses*, Cambridge/New York.

Hunter, R. (2017) 'Comedy and reperformance', in R. Hunter and A. Uhlig, eds, *Imagining reperformance in ancient culture: studies in the traditions of drama and lyric* (Cambridge/New York) 209–31.

Hunter, V. (1992) 'Constructing the body of the citizen: corporal punishment in classical Athens', *Echos du monde classique* 36: 271–91.

Hutchins, E. (1995) *Cognition in the wild*, Cambridge, MA.

Hutchinson, J. and L. Barrett (2019) 'The power of predictions: an emerging paradigm for psychological research', *Current Directions in Psychological Science* 28: 280–91.

Jackson, S. (1990) 'Myrsilus of Methymna and the dreadful smell of the Lemnian women', *ICS* 15: 77–83.

Janko, R. (1984) *Aristotle on comedy: towards a reconstruction of Poetics II*, Berkeley.

Jarbus, A. (1967) *Eye movements and vision*, New York.

Jebb, R. (1900) *Sophocles: the plays and fragments. Part 3: the Antigone*, 3rd edn, Cambridge.

Johnston, S. I. (2006) 'Antigone's other choice', *Helios* 33S: 179–86.

Kaimio, M. et al. (1990) 'Comic violence in Aristophanes', *Arctos* 24: 47–72.

Kant, I. (2017) 'Objective and subjective senses: the sense of taste', in Korsmeyer 2017b: 205–10.

Kennedy, G. (1989) 'Language and meaning in archaic and classical Greece', in G. Kennedy, ed., *The Cambridge history of literary criticism* (Cambridge) 78–92.

Ketterer, R. (1980) 'Stripping in the parabasis of *Acharnians*', *GRBS* 21: 217–21.

Kidd, S. (2019) *Play and aesthetics in ancient Greece*, Cambridge/New York.

Kierstead, J. (2017) 'Democracy's humility: a reading of Sophocles' *Antigone*', *Polis* 34: 288–305.

Kitzinger, M. (2008) *The choruses of Sophokles' Antigone and Philoktetes: a dance of words*, Leiden.

Kivy, P. (1984) *Sound and semblance: reflections on musical representation*, Princeton.

Knox, B. (1985) 'Euripides', in P. Easterling and B. Knox, eds, *The Cambridge history of classical literature. Volume I: Greek literature* (Cambridge) 316–39.

Kompridis, N., ed. (2014) *The aesthetic turn in political thought*, London/New York.

Konstan, D. (1985) 'The politics of Aristophanes' *Wasps*', *TAPA* 115: 27–46.

Konstan, D. (2001) *Pity transformed*, London.

Konstan, D. (2023) 'Finishing *Iphigenia in Aulis*', in J. Fabre-Serris, M. Formisano and S. Frangoulidis eds, *Labor imperfectus: unfinished, incomplete, partial texts in classical antiquity* (Berlin) 261–73.

Korsmeyer, C. (2002) *Making sense of taste*, Ithaca, NY.

Korsmeyer, C. (2017a) 'Introduction: perspectives on taste', in Korsmeyer 2017b: 1–8.

Korsmeyer, C., ed. (2017b) *The taste culture reader: experiencing food and drink*, New York.

Kott, J. (1973) *The eating of the gods*, Evanston.

Kovacs, D. (2002) *Euripides: Bacchae, Iphigenia at Aulis, Rhesus*, Cambridge, MA/London.

Kovacs, D. (2003) 'Toward a reconstruction of *Iphigenia Aulidensis*', *JHS* 123: 77–103.

Kowalzig, B and P. Wilson, eds, (2013) *Dithyramb in context*, Oxford.

Kranz, W. (1933) *Stasimon: Untersuchungen zu Form und Gehalt der griechischen Tragödie*, Berlin.

Kristeller, P. (1980) 'The modern system of the arts: a study in the history of aesthetics', in P. Kristeller, ed., *Renaissance thought and the arts: collected essays* (Princeton) 496–527.

Kristeva, J. (1984) *Revolution in poetic language*, trans. M. Waller, New York.

Kurke, L. (1992) 'The politics of ἁβροσύνη in archaic Greece', *ClAnt* 11: 91–120.

Kurke, L. (2013) 'Imagining chorality: wonder, Plato's puppets and moving statues', in A.-E. Peponi, ed., *Performance and culture in Plato's laws* (Cambridge) 123–70.

Lada-Richards, I. (1993) 'Empathic understanding: emotion and cognition in classical dramatic audience-response', *PCPS* 39: 94–140.

Lada-Richards, I. (1999) *Initiating Dionysus: ritual and theatre in Aristophanes' Frogs*, Oxford.

Lamari, A. (2017) *Reperforming Greek tragedy: theater, politics, and cultural mobility in the fifth and fourth centuries BC*, Berlin/Boston, MA.

Land, M. and B. Tatler, eds (2009) *Looking and acting: vision and eye movements in natural behaviour*, New York.

Lape, S. (2013) 'Slavery, drama and the alchemy of identity in Aristophanes', in Akrigg and Tordoff 2013: 76–90.

Largey, D. and G. Watson (1972) 'The sociology of odors', *American Journal of Sociology* 77.6: 1021–34

Larocco, S. (2016) 'Pain as semisomatic force: the disarticulation and rearticulation of subjectivity', *Subjectivity* 9.4: 343–62.

Lateiner, D. and D. Spatharas (2016a) 'Ancient and modern modes of understanding and manipulating disgust', in Lateiner and Spatharas 2016b: 87–102.

Lateiner, D. and D. Spatharas, eds (2016b) *The ancient emotion of disgust*, Oxford.

Lather, A. (2018) 'Olfactory theater: tracking scents in Aeschylus's *Oresteia*', *Arethusa* 51: 33–54.

Lauriola, R. (2007) 'Wisdom and foolishness: a further point in the interpretation of Sophocles' *Antigone*', *Hermes* 135.4: 389–405.

Lauriola, R. and E. Magnelli (2017) *Athens on the stage: theatre and democracy in Classical Greece*, Leiden.

Lawrens, J. (2012) 'Welcome to the revolution: the sensory turn and art history', *Journal of Art Historiography* 7.

Lebeck, A. (1971) *The Oresteia: a study in language and structure*, Washington.

Lee, K. (1982) 'The Iris–Lyssa scene in Euripides' *Heracles*', *Antichthon* 16: 44–53.

Lee, M. (2015) *Body, dress and identity in ancient Greece*, Cambridge.

Lesky, A. (1971) *Geschichte der griechischen Literatur*, 3rd edn, Bern.

LeVen, P. (2014) *The many-headed muse: tradition and innovation in late Classical Greek lyric poetry*, Cambridge.

LeVen, P. (2019) 'The erogenous ear', in Butler and Nooter 2019: 212–32.

Levi, E. (2002) 'Antigonae', *Grove Music Online*, https://doi.org/10.1093/gmo/9781561592630.article.O006002.

Levine, D. (2016) 'Disgust and delight: the polysemous exclamation αἰβοῖ in Attic comedy', in Lateiner and Spatharas 2016b: 1–42.

Ley, G. (2007) *The theatricality of Greek tragedy: playing space and chorus*, Chicago.

Liebert, R. (2017) *Tragic pleasure from Homer to Plato*, Cambridge/New York.

Lilja, S. (1972) *The treatment of odours in the poetry of antiquity*, Helsinki.

Lloyd-Jones, H. (1952) 'The robes of Iphigenia', *CR* 2: 132–5.

Lloyd-Jones, H. (1990) 'Problems of early Greek tragedy: *Pratinas and Phrynichus*', in H. Lloyd-Jones, ed., *Greek epic, lyric and tragedy* (Oxford) 225–37.

Lloyd-Jones, H. (1994) *Sophocles: Antigone, the women of Trachis, Philoctetes, Oedipus at Colonus.* Cambridge MA/London.

Lloyd-Jones, H. and N. Wilson (1990) *Sophoclis fabulae*, Oxford.

Lonsdale, S. H. (1993) *Dance and ritual play in Greek religion*, Baltimore.

Loraux, N. (1987) *Tragic ways of killing a woman*, trans. A. Forster, Cambridge, MA.

Loraux, N. (2002) *The mourning voice: an essay on Greek tragedy*, trans. E. T. Rawlings, Ithaca, NY.

Loraux, N. (2006) *The divided city: on memory and forgetting in ancient Athens*, trans. C. Pache, New York.

Louden, B. (2007) 'Reading through *The Alcestis* to *The Winter's Tale*', *Classical and Modern Literature* 27.2: 7–30.

Low, K. (2012) 'The social life of the senses: charting directions', *Sociology Compass* 6 (3): 271–82.

Lupton, D. (2017) 'Food and emotion', in Korsmeyer 2017b: 315–21.

Macedo, J. (2011) 'In between poetry and ritual: the hymn to Dionysus in Sophocles' *Antigone* (1115–54)', *CQ* 61.2: 402–11.

Mackey, J. (2019) 'Roman ritual orthopraxy and overimitation', in Meineck, Short and Devereaux 2019: 253–69.

Malafouris, L. and C. Renfrew (2010) 'The cognitive life of things: archaeology, material engagement and the extended mind', in L. Malafouris and C. Renfrew, eds, *The cognitive life of things: recasting the boundaries of the mind* (Cambridge) 1–12.

Mallory, J. and D. Adams (2006) *The Oxford introduction to Proto-Indo-European and the Proto-Indo-European world*, Oxford.

Markantonatos, A. (2013) *Euripides' 'Alcestis': narrative, myth and religion*. Berlin.

Marks, L. (2000) *The skin of the film: intercultural cinema, embodiment, and the senses*, Durham, NC.

Marks, L. (2002) *Touch: sensuous theory and multisensory media*, Minneapolis.

Marshall, C. and D. Kovacs (2012) *No laughing matter: studies in Athenian comedy*, London.

Marshall, C. (1999) 'Some fifth-century masking conventions', *G&R* 46.2: 188–202.

Marshall, C. (2000) '*Alcestis* and the problem of prosatyric drama', *CJ* 95: 229–38.

Martin, R. (1987) 'Fire on the mountain: *Lysistrata* and the Lemnian women', *ClAnt* 6: 77–105.

Martindale, C. (1993) *Redeeming the text: Latin poetry and the hermeneutics of reception*, Cambridge.

Martindale, C. (2001–2) 'The aesthetic turn: Latin poetry and the judgement of taste', *Arion* 9.2: 63–89.

Martindale, C. (2005) *Latin poetry and the judgement of taste: an essay in aesthetics*, Oxford/ New York.

Martindale, C. (2010) 'Performance, reception, aesthetics: or why reception studies need Kant', in Hall and Harrop 2010: 71–84.

Martindale, C., S. Evangelista and E. Prettejohn, eds (2017) *Pater the classicist: Classical scholarship, reception, and aestheticism,* Oxford/New York.

Martindale, C. and R. Thomas, eds (2006) *Classics and the uses of reception,* Oxford/Malden, MA.

Maxwell-Stuart, P. (1972) 'Strato and the musa puerilis', *Hermes* 100: 215–40.

McGlew, J. (2002) *Citizens on stage: comedy and political culture in the Athenian Democracy,* Ann Arbor.

McMullan, G. and J. Hope, eds (1992) *The politics of tragicomedy: Shakespeare and after,* London.

Meineck, P. (1998) *Oresteia,* Indianapolis.

Meineck, P. (2012) 'The embodied space: performance and visual cognition at the fifth century Athenian theatre', *New England Classical Journal* 39: 3–46.

Meineck, P. (2017) *Theatrocracy: Greek drama, cognition, and the imperative for theatre,* London.

Meineck, P., W. Short and J. Devereaux, eds (2019) *The Routledge handbook of Classics and cognitive theory,* London.

Merleau-Ponty, M. (1945) *Phénoménologie de la perception,* Paris.

Merleau-Ponty, M. (1962) *Phenomenology of perception,* trans C. Smith, London.

Miller, P. (2014) 'Destabilizing Haemon: radically reading gender and authority in Sophocles' *Antigone*', *Helios* 41.2: 163–85.

Mills, P. (1996) 'Hegel's *Antigone*', in P. Mills, ed., *Feminist interpretations of G. W. F. Hegel* (University Park) 59–88.

Mirhady, D. (1996) 'Torture and rhetoric in Athens', *JHS* 116: 119–31.

Mitchell-Boyask, R. (2008) *Plague and the Athenian imagination: drama, history, and the cult of Asclepius,* Cambridge.

Mitchell-Boyask, R. (2013) *Aeschylus: Eumenides,* London.

Moll J., R. Oliveira-Souza, F. Moll et al. (2005) 'The moral affiliations of disgust: a functional MRI study', *Cognitive and Behavioural Neurolology* 18.1: 68–78.

Moodie, E. (2012) 'Aristophanes, the *Assemblywomen* and the audience: the politics of rapport', *CJ* 107: 257–81.

Moss, J. (2012) *Aristotle on the apparent good: perception, phantasia, thought, and desire,* Oxford.

Most, G. (2019) 'Greek tragedy and the discourse of politics', in C. Riedweg, ed., *Philosophie für die Polis: Akten des 5. Kongresses der Gesellschaft für Antike Philosophie 2016* (Berlin/Boston, MA) 87–92.

Mueller, M. (2011) 'The politics of gesture in Sophocles' *Antigone*', *CQ* 61.2: 412–25.

Mueller, M. (2016) 'Recognition and the forgotten senses in the *Odyssey*', *Helios* 43: 1–20.

Mukherji, S. and R. Lyne, eds (2007) *Early modern tragicomedy*, Suffolk.

Mulroy, D. (2013) *Antigone: Sophocles. A verse translation by David Mulroy, with introduction and notes*, Madison.

Munteanu, D. (2012) *Tragic pathos: pity and fear in Greek philosophy and tragedy*, Cambridge/New York.

Murnaghan, S. (1986) 'Antigone 904–920 and the institution of marriage', *AJP* 107.2: 192–207.

Murphy, A. (2011) 'Corporeal vulnerability and the new humanism', *Hypatia* 26: 575–90.

Murray, P. and P. Wilson, eds (2004) *Music and the muses: the culture of 'mousike' in the classical Athenian city*, Oxford/New York.

Naerebout, F. (1997) *Attractive performances. Ancient Greek dance: three preliminary studies*, Amsterdam.

Neer, R. (1995) 'The lion's eye: imitation and uncertainty in Attic red-figure', *Representations* 51: 118–53.

Neer, R. (2002) *Style and politics in Athenian vase–painting: the craft of democracy, ca. 530–460 B.C.E*, Cambridge/New York.

Neer, R. (2010) *The emergence of the classical style in Greek sculpture*, Chicago.

Nehamas, A. (1992) 'Pity and fear in the *Rhetoric* and the *Poetics*', in Rorty 1992: 291–314.

Neitzel, H. (1967) 'Die dramatische Funktion der Chorlieder in den Tragödien des Euripides', unpublished PhD thesis, University of Hamburg.

Nelson, S. (2014) 'Aristophanes and the polis', in J. Mhire and B. Frost, eds, *The political theory of Aristophanes: explorations in poetic wisdom* (Albany) 109–36.

Neuburg, M. (1990) 'How like a woman: Antigone's "inconsistency"', *CQ* 40.1: 54–76.

Nevitt, L. (2013) *Theatre and violence*, London.

Nietzsche, F. (1999) *The birth of tragedy and other writings*, eds R. Geuss and R. Speirs, Cambridge.

Noel, A.-S. (2019) 'What do we actually see on stage? A cognitive approach to the interactions between visual and aural effects in the performance of Greek tragedy', in Meineck, Short and Devereaux 2019: 297–309.

Nooter, S. (2012) *When heroes sing: Sophocles and the shifting soundscape of tragedy*, Cambridge/New York.

Nooter, S. (2017) *The mortal voice in the tragedies of Aeschylus*, Cambridge/New York.

Nooter, S. (2019) 'Sounds of the stage', in Butler and Nooter 2019: 198–211.

Nordheider, H. (1980) *Chorlieder des Euripides in ihrer dramatischen Funktion*, Frankfurt.

Nussbaum, M. (1992) 'Tragedy and self-sufficiency: Plato and Aristotle on fear and pity', in Rorty 1992: 261–90.

O'Gorman, E. (2018) 'The noise and the people: popular *clamor* and political discourse in Latin historiography', in S. Matzner and S. Harrison, eds, *Complex inferiorities: the poetics of the weaker voice in Latin literature* (Oxford) 129–48.

O'Sullivan, N. (1992) *Alcidamas, Aristophanes and the beginnings of Greek stylistic theory*, Stuttgart.

Olender, M. (1990) 'Aspects of Baubo: ancient texts and contexts', in D. Halperin, J. Winkler and F. Zeitlin, eds, *Before sexuality: the construction of erotic experience in the ancient world* (Princeton) 83–113.

Oliver, K. (2015) 'Witnessing, recognition, and response ethics', *Philosophy & Rhetoric* 48: 473–93.

Olsen, S. (2021) 'Narrating Neoptolemus: dance and death in Euripides', in L. Gianvittorio-Ungar and K. Schlapbach, eds, *Choreonarratives: dancing stories in Greek and Roman antiquity and beyond* (Leiden) 156–79.

Olsen, S. (2017) 'Kinesthetic *choreia*: empathy, memory, and dance in ancient Greece', *CP* 112: 1–22.

Olsen, S. (2020) *Solo dance in archaic and classical Greek literature*, Cambridge.

Olson, D. (1996) 'Politics and poetry in Aristophanes' *Wasps*', *TAPA* 126: 129–50.

Olson, D. (1998) *Aristophanes: Peace*, Oxford.

Olson, D. (2002) *Aristophanes: Acharnians*, Oxford.

Opondo, S. and M. Shapiro, eds (2012) *The new violent cartography: geo-analysis after the aesthetic turn*, London/New York.

Orgel, S., ed. (1996) *The Winter's Tale*, Oxford.

Osborne, R. (2010) *Athens and Athenian democracy*, Cambridge.

Osborne, R. (2016) 'Visual evidence – of what?', in S. Hodkinson, M. Kleijwegt and K. Vlassopoulos, eds, *The Oxford handbook of Greek and Roman slaveries* (Oxford) online pagination.

Oudemans, T. and A. Lardinois (1987) *Tragic ambiguity: anthropology, philosophy and Sophocles' Antigone*, Leiden.

Padel, R. (1992) *In and out of the mind: Greek images of the tragic self*, Princeton.

Paduano, G. (1969) *Euripide. Alcesti*, Firenze.

Page, D. (1941) *Select papyri III: poetry*, Cambridge, MA/London.

Paley, F. (1857) *Euripides, vol. 1*, London.

Paley, F. (1860) *Euripides: with an English Commentary, vol. III*, London.

Panagl, O. (1971) 'Die "dithyrambischen Stasima" des Euripides: Untersuchungen zur Komposition und Erzähltechnik', unpublished PhD thesis, University of Vienna.

Papadis, D. (2018) *Περί των αισθήσεων: Αριστοτέλης και Αλέξανδρος Αφροδισιεύς*, Athens.

Papadopoulou, T. (2005) *Heracles and Euripidean tragedy*, Cambridge.

Papastamti-Von Mook, C. (2020) Ἰο "θέατρο των μεγάλων τραγικών": Αρχαιολογικά δεδομένα και λειτουργικά ζητήματα', *Logeion* 10: 1–125.

Parker, L. (2007) *Euripides: Alcestis*, Oxford.

Parry, H. (1963) 'The choral odes of Euripides: problems of structure and dramatic relevance', unpublished PhD thesis, University of Berkeley.

Parry, H. (1965) 'The second stasimon of Euripides' *Heracles* (637–700)', *AJP* 86: 363–74.

Pelling, C. (2005) 'Tragedy, rhetoric, and performance culture', in J. Gregory, ed., *A companion to Greek tragedy* (Oxford) 83–102.

Peponi, A.-E. (2012) *Frontiers of pleasure: models of aesthetic response in archaic and classical Greek thought*, Oxford.

Peponi, A.-E. (2013) 'Theorizing the chorus in Greece', in J. Billings, F. Budelmann and F. Macintosh, eds, *Choruses, ancient and modern* (Oxford/New York) 15–34.

Pernerstorfer, M. (2005) 'Carl Orffs hesperische Musik', in S. Hagel and C. Harrauer, eds, *Ancient Greek music in performance* (Vienna) 121–30.

Pezzulo, G. et al. (2015) 'Active inference and cognitive–emotional interactions in the brain', *Behavioral and Brain Sciences* 38: 85.

Pitcher, J., ed. (2010) *The Winter's Tale*, London.

Platter, C. (2007) *Aristophanes and the carnival of genres*, Baltimore.

Platts, H. (2020) *Multisensory living in ancient Rome: power and space in Roman houses*, London, New York.

Podlecki, A.J. (1989) *Aeschylus, Eumenides*, Warminster.

Pohlenz, M. (1954) *Die griechische Tragödie*, 2nd edn, Göttingen.

Pollard, T. (2013) 'Greek playbooks and dramatic forms in early modern England', in A. Deuterman and A. Kisery, *Formal matters: reading the materials of English renaissance literature* (Manchester) 99–123.

Pollard, T. (2017) *Greek tragic women on Shakespearean stages*, Oxford.

Porter, J. I. (2010) *The origins of aesthetic thought in ancient Greece: matter, sensation, and experience*, Cambridge.

Power, T. (2010) *The culture of kitharôdia*, Cambridge, MA.

Power, T. (2011) 'Cyberchorus: Pindar's Κηληδόνες and the aura of the artificial', in L. Athanassaki and E. Bowie, eds, *Archaic and classical choral song: performance, politics and dissemination* (Berlin) 67–113.

Power, T. (2013) 'Kyklops *kitharoidos*: dithyramb and nomos in play', in Kowalzig and Wilson 2013: 237–56.

Prins, Y. (1991) 'The power of the speech act: Aeschylus' Furies and their binding song', *Arethusa* 24: 177–95.

Pritchard, D. (2004) 'Kleisthenes, participation, and the dithyrambic contests of late archaic and classical Athens', *Phoenix*: 208–28.

Purves, A., ed. (2017) *Touch and the ancient senses*, London/New York.

Rancière, J. (1999) *Disagreement: politics and philosophy*, trans. J. Rose, Minneapolis.

Rancière, J. (2009) *The emancipated spectator*, trans G. Elliott, London/New York.

Rancière, J. (2010) *Dissensus: on politics and aesthetics*, trans. S. Corcoran, New York.

Rancière, J. (2013) *The politics of aesthetics: the distribution of the sensible*, trans G. Rockhill, London.

Randhawa, B. (2014) 'The unblest room: Kristeva's chora in Sophocles's *Antigone*', *Philosophy and Literature* 38.2: 293–313.

Rayor, D. (2011) *Sophocles' Antigone: a new translation*, Cambridge.

Reason, M. and D. Reynolds (2010) 'Kinesthesia, empathy, and related pleasures: an inquiry into audience experiences of watching dance', *Dance Research Journal* 42: 49–75.

Reckford, K. (1987) *Aristophanes'old -and-new-comedy, vol. 1: six essays in perspective*, Chapel Hill/London.

Reeve, C. (2009) 'Luck and virtue in Pindar, Aeschylus, and Sophocles', in W. Wians, ed., *Logos and muthos: philosophical essays in Greek literature* (Albany) 215–32.

Rehm, R. (1988) 'The staging of suppliant plays', *GRBS* 29.3: 263–307.

Rehm, R. (2002a) *Understanding Greek tragic theatre*, 2nd edn, London.

Rehm, R. (2002b) *The play of space: spatial transformation in Greek tragedy*, Princeton.

Rehm, R. (2006) 'Sophocles' *Antigone* and family values', *Helios* 33S: 187–218.

Reig, M. and X. Riu, eds (2014) *Drama, philosophy, politics in ancient Greece: contexts and receptions*, Barcelona.

Reinke, A. (2019a) 'Concepts of (un)dressing in Greek drama', unpublished PhD thesis, University of Cambridge.

Reinke, A. (2019b) 'It takes a fraud to catch a fraud: on the exposure of imposture in ancient Greek comedy', in S. Hobe, V. Mastellari and N. Hatton, eds, *Hacks, quacks & impostors: affected and assumed identities in literature* (Freiburg) 37–59.

Revermann, M. and P. Wilson, eds (2008) *Performance, iconography, reception: studies in honour of Oliver Taplin*, Oxford/New York.

Robert, W. (2010) 'Antigone's nature', *Hypatia* 25.2: 412–36.

Robson, J. (2013) 'Beauty and sex appeal in Aristophanes', *Eugesta* 3: 43–66.

Rorty, A. ed. (1992) *Essays on Aristotle's Poetics*, Princeton.

Rosen, R. and H. Foley (2020) *Aristophanes and politics: new studies*, Leiden/Boston, MA.

Rosenbloom, D. (2014) 'The politics of comic Athens', in Fontaine and Scafuro 2014: 297–320.

Ruck, C. (1976) 'Duality and the madness of Herakles', *Arethusa* 9: 53–75.

Rudolph, K., ed. (2018a) *Taste and the ancient senses*, London/New York.

Rudolph, K. (2018b) 'Introduction: on the tip of the tongue: making sense of ancient taste', in Rudolph 2018a: 1–21.

Ruffell, I. (2011) *Politics and anti-realism in Athenian old comedy: the art of the impossible*, Oxford/New York.

Ruffell, I. (2013) 'Humiliation?: voyeurism, violence, and humor in old comedy', *Helios* 40: 247–77.

Scarry, E. (1985) *The body in pain: the making and unmaking of the world*, Oxford.

Scharffenberger, E. (2006–7) '*Deinon eribremetas*: the sound and sense of Aeschylus in Aristophanes' Frogs', *CW* 100.3: 229–49.

Schein, S. (1988) 'ΦΙΛΙΑ in Euripides' *Alcestis*', *Métis: Anthropologie des mondes grecs anciens*, 3.1/2: 179–206.

Scodel, R. (2018) 'Antigone's change of heart', in Stuttard 2018: 88–100.

Scott, N. (2017) 'Women and the language of food in the plays of Aristophanes', *Mnemosyne* 70: 666–75.

Scullion, S. (1998) 'Dionysus and katharsis in *Antigone*', *ClAnt* 17.1: 96–122.

Seaford, R. (1996) *Euripides: Bacchae*, Warminster.

Segal, C. (1971) 'The two worlds of Euripides' Helen', *TAPA* 102: 553–614.

Segal, C. (1993) *Euripides and the poetics of sorrow: art, gender and commemoration in Alcestis, Hippolytus, and Hecuba*, Durham, NC.

Segal, C. P. (1961) 'The character and cults of Dionysus and the unity of the *Frogs*', *HSP* 65: 207–42.

Segal, C. (1964) 'Sophocles' Praise of Man and the conflicts of the *Antigone*', *Arion* 3.2: 44–66.

Sells, D. (2012) 'Eleusis and the public status of comedy in Aristophanes' *Frogs*', in Marshall and Kovacs 2012: 83–100.

Sells, D. (2019) *Parody, politics, and the populace in Greek old comedy*, London/New York.

Seth, A., and H. Critchley (2013) 'Extending predictive processing to the body: emotion as interoceptive inference', *Behavioral and Brain Sciences* 36: 227–8.

Sharratt, P. and P. Walsh, eds (1983) *George Buchanan: Tragedies*, Edinburgh.

Shepherd, S. (2006) *Theatre, body and pleasure*, London/New York.

Shipton, M. (2018) *The politics of youth in Greek tragedy: gangs of Athens*, London.

Sifakis, G. (1971) *Parabasis and animal choruses: a contribution to the history of Attic comedy*, London.

Silk, M. (1993) 'Aristophanic paratragedy', in Sommerstein, Halliwell, Henderson and Zimmermann 1993: 477–504.

Simas, A. (2020) 'Aeschylus and the iconography of the Erinyes', in H. Marshall and C. Marshall, eds, *Greek drama V: studies in the theatre of the fifth and fourth centuries* BCE (London) 145–59.

Sklar, D. (2008) 'Remembering kinesthesia: an inquiry into embodied cultural knowledge', in C. Noland and S. Ness, eds, *Migrations of gesture* (Minneapolis) 85–111.

Slater, N. (1985) *Plautus in performance: the theatre of the mind*, Princeton.

Slater, N. (1999) 'Making the Aristophaniuc audience', *AJP* 120.3: 351–68.

Slater, N. (2002) *Spectator politics: metatheatre and performance in Aristophanes*, Philadelphia.

Slater, N. (2013) *Euripides: Alcestis: companions to Greek and Roman tragedy*, London.

Sluiter, I. and R. Rosen, eds (2012): *Aesthetic value in Classical antiquity*, Leiden/ Boston, MA.

Smith, D. (2012) *Essays on Deleuze*, Edinburgh.

Smith, R. et al. (2021) 'Recent advances in the application of predictive coding and active inference models within clinical neuroscience', *Psychiatry and Clinical Neurosciences* 75: 3–13.

Smith, W. (1960) 'The ironic structure in "Alcestis"', *Phoenix* 14.3: 127–45.

Sobchack, V. (1992) *The address of the eye: a phenomenology of film experience*, Princeton.

Sobchack, V. (2004) *Carnal thoughts: embodiment and moving image culture*, Berkeley.

Sommerstein, A. (1981) *Aristophanes: Knights*, Liverpool.

Sommerstein, A. (1985) *Aristophanes: Peace*, Warminster.

Sommerstein, A., ed. (1989) *Aeschylus: Eumenides*, Cambridge.

Sommerstein, A. (1990) *Aristophanes: Lysistrata*, Warminster.

Sommerstein, A. (1992) 'Old comedians on old comedy', in B. Zimmermann, ed., *Antike Dramentheorien und ihre Rezeption* (Stuttgart) 14–33.

Sommerstein, A. (1996) *Aristophanes: Frogs*, Warminster.

Sommerstein, A. (1998) *Aristophanes: Ecclesiazusae*, Warminster.

Sommerstein, A. (2005) 'A lover of his art: the art-form as wife and mistress in Greek poetic imagery', in E. Stafford and J. Herrin, eds, *Personification in the Greek world: from antiquity to Byzantium* (Aldershot) 161–71.

Sommerstein, A. (2008) *Aeschylus: Oresteia. Agamemnon, Libation–Bearers, Eumenides*, Cambridge MA/London.

Sommerstein, A. (2009a) 'Talking about laughter in Aristophanes', in Sommerstein 2009c: 104–14.

Sommerstein, A. H. (2009b) 'Slave and citizen in Aristophanic comedy', in Sommerstein 2009c: 136–54.

Sommerstein A. (2009c) *Talking about laughter and other studies in Greek comedy*, Oxford.

Sommerstein, A. (2014) 'The politics of Greek comedy', in M. Revermann, ed., *The Cambridge companion to Greek comedy* (Cambridge/New York) 291–305.

Sommerstein, A. (2018) 'Antigone as others see her', in Stuttard 2018: 29–41.

Sommerstein, A., S. Halliwell, J. Henderson and B. Zimmermann, eds (1993) *Tragedy, comedy and the polis. papers from the Greek drama conference. Nottingham, 18–20 July 1993*, Bari.

Sontag, S. (2009) *Against interpretation and other essays*, London.

Sourvinou-Inwood, C. (1989) 'Assumptions and the creation of meaning: reading Sophocles' *Antigone*', *JHS* 109: 134–48.

Sourvinou-Inwood, C. (2003) *Tragedy and Athenian religion*, Lanham, MD.

Spatharas, D. (2008) 'ταῦτ' ἐγὼ μαρτύρομαι: bystanders as witnesses in Aristophanes', *Mnemosyne* 61: 171–91.

Spencer, N. (1995) *Time, tradition and society in Greek archaeology: bridging the 'great divide'*, London.

Squire, M., ed. (2016) *Sight and the ancient senses*, London/New York.

Staley, G. A. (1985) 'The literary ancestry of Sophocles "Ode to Man"', *CW* 78.6: 561–70.

Stallsmith, A. (2008) 'The name of Demeter Thesmophoros', *GRBS* 48: 115–31.

Stalpaert, C. (2008) 'The mind taken hostage: Antigone's corporeal memory in *Mind the Gap*', *Mosaic* 41.3: 137–52.

States, B. (1992) 'The phenomenological attitude', in J. Reinelt and J. Roach, eds., *Critical theory and performance* (Ann Arbor) 369–79.

States, B. 1985. *Great reckonings in little rooms: on the phenomenology of theater*, Berkeley.

Stein, G. (1891) *Scholia in Aristophanis Lysistratam*, Göttingen.

Steiner, D. (2011) 'Dancing with the stars: choreia in the third stasimon of Euripides' *Helen*', *CP* 106.4: 299–323.

Steiner, D. (2014) 'Greek and Roman theories of art', in C. Marconi, ed., *The Oxford handbook of Greek and Roman art and architecture* (New York) 21–40.

Steiner, D. (2021) *Choral constructions in Greek culture: the idea of the chorus in the poetry, art and social practices of the Archaic and early Classical period*, Cambridge/New York.

Steiner, G. (1984) *Antigones: how the Antigone legend has endured in Western literature, art, and thought*, New Haven.

Stern, J. (1996) *Palaephatus: On Unbelievable Tales*, Wauconda.

Stieber, M. (1998) 'Statuary in Euripides' *Alcestis*', *Arion* 5.3: 69–97.

Stieber, M. (2011) *Euripides and the language of craft*, Leiden.

Stockert, W. (1992) *Iphigenie in Aulis*, 2 vols, Vienna.

Stocking, D. (2008) 'Antigone, désoeuvrée: tragedy, finitude, and community', *Mosaic* 41.3: 153–68.

Stone, L. (1981) *Costume in Aristophanic poetry*, New York.

Strejcek B. and C. Zhong (2014) 'Morality in the body', in L. Shapiro, ed., *The Routledge handbook of embodied cognition* (Abingdon/New York) 220–30.

Stuttard, D., ed. (2018) *Looking at Antigone*, New York.

Swift, L. (2010) *The hidden chorus: echoes of genre in tragic lyric*, Oxford.

Taaffe, L. (1991) 'The illusion of gender disguise in Aristophanes' *Ecclesiazusae*', *Helios* 18.2: 91–112.

Taaffe, L. (1993) *Aristophanes and women*, London/New York.

Taillardat, J. (1965) *Les images d'Aristophane: études de langue et de style*, Paris.

Taplin, O. (1972) 'Aeschylean silences and silences in Aeschylus', *HSP* 76: 57–97.

Taplin, O. (1977) *The stagecraft of Aeschylus: the dramatic use of exits and entrances in Greek tragedy*, Oxford.

Tatum, W. J. (2015) 'Anarchy and administration in Sophocles *Antigone* 259–77', *CP* 110.2: 91–8.

Telò, M. (2009) 'Slavery, freedom and citizenship in classical Athens: beyond a legalistic approach', *European Review of History* 16: 347–63.

Telò, M. (2013) 'Aristophanes, Cratinus and the smell of comedy', in Butler and Purves 2013: 53–69.

Telò, M. (2018) 'The boon and the woe: friendship and the ethics of affect in Sophocles' *Philoctetes*', in Telò and Mueller 2018a: 133–52.

Telò, M. (2020a) *Archive feelings: a theory of Greek tragedy*, Columbus.

Telò, M. (2020b) 'The politics of *dissensus* in Aristophanes' *Birds*', in Rosen and Foley 2020: 214–47.

Telò, M. (2020c) 'Laughter, or Aristophanes' joy in the face of death', in E. Hall and P. Swallow, eds, *Aristophanic humour: theory and practice* (London) 53–68.

Telò, M. (Forthcoming) 'Literary–critical intensities: pathos, affect, and Greek tragedy', in J. Connolly and N. Worman, eds, *The Oxford handbook of ancient literary theory and criticism* (Oxford).

Telò, M. and M. Mueller (2018a) *The materialities of Greek tragedy: objects and affect in Aeschylus, Sophocles and Euripides*, London/New York.

Telò, M. and M. Mueller (2018b): 'Introduction: Greek tragedy and new materialisms', in Telò and Mueller 2018a: 1–16.

Thatcher, M. (2019) 'Aeschylus' *Aetnaeans*, the Palici and cultural politics in Deinomenid Sicily', *JHS* 139: 67–82.

Thiercy, P. (1993) 'Les odeurs de la polis ou le nez d' Aristophanes', in Sommerstein, Halliwell, Henderson and Zimmermann 1993: 505–26.

Thür, G. (1996) 'Reply to D. C. Mirhady: torture and rhetoric in Athens', *JHS* 116: 132–4.

Toner, J., ed. (2014) *A cultural history of the senses in antiquity*, London/New York.

Tordoff, R. (2011) 'Excrement, sacrifice, commensality: the osphresiology of Aristophanes' *Peace*', *Arethusa* 44: 167–98.

Torrance, I. (2013) *Metapoetry in Euripides*, Oxford.

Tulard, J., ed. (1981) *Napoleon: lettres d'amour à Joséphine*, pref. J. Favier, Paris.

Turner, S. (2016) 'Sight and death: seeing the dead through ancient eyes', in Squire 2016: 143–60.

Tyrrell, W. and L. Bennett (1990) 'Sophocles' *Antigone* and Funeral Oration', *AJP* 111: 441–56.

Tyrrell, W. and L. Bennett (2008) 'Sophocles's enemy sisters: Antigone and Ismene', *Contagion* 15/16: 1–18.

Uhlig, A. (2018) 'Noses in the orchestra: bodies, objects and affect in Sophocles' *Ichneutae*', in Telò and Mueller 2018a: 153–292.

Ustinova, Y. (2017) *Divine mania: alteration of consciousness in ancient Greece*, London.

Vernant, J.-P. (1985) 'Figuration de l'invisible et catégorie psychologique du double: le colossus', in J.-P. Vernant, ed., *Mythe et Pensée chez les Grecs* (Paris) 325–38.

Verrall, A. (1895) *Euripides the rationalist*, Cambridge.

Vlassopoulos, K. (2007) 'Free spaces: identity, experience and democracy in classical Athens', *CQ* 57: 33–52.

Vlassopoulos, K. (2009) 'Slavery, freedom and citizenship in classical Athens: beyond a legalistic approach', *European Review of History* 16: 347–63.

Vlassopoulos, K. (2010) 'Athenian slave names and Athenian social history' *ZPE* 175: 113–44.

Walsh, G. (1974) '*Iphigenia in Aulis*, third stasimon', *CP* 69: 241–8.

Webb, R. (2016) 'Sight and insight: theorizing vision, emotion and imagination in ancient rhetoric' in Squire 2016: 205–19

Weiss, A. (1997) 'Paradigms of taste', in A. Weiss, ed., *Taste nostalgia* (New York) 7–12.

Weiss, N. (2017) 'Noise, music, speech: the representation of lament in Greek tragedy', *AJP* 138.2: 243–66.

Weiss, N. (2018a) *The music of tragedy: performance and imagination in Euripidean Theater*, Oakland.

Weiss, N. (2018b) 'Speaking sights and seen sounds in Aeschylean tragedy', in Telò and Mueller 2018a: 169–84.

Weiss, N. (2018c) 'Performing the wedding song in Euripides' *Iphigenia in Aulis*', in R. Andújar, T. Coward and T. Hadjimichael, eds, *Paths of song: the lyric dimension of Greek tragedy* (Berlin/Boston, MA) 315–41.

Weiss, N. (2023a) *Seeing theater: the phenomenology of classical Greek drama*, Oakland.

Weiss, N. (2023b) 'Music, dance, and meter in Aeschylean tragedy', in J. Bromberg and P. Burian, eds, *A companion to Aeschylus* (Chichester) 242–53.

Weiss, N. (Forthcoming) 'Music and *pathos* in Aeschylean tragedy', in D. Creese and P. Destrée, eds, *The beauties of song: aesthetic appreciations of music in the Greek and Roman world* (Cambridge).

West, M. (1990) *Aeschyli tragoediae cum incerti poetae Prometheo*, Stuttgart.

Wiles, D. (2007) *Mask and performance in Greek tragedy: from ancient festival to modern experimentation*, Cambridge.

Wilkins, J. (2000) *The boastful chef: the discourse of food in ancient Greek comedy*, Oxford.

Willi, A. (2003) 'New language for a new comedy: a linguistic approach to Aristophanes' *Plutus*', *CCJ* 49: 40–73.

Wilson, D. (1984) 'Euripides' *Alcestis* and the ending of Shakespeare's *The Winter's Tale*', *Iowa State Journal of Research* 58.3: 345–55.

Wilson, N. (2007) *Aristophanis fabulae*, 2 vols, Oxford.

Wilson, P. (1999-2000) 'Euripides' Tragic Muse', *ICS* 24-5: 427–49.

Winchester, J. (1994) *Nietzsche's aesthetic turn: reading Nietzsche after Heidegger, Deleuze, Derrida*, New York.

Winkler, J. and F. Zeitlin, eds (1990) *Nothing to do with Dionysos? Athenian drama in its social context*, Princeton.

Winnington-Ingram, R. P. (1980) *Sophocles: an interpretation*, Cambridge.

Wohl, V. (2002) *Love among the ruins: the erotics of democracy in Classical Athens*, Princeton.

Wohl, V. (2015) *Euripides and the politics of form*, Princeton.

Worman, N. (2008) *Abusive mouths in Classical Athens*, Cambridge.

Worman, N. (2017) 'Touching, proximity, and the aesthetics of pain in Sophocles', in Purves 2017: 34–49.

Worman, N. (2018) 'Electra, Orestes, and the sibling hand', in Telò and Mueller 2018a: 185–202.

Worman, N. (2020) *Tragic bodies: edges of the human in Greek drama*, London/ New York.

Wrenhaven, K. (2013) 'A comedy of errors: the comic slave in Greek art', in Akrigg and Tordoff 2013: 124–43.

Wright, M. (2005) *Euripides' escape-tragedies: a study of Helen, Andromeda, and Iphigenia among the Taurians*, Oxford/New York.

Wright, M. (2012) *The comedian as critic: Greek old comedy and poetics*, London.

Zangwill, N. (2001) *The metaphysics of beauty*, Ithaca, NY.

Zeitlin, F. (1978) 'The dynamics of misogyny: myth and mythmaking in the *Oresteia*', *Arethusa* 11: 149–84.

Zeitlin, F. (1982) 'Cultic models of the female: rites of Dionysus and Demeter', *Arethusa* 15: 129–57.

Zeitlin, F. (1994) 'The artful eye: vision, ecphrasis and spectacle in Euripidean theatre', in S. Goldhill and R. Osborne, eds, *Art and text in ancient Greek culture* (Cambridge) 138–96.

Zumbrunnen, J. (2012) *Aristophanic comedy and the challenge of democratic citizenship*, Rochester, NY.

Zweig, B. (1992) 'The mute nude female characters in Aristophanes' plays', in A. Richlin, ed., *Pornography and representation in Greece and Rome* (Oxford/New York) 73–89.

# Index locorum

# General index

# *Cambridge Classical Journal* Supplements

22  *Amor: Roma. Love and Latin literature (essays presented to E. J. Kenney)* ed. Susanna Morton Braund and Roland Mayer (1999)

23  *Ovidian transformations: essays on the Metamorphoses and its reception* ed. Philip Hardie, Alessandro Barchiesi and Stephen Hinds (1999)

24  *Classics in 19th and 20th century Cambridge* ed. Christopher Stray (1999)

25  *Pyrrhonian inquiry* Marta Anna Włodarczyk (2000)

26  *Production and public powers in classical antiquity* ed. E. Lo Cascio and D. W. Rathbone (2000)

27  *Economy and politics in the Mycenaean palace states* ed. Sofia Voutsaki and John Killen (2001)

28  *The owl of Minerva: the Cambridge praelections of 1906* ed. Christopher Stray (2005)

29  *Greeks on Greekness: viewing the Greek past under the Roman empire* ed. David Konstan and Suzanne Saïd (2006)

30  *Paideia Romana: Cicero's Tusculan Disputations* Ingo Gildenhard (2007)

31  *Ennius perennis: the Annals and beyond* ed. William Fitzgerald and Emily Gowers (2007)

32  *Greek and Latin from an Indo-European perspective* ed. Coulter George, Matthew McCullagh, Benedicte Nielsen, Antonia Ruppel and Olga Tribulato (2007)

33  *Theophrastus and his world* Paul Millett (2007)

34  *Unclassical traditions I: alternatives to the classical past in late antiquity* ed. Christopher Kelly, Richard Flower and Michael Stuart Williams (2010)

35  *Unclassical traditions II: perspectives from east and west in late antiquity* ed. Christopher Kelly, Richard Flower and Michael Stuart Williams (2011)

36  *Ratio et res ipsa: classical essays presented by former pupils to James Diggle on his retirement* ed. Paul Millett, S. P. Oakley and R. J. E. Thompson (2011)

37  *Menander: eleven plays* Colin Austin (2012)

38  *Sophocles' Jebb: a life in letters* Christopher Stray (2013)

39  *Varro varius: the polymath of the Roman world* ed. D. J. Butterfield (2015)

40  *Word and context in Latin poetry: studies in memory of David West* ed. A. J. Woodman and J. Wisse (2017)

41  *Augustus and the destruction of history: the politics of the past in early imperial Rome* ed. Ingo Gildenhard, Ulrich Gotter, Wolfgang Havener and Louise Hodgson (2019)

42  *Simonides lyricus: essays on the 'other' classical choral lyric poet* ed. Peter Agócs and Lucia Prauscello (2020)

Most past Supplements are available through Oxbow Books (www.oxbowbooks.com) or direct from the Cambridge Philological Society (www.classics.cam.ac.uk/seminars/philological). All are also available as ebooks.